Blues in the 21ˢᵗ Century

Myth, Self-Expression and Trans-Culturalism

Edited by

Douglas Mark Ponton
University of Catania, Italy
and
Uwe Zagratzki
University of Szczecin, Poland

Series in Music
VERNON PRESS

In the Americas:
Vernon Press
1000 N West Street,
Suite 1200, Wilmington,
Delaware 19801
United States

In the rest of the world:
Vernon Press
C/Sancti Espiritu 17,
Malaga, 29006
Spain

Series in Music

Library of Congress Control Number: 2019951782

ISBN: 978-1-64889-073-4

Also available: 978-1-62273-634-8 [Hardback]; 978-1-62273-956-1 [PDF, E-Book]

Cover design by Vernon Press. Cover image by Jean-Charles Khalifa.
Cover font (main title): Free font by Tup Wanders.

Table of contents

List of Figures

List of Tables

Preface

Since its beginnings in the late nineteenth century, the Blues has been more than a music style with a seminal impact on twenty-first-century popular music. As a medium of social expression, it articulated the tribulations of an entire black culture, male and female. Discourses about race were as much an integral part of the evolution of the Blues as were those of class, when young white kids–in America and Europe, especially the UK–adopted the music for their political and social ends. Idealising black models of culture, white interpretations verged on myths on the one hand, but on the other brought out transcultural features of the Blues in their performative acts. Other realms of performing arts, such as literature, films and photography speak of the flexibility of the Blues. Its commercialisation by white and black record companies, or annual festivals around the world, is another proof of its durability. Bearing this in mind, any doubts about the survival of the Blues in the twenty-first century are rendered obsolete.

The flexibility and changeability of the music and the culture it is embedded in are paralleled by the versatility of academic discourses about the Blues. Early studies of the Blues, chiefly by US-American authors (with the exception of *Blues Fell this Morning: The Meaning of the Blues* 1960 or *The Story of the Blues* 1969 by the British scholar Paul Oliver), emphasise the evolution of the genre against the background of structural racism in the US, and further illuminate the counter-cultural features the producers of the music incorporated. They made an important contribution to the documentation and survival of this feature of black Blues culture. Of outstanding importance is Samuel Charters' *The Bluesmen* (1967), *The Roots of the Blues; An African Search* (1981) or his *The Blues Makers* (1991), which come to mind here.[1]

The chapters in this volume are representative of the papers presented at the conference "Blues in the 21st Century: Myth, Self-Expression and Trans-Culturalism", held at the University of Catania, Sicily, in November 2018. The conference focused on, among other topics, specific features of corpora of classic Blues lyrics, Blues tourism (not represented in the book, though it was

---

[1] The tradition has continued, as recent studies have shown: Lynn Abbott. 2017. *The original Blues: the Emergence of the Blues in African American Vaudeville.* Jackson: University Press of Mississippi. Alan Harper. 2016. *Waiting for Buddy Guy: Chicago Blues at the Crossroads.* Urbana: University of Illinois Press.

included in the conference)[2] and national, regional and other varieties of (European) Blues.[3]

There are three sections of the book: the first, *Blues impressions: responding to the music,* is informed by a variety of analytical perspectives including Cultural/Film Studies, Literary Criticism and Musicology, and presents studies that focus either on the works of individual artists, including Jimi Hendrix, Lightnin' Hopkins, Ali Farka Touré ; or on specific features of the Blues as a genre. The second group of studies, *Blues on the page: perspectives from literary criticism,* focuses on the Blues in contemporary literature, especially in the work of the prominent poet and activist Langston Hughes, who found in the Blues a language and a body of cultural practices, appropriate for his needs as an African American intellectual seeking social freedom, in the period before the Civil Rights movement. A third section, *Scientific perspectives: Authenticity and identity in contemporary Blues studies,* presents studies that use analytical techniques, from musicology and corpus linguistics, to explore a variety of issues that include authenticity, vocal technique, emotions in Blues lyrics and the themes of Robert Johnson.

One of the themes that will be seen to run through the diverse contributions to this book, whatever their methodological approach, is *authenticity.* This is only natural, since it is an issue for the Blues itself. Legend has it that the Blues began on Dockery's cotton plantation in Mississippi, in a far-off time of black slaves, of cultural and religious syncretism, of moonshine whiskey; when Charlie Patton's inspired exhibitions were the evening release for a burdened people. Its first, most truly authentic performers, before the turn of the 20th century, came from this problematic social setting, and many took to music, it is said, as a way of escaping from their lives of drudgery. The early Blues singers, whose names have mostly disappeared, drew on such experiences to provide material for their songs, and sang them to a mainly black audience, who would gather on street corners or at informal dances in farmhouses, to hear them play. From the musical point of view, the rhythms of the songs had to respond to the needs of dancers. The lyrics consisted, initially, of stock references to shared experiences; they used in-jokes, jargon, veiled social criticism and so on, in a recipe that gave rebelliousness a compelling voice, that has echoed down the years.

---

[2] An example from the States: Steve Cheseborough. 2018. *Blues Traveling: The Holy Sites of Delta Blues.* 4th edition. Jackson: University Press of Mississippi.

[3] For Germany: Winfried Siebers, Uwe Zagratzki, eds. 2010. *Das Blaue Wunder. Blues aus deutschen Landen.* Eutin: Lumpeter und Lasel. Michael Rauhut. 2016. *Ein Klang – zwei Welten. Blues im geteilten Deutschland.* Bielefeld: Transcript.

The names who first emerged as significant artists in the field—Patton himself, Bessie Smith, Robert Johnson, Son House, Sonny Boy Williamson and the rest—all knew the tropes of the Blues backwards, both from a musical and a textual point of view. With these names, we are already approaching a later period, when advances in technology such as the radio and the phonograph had begun to bring their music to a wider audience. With the mass exodus to Chicago in the early 20th century, we find a new form of Blues, one that took the name of the city, a pulsating electric music that already feels worlds away from its antique country cousin. Is that music still the Blues, still authentic? Muddy Waters, one of the great names whose life and work straddles both periods, talked about the mojo, an amulet or talisman that features in one of his classics 'Got my mojo working':

> "When you're writin' them songs that are coming from down that way, you can't leave out somethin' about that mojo thing...I didn't believe in it, no way. But even today, when you play the old Blues like me, you can't get around from that."[4] (Palmer 1982, 98-99)

In other words, Muddy himself was engaged in a kind of cultural sleight of hand, using outdated symbols because the genre demanded it. His dilemma concerns authenticity, too; how far such country superstitions, which the singer himself had grown away from, could be relevant to listeners on the streets of the windy city. If even one of the undisputed masters of both Delta and Chicago schools could have issues with authenticity, it is understandable that the music's adoption by white stars like Eric Clapton and Mick Jagger, in the 1960s, provoked such a storm. Though many black artists have expressed their approval for white performers, some would still agree with critic Paul Garon's complaint that "Blues as purveyed by whites appears unauthentic and deeply impoverished."[5]

As a white Blues enthusiast, whose interest was kindled long ago and grew up revering these great figures, I have often pondered these issues. For the South of England, white and middle class, what possible relevance could this powerful magic have held, what message could pass from the Delta of the Mississippi to our own less mighty rivers? In Randolph Lewis's chapter, he quotes film-maker Les Blank's phrase, saying that the Blues would "calm somewhat the inner terror of my chaotic soul." Perhaps this comes close to an explanation, or an answer. Sadly, we will never know what it was like to be a young black teenager in the audience while Lightnin' Hopkins was telling the

---

[4] Robert Palmer. 1982. *Deep Blues*. New York and London: Penguin.
[5] Paul Garon. White Blues. https://ourBlues.files.wordpress.com/2012/02/microsoft-word-white-Blues.pdf. Last access 18/9/2019.

story of Mister Charlie. We will never be in the same room as Howling' Wolf, laying down his powerful, irresistible sounds. The popularity of the Blues among white audiences is testimony that its message, whatever it is, speaks not just to the skin but to the soul. To the extent that we share that immediate feeling, the paradoxes and doubts melt away, and the music is still able to offer us an authentic experience. Uwe Zagratzki, co-editor of this volume, writes: "I had to clear the language hurdle, as English is not my native tongue. Yet my first encounter with the Blues, in a 1970s North-western town in Germany, via a then-popular radio programme, caught me unawares and captured me for good. Not by words but by 'magic' chords, that struck a chord with me. When words became comprehensible in the course of time, and with them came increasing knowledge and–much later–professional ambition, still the original feelings have prevailed."

Some of the above themes are picked up directly by our contributors; other chapters explore different facets of the story of the music, to comprise a work divided into three thematic sections. The first section is entitled *Blues impressions: responding to the music*:

Randolph Lewis argues that authenticity was found, by film-maker Les Blank, in the life and music of Texas Bluesman Lightnin' Hopkins. Centring on Blank's documentary "Trouble in Mind: The Blues According to Lightnin' Hopkins", he explores the affinity between the representation (film) and the represented (Lightnin' Hopkins), in a "film that moves and feels like the music it represents." He discusses how Blank was drawn to the gritty realities of Hopkins' life as they contrasted with his own milieu, the superficial, materialistic world of white American culture.

Iain Halliday's chapter discusses the transcultural transformations of the Blues in time and space, and reflects on its paradoxical capacity for speaking to listeners from social contexts that are worlds away from its starting points. He considers the metaphorical and emotional dimensions of the colour "Blue", which stands for an art form that has endured, and still has the potential to be associated with authentic human experience and music of significant quality.

In her study of Ali Farka Touré, **Diana Sfetlana Stoica** poses the authenticity question from another angle. Touré is an African musician, and his colour credentials are therefore impeccable; however, it is questioned how far his music, in which African sounds and rhythms are perceptible, can be heard as Blues, and how far it is representative of a kindred, though distinct, tradition. The Malian musician's work, she suggests, represents an African counter-discourse to the African American definition of the roots of the Blues.

Daniel Lieberfeld focuses on an artist not generally thought of as a Bluesman—Jimi Hendrix—and convincingly presents him as a true pioneer of the genre, whose work may be seen as a departure from older Blues patterns, but nevertheless reproduces the real sounds and feelings of the form. Hendrix's whole sound, he suggests, was deeply rooted in the Delta sounds of Hooker and Waters, and their influences are felt in the song "Machine Gun", analysed here.

Uwe Zagratzki raises the issue that the authenticity of the Blues consists in its alternative cultural features (see Raymond Williams), which have survived post-modernist mainstreaming. Modern listeners adapt the Blues to their personal experience and thus manage to "reproduce" a plethora of individual alternatives, which negate the original "aura" (Walter Benjamin's term), that is the unique specificity of a work of art. He argues that the Blues, owing to its de-constructiveness and flexibility, empowers the recipient to retain the music's alternative gestures, also under the conditions of technical reproduction.

In the second part of the book, *Blues on the page: perspectives from literary criticism;*

Chiara Patrizi underlines the political potential in Langston Hughes' last Blues poem "The Backlash Blues" (1967), and explores the interplay between the written text and the sung version by Nina Simone. Recapturing and intensifying the denunciatory spirit of the original, Simone's version expressed the poem's latent militancy for a global audience of black and white, and Patrizi shows how its message still resonates in contemporary America.

Valerio Massimo De Angelis reflects upon Langston Hughes' long writing career and the poet's purposeful return to political engagement, which especially emerged in his work "the Backlash Blues". He explores the roots of the poem in a lifetime of experience dating from the poet's days at the centre of the Harlem Renaissance, and argues that it represents his most complete attempt to infuse an authentic poetic discourse with the slave language and "signifying" common in the plantation context.

Irene Polimante's starting point is Hughes' work on such poems as "The Weary Blues", which left a legacy for poetic strategies in contemporary African American poetry. The performativity of experimental poets such as Willie Perdomo, she argues, explores analogous terrain, in terms of authenticity and identity, to that mapped out by Langston Hughes. Thus, the Blues is seen as a continual influence, changing form in response to circumstances, linking past and present, abolishing distinctions between high and low cultural forms.

Authenticity was an issue for Langston Hughes, as he sought for a bridge between the élite cultural form of poetry and the popular symbols and patterns of speech and action of his community. As early as 1925, as **Adriano**

Elia says in his chapter, Hughes produced the first poem that incorporated actual Blues lyrics. In his study of "The Weary Blues", he explores Hughes' conception of music and poetry as possessing a cathartic potential and healing power. He also shows the extent to which Hughes' poetical techniques drew on the forms and features of the field experiences of the American South.

The final part of the book, *Authenticity and identity in contemporary Blues studies*, presents some scientific perspectives:

Authenticity in the Blues is the topic of **Thomas Claviez**'s contribution. He recognises the increasing importance of the concept in today's corporate business context. He asks, not only whether white boys—and girls—can play the Blues, but whether "electrified, popular, successful" Blues can be considered authentic, whether played by black or white. Claviez even questions the authenticity of one of the foundation myths of the Blues, the legend of Robert Johnson selling his soul to the Devil in return for musical knowledge.

Jean Charles Khalifa also uses corpus techniques to compare black and white Blues singers, but focuses on features of the texts. A quantitative analysis of word frequencies and a qualitative grouping of speech patterns lead to a deeper understanding of the "unconscious" layers of the black Blues. Their emotional patterns oscillate between feelings of fear, loathing and curiosity, which depend on complex responses to factors in their immediate social situations.

Giulia Magazzù applies critical discourse analysis to the lyrics of one of the best-known traditional Bluesmen, Robert Johnson. As the quintessential representative of the authentic, "Delta" Blues, Johnson's texts were both collections of standard verses that circulated at the time, as well as personal lyrics reflecting his own preoccupations. The chapter therefore sheds light on the whole genre, distinguishing between types of lexical units and semantic structures, and attempting to identify the source of the subversive potential of the texts.

From a musicological perspective, **Emiliano Bonanomi** and **Jack Dandy** explore the question of authenticity in the digital age, asking how far the presence of digital recording techniques and new patterns of instrumentation impact these questions. Communication through social media with a virtual fan base shows how far the Blues has moved from the earliest periods in its evolution. A comparison is made between the way a modern artist such as Joe Bonamassa establishes a sense of community with his public, and more traditional patterns of old-style Delta relations.

Douglas Mark Ponton traces the differences in vocal techniques and other aspects of performance between black and white singers, exploring Garon's claim that whites are incapable of achieving authenticity. It is by now acknowledged that certain white guitarists (Clapton, Stevie Ray Vaughan, Ry Cooder, etc.) are capable of playing the Blues in an authentic way, but what about white vocal performers? In a corpus study, the author outlines the features of authentic Delta Blues singing, and suggests that there are some white performers able to reproduce them to a degree.

This brief outline highlights the variety of approaches, methodologies and points of view in this volume. Such diversity is natural in a multi-disciplinary scientific endeavour. However, the reader will also find many points of contact between the different chapters, and a common fascination with this extraordinary musical and cultural phenomenon. It is indeed our hope, with this volume, to make a contribution to the continuation of scholarly interest in the Blues.

The two-day conference left many vivid memories. The stimulating talks from our speakers, performances by Catania-based Blues band "Hot Shanks", and the viewing of a film by John Baily on British Blues drummer Hughie Flint, "Beyond the Blues", an intense and personal document that shared Flint's love of the Blues, as well as his developing interest in Irish music. Perhaps it is appropriate to end this preface—and begin our book—with Flint, moving on from the Blues, seeking trans-cultural connections, the emotional sensibility that underlies all folk music. Not forgetting to include some lines from Robert Johnson:

> From Memphis to Norfolk is a thirty-six-hour ride
> A man is like a prisoner, and he's never satisfied

Acknowledgements

Thanks to all those who made the conference at Catania such a memorable occasion.To all contributors to this volume. To Winfried Siebers for his vital contributions to the copy-editing. To Céline Longin-Khalifa for the cover artwork.

Part One:
**Blues impressions:
responding to the music**

1.

Trouble in mind:
the Blues according to Lightnin' Hopkins

Randolph Lewis

University of Austin, Texas, USA

No one writes about the Blues without writing about feeling, and that is what I want to explore as well—the feeling of the Blues, in particular, the feeling of *The Blues According to Lightnin' Hopkins*. More than a description of the great East Texas guitarist and vocalist Lightnin' Hopkins, it's also the title of a nonfiction film made in 1968 by the American director Les Blank. Even though the film was made fifty years ago, and both its maker and its subject have long since passed on, this wry look at Lightnin' Hopkins is still one of the most vital and evocative films about the Blues ever made in the United States.

I make this claim with full recognition that there are many films about the Blues and many films that prominently feature the Blues. From *Sounder* to *The Blues Brothers*, from Martin Scorsese's documentary series to the Coen Brother's *Brother, Where Art Thou?*, American soundtracks have long been a welcome home for Blues music. But here I want to suggest that Les Blank's film about Hopkins is unusual because it has a distinct *feeling for the Blues*: it is not simply a film about a Bluesman, but rather a film that reflects and embodies the feelings, the places, and even the structure of Lightnin' Hopkins's music. What I am suggesting is that Les Blank created a rare film that moves and feels like the music it represents.

Hopkins and Blank: they may not be household names, but they were giants of their respective forms who came together in the late sixties to collaborate on a small film—and what a strange collaboration it was. The result of their brief time together was a lyrical, gentle, wry, almost anthropological documentary shot on an Eclair NPR, a film that remains an unusual model of how to put music on film with appreciation and insight.

And we're fortunate that the subject was Lightnin' Hopkins, who was an extraordinary figure in the history of the Blues. Born in Centerville, Texas, in 1912, died in Houston, Texas in 1982, Hopkins had a remarkable career that rose and fell over the course of four decades, but his influence is still felt. *Rolling Stone* magazine named him number 71 on a list of the 100 greatest guitarists of all time, while Houston-based Blues guitarist Rayfield Jackson said, "Lightnin' is important to American music because of the era he came up in, for black America, the style that reaches back to the old days while being modern too…" (Wood 2003, 18).

But this essay is about Lightnin' on film, not Lightnin' on the radio or on record. Which makes sense because I am someone who writes mostly about visual culture, even though I have a passionate interest in the Blues as a musician and as someone who teaches courses on American popular music. However, I am eager to say something about post-war American visual culture in general and documentary cinema in particular, because it is a subject about which I have written three books. By looking closely at nonfiction cinema, I have always focused on what we might learn about American life through *unpopular culture*, as it were, through little films that are far from Hollywood and often much more personal and interesting to me. That is how I bumped into the work of the late California-based independent filmmaker Les Blank, who has fascinated me since the 1980s when I corresponded with him as a young graduate student interested in documentary expression.

Then as now, I approached the subject from an interdisciplinary perspective that combines elements of Cinema Studies, Cultural Studies, and standard cultural history, though readers may detect something more than the usual blend of textual and extra-textual analysis that drives most of the work in my field (American Studies). For the more personal elements, I should give credit to the world of creative nonfiction: writers such as Mark Dery, Zadie Smith, Rebecca Solnit, and Meghan Daum have turned cultural criticism into an art form that is intoxicating and illuminating. Like them, I want to dig into odd corners, and then sift, muse, and mull. And I want to write in a mode—clearly essayistic, personal, reflective, a bit idiosyncratic—that lets the reader know where the scholarship is rooted.

The importance of Lightnin' Hopkins is well established. So let me start with a bold claim for Les Blank's cinema before focusing on Hopkins. If you want to understand American culture since the 1960s, especially the subcultures where real American beauty, eccentricity, and originality thrives, you would be well advised to look at the work of Les Blank. And especially if you want to understand the Blues, Les Blank is a perfect guide to the sticky, humid landscape of East Texas in the late sixties where a brutal kind of apartheid was very much still in place. Even in 2018, Texas is too often a place of structural immiseration for brown and black people, but in the mid-century heyday of Lightnin' Hopkins, it was even more dangerous. As a child, Hopkins knew that his grandfather had killed himself rather than endure the agony of slavery; he knew that his father was a sharecropper who was murdered; he knew there was a "hanging tree" in front of the town courthouse where African American men were lynched and left where even school children could see this violent spectacle of white supremacy (O'Brien 2014, 6-8). You can understand why he sings, "I'm gonna get my shotgun and be a slave no more." (Much of this information comes from research I conducted in the papers of folklorist John Lomax in Austin as well as the Academy of Motion Pictures library in Los Angeles).

In the 1930s, as a young man, Lightnin' found himself tossed in jail for sassing a white judge, leaving him wary of white people for the rest of his days. Certainly, East Texas is a hard, mean place, but not in the way outsiders imagine. It is not the flat dry desert of West Texas; instead, it is the densely forested rolling hills known as the "the big thicket" that gets denser as you approach the Louisiana border. It is a sweltering hot place for much of the year, and it is still a place that African Americans do not feel safe driving through. For Hopkins, growing up Black in East Texas in the twenties and thirties was a constant education in the affective burden of structural racism, the heaviness of institutionalized cruelty and hierarchy.

Les Blank had a much luckier path. Born into privilege in the south in 1935, attending college in the late fifties in New Orleans, then heading to California for film school, Blank was a Southern boy who turned into a flower child. He grew up with black music, fell deeply into it in New Orleans, where he heard Fat Domino and Professor Longhair, and found his way back to it throughout his career as a filmmaker. Best known for *Burden of Dreams*, a revelatory look at Werner Herzog's making of *Fitzcaraldo*, Blank was a folkloric filmmaker with a gentle, open mind: he was curious to learn about the world he didn't know first-hand and he wanted to share in the experience of people quite different from himself. As one scholar put it in 1973, he would show us the South "as conventional media rarely sees it" (Kernan 1973, 322). Starting in 1968 with his Lightnin' Hopkins film when he was a few years out of film school at USC, Les Blank compiled a remarkable filmography over four decades, making invaluable portraits of musicians and artists including Dizzy Gillespie, lap steel guitarist Sonny Rhodes, Texas Bluesman Mance Lipscomb, Zydeco King Clifton Chenier, Conjunto genius Flaco Jimenez, as well as clever films on garlic lovers (*Garlic Is As Good As Ten Mothers*) and gap-toothed women (*Gap-Toothed Women*). He also made an epic film about Leon Russell, based on two years of filming in Oklahoma, that was not released for 40 years. As a result of this beautifully eccentric body of work, *The New York Times* once wrote:

> "Les Blank is a documentarian of folk cultures who transforms anthropology into art," while a writer in *Time* magazine claimed, "I can't believe that anyone interested in movies or America...could watch Blank's work without feeling they'd been granted a casual, soft-spoken revelation" (Les Blank Films website).

Many viewers seem to agree whenever they have a chance to see Blank's careful treatment of Hopkins, one of the greatest Blues musicians in the history of Texas, which makes him one of the greatest Blues musicians ever. Although I have lived in Austin for much of my life, I am by no means a Texas nationalist—far from it. Texas has many serious problems and many shortcomings, but not when it comes to the Blues. Texas produced "poor old Lightnin'," as Hopkins ironically called himself, but also Freddie King, Blind Lemon Jefferson, Albert Collins, Stevie Ray Vaughan, T Bone Walker, Johnny Winter, and many others without whom the Blues is unthinkable. So when Les Blank came to Texas with his camera and a few thousand dollars looking for the great Lightnin' Hopkins, he was in the right place at the right time.

How did this come about? Les Blank came across Lightnin' the same way many others did in the sixties: as part of the Blues and folk revival of the sixties, which brought many neglected musicians to a new and very appreciative audience. After hitting a commercial peak in the early fifties, Hopkins languished commercially as his country Blues style seemed to go out of fashion in the late fifties surge of rock and roll. But the folk revival of the early sixties brought country Bluesmen like Hopkins to new audiences—largely white, coastal, urban, and college.

Like many young college-educated whites on the edge of the sixties counterculture, Les Blank was looking for something missing in his life, something that he eventually found in the Blues. Blank explained where he was at as an artist and as a human being in 1967 when he first saw Lightnin' perform in LA:

> At the time, my second marriage had recently collapsed and I felt myself a failure as a father, a human and an artist. My future as a filmmaker seemed a hollow, hopeless void. Listening to the Blues being performed by those who had truly lived the Blues, provided an escape from my problems and also gave me a strong sense of connection to pain and suffering, even though I had not been born into a world beleaguered for generations by racism, poverty and gross injustice. I found that really listening to Blues music provided a kind of comfort not experienced since my younger days as a believer in organized religion. A couple shots of whisky and a beer or two helped the process along, numbing the fears of getting close to the source of my deepest sorrows and anxieties. When Lightnin' sang about how bad he felt when his woman left him, I was able to cry in my beer and also calm somewhat the inner terror of my chaotic soul (Blank, "On the Making...").

I love that phrase: "calm somewhat the inner terror of my chaotic soul." That, in a nutshell, is the Blues according to Lightnin' Hopkins—and Les Blank as well, who turned to the Blues for authenticity, depth, and comfort that he found lacking in mainstream American culture in the sixties. The music scholar Dick Weissman argues that the Blues surged in popularity in the sixties for several reasons (Weissman 2004, 112). The sound of the Blues was compelling to many middle-class white listeners, for whom it represented a complex blend of sonic bliss, sexual frankness, and social rebellion. Pushing guitars, both electric and acoustic, in new directions that would find their most popular expression in the songs of Jimi Hendrix and Eric Clapton, Blues artists "talked about sex, not romance, and highlighted the dynamics of a culture that was relatively exotic" to white college students. Moreover, "the dilemmas discussed in Blues songs—failed romances, hard times, and traveling to new and unknown destinations—were all fascinating to the mostly college-age audiences." As a white counterculture sympathizer a few years out of college, Les Blank was perfectly positioned to make this film in 1968, which one writer called "more of a spiritual journey than a factual account of the man." Finding the Blues was a spiritual experience for the filmmaker.

Not that Lightnin' made it easy to film him and his world. Once Blank got into contact with the Bluesman at his home in East Texas, he learned that Lightnin' was as tricky as he was charismatic. Lightnin' demanded money up front to appear in the film. When the musician got the funds, he only allowed Blank to shoot for one day before refusing any more interviews. The young filmmaker was lost and depressed: his idea for a film was falling apart after just one day in Texas. But then he caught a lucky break. Lightnin' started playing cards with the filmmaker, who kept losing at a game called "pitty-piar" which Blank said "is something like gin rummy except it involves no skill. It's strictly mental telepathy or cheating" (Blank 1972, 22). The more money the filmmaker lost, the more Lightnin' wanted to keep him around. And that's why Lightnin' let Les Blank into his world in East Texas for a few more weeks. It was mostly about gambling.

I cannot help but feel a close regional connection to the world of this film. My family has been in East Texas, not far from where Lightnin' was born, for 150 years, which in non-indigenous Texas is a long time. In 2005 I made a documentary film called *Muleskinner Blues*, a documentary about my East Texas grandfather and a man that he killed in the logging woods during the Great Depression. Even though I live in the fairly cosmopolitan setting of Austin, I have spent some time in the rough and tumble world of rural East Texas, not far from the humid landscape around Lightnin's birthplace of Centerville, Texas, though he spent most of his adult life in the chaotic sprawl of Houston, a port city long famous for Blues, rap, ZZ Top, and of course now Beyoncé. So the film resonates with me in complex ways because it occupies a sweet spot between creative nonfiction cinema, great musicianship, and the sticky, vibrant culture of East Texas where my family has lived for 150 years.

But I suspect that the film has something to offer anyone interested in the Blues—and especially those interested in making documentaries about music. As Blank said:

> I started off trying to write a standard script for the *Lightnin'* film and it just never worked. Finally, in desperation, I just started throwing scenes together. I found that there was something pleasurable in just cutting pictures like you would notes of music in a music score (Blank 1972, 22).

Not wanting to make a traditional biopic about Hopkins, Blank gives us something more rambling and curious—no narration, no maps, no argument, no clear position to adopt, none of the "discourse of sobriety" that characterizes much of post-war nonfiction cinema. We do not even hear Hopkins talk about himself very much.

Instead, the film lets us see through the roving eye of a curious guest following Lightnin' around East Texas, watching him play and walk and joke and drink with his buddies, and keeping the smallest details in the frame: roses, stray dogs, trees, kids playing, rodeo dancers, barbed wire. The movie takes unexpected twists and turns, just like Hopkins' improvised lyrics and even his work on the fretboard. We sometimes lose sight of Hopkins, like when the camera follows a stylish young African American couple strolling through the "little old one horse town" of Centerville. But we keep coming back to Hopkins, as he is telling stories, trying to kill something on the train tracks that they call a "snake snake," and of course singing. And as in all of Blank's films, there is plenty of barbeque—food is his obsession as much as music.

Blank might sound like an ethnomusicologist working with a camera, but film scholars such as Brad Prager and Andrew Horton have disagreed with this assessment. "Blank's cinematic imprint is the poetic representation of the pleasures typical of minor cultures, languages and cuisines," says Prager, before noting that his work does not offer an "objective" study of a subculture like East Texas Blues (Prager 2010, 126). They are instead intensely felt, closely observed, and carefully edited experiences he has had with people he enjoys—documentary as a kind of sharing, not "capturing" (Horton 1982, 28).

This ethic of "sharing" invites a form of empathetic engagement from the audience, both in terms of the film as well as the music it captures. Like so many Blues artists, Lightnin' gives us a way of feeling the indignities and dangers of segregation and does so with an invitation to profound empathy: *hear my story, share my burden, ease my pain*— these are the essential impulses of the Blues in America, and Les Blank honours that fact with a point of view that is equal parts empathy and curiosity, with none of the moralizing of mainstream documentary in the 1960s. As a result, this film gives us a way to access the structure of feeling of segregated America, most especially in the strange, hot, violent, and humid world of East Texas where he lived. "Yes, bring me my shotgun and a pocket full of shells," he famously sang about a woman, and when he was filming with Les Blank, Hopkins was carrying a pistol because a man was looking for him. He needed a pocket full of shells to survive East Texas.

It is not all heavy Blues in Les Blank's film, far from it. We also see the lightness of Lightnin' Hopkins, and we feel that great Blues spirit of laughing at the absurdity of life and the tragi-comedy of surviving it all. Houston musician Kinney Abair said that "Lightnin' was a comic, a real joker, onstage too—always cracking wise," and that humour is a big part of his on-screen charisma (Wood 2003, 18). And along with laughter, the film gives us the style, the cool, the dignity of the black artist in an apartheid society. As the singer Steve Earle said, "Lightnin' had a lot of gold in his mouth. He figured it was a good investment" (18).

And maybe just as importantly, the film gives us Lightnin' in context: this film has a strong sense of place, though it gives us the texture of place more than the specifics of where and when. Blank is attentive to the emotional geography of the Blues, the farms, the streets, the simple living rooms in Centerville and in Houston where Hopkins had his little shotgun house (Wood 2003, 16). His freedom of movement is limited. Geographers such as Rashad Shabazz (2015) have described the ways that Black men experienced life in places like the South Side of Chicago as a form of imprisonment, and similarly, Lightnin' often seems free in the film, but we do not see him on the white side of town, as it were. He is only seen in segregated spaces, where he is a regal, if somewhat tipsy, presence.

Which brings me to my last point. One scholar of black cinema, Terri Simone Francis, has asked: "What do motion pictures mean for people whose sense of home has been dislocated by migrations and characterized by attacks on their citizenship and humanity, largely through visual representation?" She goes on to wonder if cinema could ever

> ...find a Blues that responds specifically to the experiences and histories of black people in the Americas, such as migrations, floods, and the precariousness of black life in countries where black folks' citizenship and sovereignty as human beings have been catastrophically in question? (Francis 2010, 8).

Are there filmmakers who can reckon with this? Who can honour, explore, and assess the cultural weight of Blackness in the United States? Correctly, I think, she points to Spike Lee, Melvin Van Peebles, Gordon Parks, and other African American filmmakers since the sixties. We might also add the respectful, folkloric gaze of Les Blank to the list. His work with Lightnin' Hopkins is nothing if not respectful, appreciative, and thoughtful, even as it hints at the "precariousness of black life" that was, after all, one of Lightin's great subjects.

And on a related note, the film also has something to contribute to the image of African American masculinity. In an essay about the American visual artist Romaire Beardon, literary scholar Kimberly Lamm explores ways to untie black masculinity in the US from the weight of racism, with a particular emphasis on

> the role visual art can play developing a malleable perceptual apparatus that can register moments of destabilizing fluidity, subversion, and innovation as black masculinity makes and remakes itself within the collaged canvas of American visual culture. (Lamm 2003, 832).

Les Blank is doing more than documenting an aging Bluesman whose music excites him. He is also honouring a subversive form of black masculinity: defiant, creative, rowdy, unknowable, and cool as ice. Just as cool as the Blues.

After all, the Blues is a hip, knowing, creative mode of surviving the rigors of American life. It is a way of living through the "trouble in mind" that haunts all vulnerable people lodged in a violent world of racial hierarchy and economic dislocation. The Blues is a way of living through the pain and fear of America with grace, rhythm, wit, and dignity. If *The Blues According to Lightnin' Hopkins* sometimes seems like an artefact of an older time, an antique from the tail end of Jim Crow America, it is not. As a careful viewing of this film suggests, the Blues might even be a powerful way of responding to the challenges of America in 2018, just as it was for Lightnin' Hopkins and his audiences fifty years ago. When I spoke about Hopkins in Catania in November 2018, we were beginning a conference that happened to fall on the 50th anniversary of this extraordinary small film. It was the product of a time when a remarkable Blues musician collaborated with a unique cinematic documentarian, one black, one white, one old, one young, but both Southerners, both more interested in the backroads of American culture than in the plastic American mainstream, both in love with the endless creative possibilities of the Blues. And though the film was made 50 years ago, not enough has changed in America in that half-century for us to see the film as a relic of the folkloric past. Lightnin' Hopkins is long gone, and so is Les Blank, but the Blues endures in Texas. It is more integrated, sometimes more commercial, maybe a little less gritty and folkloric, but it is very much alive in places like my hometown of Austin, Texas. Yet we still need creative filmmakers to document, preserve, and share the artistry of Blues musicians, even those less famous than Lightnin' Hopkins. After all, the Blues "calms the inner terror of our chaotic souls," as Blank put it, and it speaks the truth of American life with pathos and passion. It is an essential American art form that speaks to a global audience, where it has assumed new local flavours and meanings. And in the age of YouTube, when the most obscure performance footage and nonfiction films are finally easy to find, a film such as *The Blues According to Lightnin' Hopkins* may find new ways to inspire musicians and filmmakers alike.

References

Blank, Les. 1972. Interview. *Filmmakers Newsletter* (June), 21-23.

Francis, Terri Simone. 2010. "Flickers of the Spirit: Black Independent Film, Reflexive Reception, and a Blues Cinema Sublime." *Black Camera* 1 (2), 7-24.

Horton, Andrew. 1982. "A Well Spent Life. Les Blank's Celebrations on Film." *Film Quarterly* 35 (3) (Spring), 25-34.

Kernan, Margot S. 1973. "Les Blank". In: *International Film Guide*. New York: A. S. Barnes: 322.

Lamm, Kimberly. 2003. "Visuality and Black Masculinity in Ralph Ellison's Invisible Man and Romare Bearden's Photomontages." *Callaloo* 26 (3), 813-835.

O'Brien, Timothy. 2014. *Mojo Hand: The Life and Music of Lightnin' Hopkins*. Austin: University of Texas Press.

Prager, Brad. 2010. "On Blank's Screen: Les Blank's Werner Herzog Eats His Shoe and the Gravity of the Director's Subject." *Studies in Documentary Film* 4 (2), 119-135.

Shabazz, Rashad. 2015. *Spatializing Blackness: Architectures of Confinement and Black Masculinity in Chicago*. Chicago, IL: University of Illinois Press.

Weissmann, Dick. 2004. *Blues: the Basics*. London: Routledge.

Wood, Roger. 2003. *Down in Houston: Bayou City Blues*. Austin: University of Texas Press.

Acknowledgements

The author would like to thank the conference organizers, Professors Douglas Ponton and Uwe Zagratzki, for creating a unique international conference, "Blues in the 21st Century: Myth, Self-Expression, and Trans-culturalism," at the University of Catania on November 23-24, 2018.

Further Reading

Blank, Les. "On the Making of the Blues According to Lightnin' Hopkins." Accessed 23 June 2019. https://www.documentary.org/feature/making-Blues-accordin-lightnin-hopkins.

Les Blank Films website. Accessed 23 June 2019. https://lesblank.com/les-blank-director-producer-and-cinematographer/

2.

Scales of Blue: the contagion and dissemination, the persistence and transformations of a form and a name

Iain Halliday

University of Catania, Italy

In this chapter, I seek to describe the history of my own awareness of the Blues as a musical form in parallel with a summary consideration of the form's history, its development and diffusion, together with its heritage for other musical forms and for the cultures it has influenced and continues to influence. As will become evident below, I am particularly indebted to the work of the English Blues scholar Paul Oliver (1927—2017).

It is a difficult undertaking, tracing a musical form and tracing a particular use of language back to their origins, reconstructing the history of words and music, because, of course, if done properly this activity is akin to reconstructing the lives of so many people—lives lived in one way and another, lives expressed in one way and another; stable lives, diasporic lives; hegemonic lives, subaltern lives.

The Blues, perhaps more than any other musical genre, consistently regard lived life and consistently offer an antidote to the existential difficulties that life presents. British musician Mick Fleetwood had this to say about the Blues in 2008 when he provided a playlist of his favourite five Blues tracks to *The Guardian*:

> To me, the Blues is an infection. I don't think it's necessarily a melancholy thing, the Blues can be really positive and I think I think anyone and everyone can have a place for the Blues. It need not always [be] a woeful, sorrowful thing. It's more reflective, it reminds you to feel. And that feeling could be anything, from sadness to joy and inspiration. So long as it triggers a passion, a feeling (Fleetwood 2008).

An infectious, contagious form, then, steeped in life's contradictions between the melancholic and the positive, between depressing and uplifting feelings.

But before dedicating some attention to the music, it will be useful to consider its name—the word "blue" and its associations with the melancholic.

In my own life my mother has always been a particularly rich source for language-learning with particular regard for idiomatic phrases: "fur coat and no knickers," "what's for you won't go by you," and, I distinctly recall, "between the devil and the deep blue sea," imparted to me sometime during my school years, though I don't recall what my adolescent quandary was at that precise moment. Those words "devil" and "blue" in the idiom, together with its metaphoric load of existential predicament (the fount of all Blues) led me to wonder if the blue in this phrase bears some etymological significance to our present-day conception of being blue.

It is almost certain, however, that there is absolutely no link between the blue in "between the devil and the deep blue sea"—the rock and the hard place, the hammer and the anvil—and the "blue-devils", synonymous with a melancholic and/or alcohol-induced depression in English in the eighteenth and nineteenth centuries and used by John Keats among others. (Jacobs 1958, 42). Probably no link at all, because that "blue" in "between the devil and the deep blue sea" did not actually make its appearance until 1931 when Koehler and Arlen wrote the song of the same title (presumably inserting "blue" for purely euphonic purposes), a song that Cab Calloway made famous. Prior to this, the idiom involved just the devil and the (deep) sea. And that "devil" in the expression may be the nautical term denoting a difficult-to-caulk seam on a ship's hull, or it may simply be Old Nick in person. Such are the intricacies, the false leads in all their deceptive allure, that lie in the path of historical language research. To be truly precise in this endeavour we would have to travel back almost three centuries and live through all those years listening, reading, attempting to understand the ways in which the language is used and the ways in which it develops. We obviously cannot do this, but we can read and listen to the naturally limited material that is available to us, though even this job in itself has to be done selectively and is thus limited even further by our choices, dictated in their turn by limited time and limited attention spans to name just two extremely important resources.

But to return to the devil, which on this occasion certainly is Old Nick, Robert Johnson, of course, provides a direct link between the devil and the Blues with his famous "Me and the Devil Blues", first released on a recording in 1937, but subsequently covered by many artists, including Eric Clapton and Gil Scott Heron. Johnson is perhaps today the most representative figure in the history of the Blues and his widespread success is entirely posthumous. He is an example of one of the culture industry's favourite commodities—a conveniently dead artist and hero. As Marybeth Hamilton put it in a talk delivered to the Royal Historical Society at the University of Warwick in the year 2000, "The Blues, The Folk, and African-American History":

> Today, Robert Johnson has become a major pop music phenomenon. The first stirrings of this were felt in the 1960s, when Johnson's recordings were reissued on a two volume LP, but it crested in 1990 with the release of *Robert Johnson: the Complete Recordings*, a CD anthology that brought together all of Johnson's songs and two recently discovered photographs of the man himself, the only photos of Johnson known to exist. Alongside the CD came extensive publicity chronicling Johnson's brief, violent, mysterious life: his death by poisoning at age twenty-seven, and the legend that he had sold his soul to the Devil at a Delta crossroads in return for prowess on the guitar. The anthology sold one million units, with the first 400,000 bought up in only six months. Johnson's face can now be found on postcards, t-shirts, posters, and guitar polishing cloths; it also stares out from the covers of recent popular musical history: Greil Marcus's *The Dustbin of History* and Francis Davis's *The History of the Blues*. (Hamilton 2001,17–18)

Hamilton's talk opens with a description of Johnson's second (and final) recording session, which took place in Dallas in June 1937, just less than a year before his death. The music he had been playing and singing itinerantly for six years, between the age of 21 and 27, throughout the small towns of the Mississippi Delta, was a musical form that had been developing in the southern United States since the 1870s and which would continue to evolve and influence musicians throughout the twentieth century and throughout the world up to the present day.

The origin and evolution of the Blues as musical form are just as complex as the origin and evolution of its given name. Here is a summary from Michael Theodore Coolen:

> Blues scholars generally regard the American Blues tradition as consisting of musical components of either African or European origin. Such distinctive features as response, Blues scales and intonation, and the *aab* form of the text are identified as reflecting the African heritage, while the harmonic character and musical structure are considered the European contributions. (Coolen 1982, 69)

Coolen's words come from the opening of an article in which he makes a very specific and detailed contribution to the debate on the musical origin of the Blues, concentrating on the Senegambia, a key African region in the North American slave trade. Senegambian peoples, particularly the Wolof people, were particularly well represented in the New World and Coolen describes and traces the musical tradition of the Wolof, particularly the use of the *xalam*, a four- or five-string plucked-lute. He speculates intelligently that the *xalam* may well have been a prototype banjo and remarks on the similarities between typical Senegambian instrument ensembles and the "fiddle, banjo, and tambourine ensembles popular in the United States from the late seventeenth through the nineteenth centuries." (74) His speculation includes an acknowledgment of the fact that the fiddle was also present in the United States due to British influence, but this fact by no means precludes influence from African musicians familiar with the Wolof *riti* and other African bowed-lutes.

However, apart from his speculation on the diffusion of instruments and musicians across the Atlantic with diasporic immigration and slave trafficking, the crucial part of Coolen's article regards a consideration of the classic twelve-bar Blues form in comparison with the classic *xalam* tradition of the *fodet*, a cyclic, repetitive musical structure with a tonal character that makes use of primary and secondary pitches. He provides a great deal of musical detail to support this comparison and then concludes:

> Syncretism has been observed in many aspects of American civilization—in language, religion, burial customs, and music. Whether or not the *xalam* tradition was the archetype for the Blues, its similarity to the Afro-American Blues is so close that it would have been predisposed to combine syncretically with whatever elements helped to shape the Blues. Functioning as a musical calque, the *xalam* tradition of the Senegambia could well have contributed to the evolution of the Blues tradition in the United States. (Coolen 1982, 82)

Syncretism may not be the correct word here, because to syncretize is, by definition, a conscious process, the implementation of a conscious desire to meld, to reconcile, differing elements. In the true and natural development of cultures, this melding, this reconciliation, this *evolution* is never the result of a conscious application of policy, but is rather the natural fusion of elements that are to hand and which contribute to cultural development while people live their lives.

The Blues as a form is and continues to be a cultural fusion that carries with it a long history. When Douglas Ponton told me he was organizing a conference on the Blues here in Catania, I was immediately interested and enthusiastic, because while by no means an expert in the genre, I am very much aware of its legacy and I have enjoyed listening to various forms of Blues over the years. There was also the matter of a small part of my own personal history—the double album I bought in my early twenties when a student in Manchester—*The Story of the Blues*—which I listened to a lot back then and which has somehow survived through the years together with a dozen or so other vinyls: an album I hadn't listened to in decades.

As a twenty-something student, I was more interested in listening to the music than in considering the music's history and I confess I hadn't fully understood that the double album, compiled by Paul Oliver, was in fact a companion to his seminal book of the same title. So, at a distance of some thirty-five years, the book was procured and read and there, in the very first lines of the first chapter of *The Story of the Blues*, "Long Hot Summer Days", I found the fruits of Oliver's own research into the naming of the genre, into the way language was first used to define it in the way we are all familiar with now. The lines are quoted from a diary entry written on December 14, 1862, in the very midst of the American Civil War, by Charlotte Forten, a "young black woman who had been born free in the North and having qualified as a teacher had come to Edisto Island in South Carolina to instruct the slaves." Forten is disturbed by the screams and noises she hears coming from the slaves' quarters and on that Sunday, she goes to church where:

> Nearly everybody was looking gay and happy; and yet I came home with the Blues. Threw myself on the bed and for the first time since I have been here, felt very lonesome and pitied myself. But I have reasoned myself into a more sensible mood and am better now. (Oliver 1969, 5)

Forten, a young African American freewoman, turned to reasoning in dealing with her existential predicament, other African Americans—first in slavery, then in the racist society of the southern United States—gradually turned to musical expression to deal with their own predicaments, one of the few means of artistic expression allowed to them. As Oliver explains, the Blues as musical form did not appear immediately in the years of slavery, or even in the years of Reconstruction following the Civil War. One of the first things to be aware of when talking about the Blues is the apparently simple fact that it was, it is a form of folk music; an apparently simple fact because being true folk music in reality its genesis and its evolution were actually very complex and received little attention from researchers through the years of its initial development. As Oliver explains in his introduction to the book:

> Blues singers were part of the total scene, no more to be remarked on than were the mules that drew the wagons to the cotton gin, or the watermelons ripening on the vines in the spreading patches. There's a certain appropriateness in this for it's in the nature of a folk music that it is the creation of the people and not separate from the whole fabric of living. (Oliver 1969, 2)

Indeed there was, there is, something elemental, immediate and urgent in the form. It is a form that eschews conventional musical refinement and elevates the elemental, the voice and the other sounds that surround us, to a position of primacy. This characteristic may well derive from the African heritage, but the immediacy and the urgency of the Blues were to ensure not just the form's survival, but its dissemination and its influence through the years and across borders.

The only borders in Paul Oliver's book, however, are state lines. I confess I was somewhat overwhelmed by the general level of detail and the sheer quantity of information about individual Blues performers, but it certainly opened my eyes to the extent and the variety of the origins. I read *The Story of the Blues* in August 2018, during a two-week stay with my parents, near Liverpool and I decided while there to visit the Slavery Gallery of Merseyside's Maritime Museum, something I hadn't done for some fifteen years.

On arriving in Liverpool, a city whose great eighteenth-century wealth was largely founded on the slave trade, I discovered that things had changed—the Slavery Gallery is now the International Slavery Museum in its own right, and one whole floor of the mid-nineteenth-century Royal Albert Dock building that houses the city's Maritime Museum is dedicated to it. There is a great array of information about Africa and African peoples, about the trade, about the shackles and the ships, about the heritage. There is even a small section dedicated to music, where, headphones on, you can press buttons and trip through American black music in all its genres and all its successes, the Blues included.

But the one thing that really sticks in my mind from the visit was a large photograph on a wall in a gallery dedicated to plantation life—its title, "1923 / BADAGRY / MERRY XMAS", the 20 letters of which written in white on the chests of three descending rows of black men standing upright, 20 in total. In the foreground, seated, four white people, three men and a woman in two groups of two with a small black boy seated between them. The British, I presume, in Africa, in Nigeria, where— irony of ironies—in 1923 slavery was still legal. Nobody smiles, nobody's joyful. Everyone, despite the season, seems to have the Blues, and I guess it's no wonder under the circumstances. You can find reproductions of the photograph quite easily on the net using its grotesque caption. One occurrence of it came from a website known as Nairaland Forum, a large and popular Nigerian forum. It was posted there on Christmas Day 2014 and the many comments it attracted are a catalogue of historical misunderstanding and confusion over what racism was and is.

I also remember turning from the photograph on the wall that day in Liverpool to find that there had been another solemn observer behind me—a black woman, a pained look on her face and in her eyes behind her studious-looking glasses. "Incredible," she said in an American accent as she gave me half a smile and I nodded in embarrassed silence.

And out of such horrors of history came the need for blue notes, for Blues scales, for things out of kilter on this the blue planet, where blue is everywhere—the colour of the sky, the colour of the sea, the colour (together with black) of our bruises. The music itself, of course, acknowledges in its very structure that things are awry in the world of its creators and performers, as scholar William Tallmadge wrote in a 1984 article for the journal, *The Black Perspective in Music*:

> Nearly all forms of Afro-American music in North America, including worksongs, hollers, ballads, spirituals and hymns, chanted sermons with congregational response, Blues, jazz, and rock contain pitches that are inflected by performers in ways quite foreign to regular melodic practice in Western art music. (Tallmadge 1984, 155)

But in its very unconventionality lies, of course, an important element of the Blues' quality and power of transcendence, in the form's function as a coping mechanism, taking its exponents and its listeners beyond the grief and the pain of their predicaments. In the words of Bluesman John Lee Hooker, responding to questions from journalist Jas Obrecht in 1997:

> Are there times it makes you happy?
> All the time, yes. Real happy. Sometimes I'm so happy that that's what cause the tears – feelin' so good. They not hurtin' tears. They happy tears.
> *Being able to express yourself with Blues songs is a good way to let go of stress.*
> Very easy. That's what I do. You can pick up a guitar and sing—it heals you. There's a song called "The Healer" —"Blues is a healer." You play that song, and it heals your mind. Just keep on doin' that, and it takes away a lot of the evil and the stress, because you know you can't change nothin', but you can try to forget it or live with it through your music. The name of my new album is called *Don't Look Back* [1997]. Don't look back to the things that happened to you in the past—the bad, the ugly. Leave it behind. You can't change it. When you think of some of the good things you did, you hope that you keep on doing good things in life, like lovin' people. I believe in one race—that's the human race. God made us all. We's all different colors and different languages, but we all God's children. He created us all. Everyone. (Obrecht 1997)

We may interpret that "everyone" as a hyperbolic, even utopian and evangelical expression of the power of the Blues and John Lee Hooker's faith in it, but there is no denying the form's universal range, its capacity to involve many over many years and over many international borders. Langston Hughes, writing in 1941 in his brief essay, "Songs Called the Blues" suggested:

> The most famous Blues, as everybody knows, is the *St. Louis Blues*, that Mr. W. C. Handy wrote down one night on the corner of a bar on a levee street in St. Louis thirty years ago, and which has since gone all over the world. The *St. Louis Blues* is sung more than any other song on the air waves, is known in Shanghai and Buenos Aires, Paris and Berlin—in fact, is heard so often in Europe that a great many Europeans think it must be the American National Anthem. (Hughes 1941, 144–45)

Hughes himself drew great inspiration from the Blues for his own work, as did W.H. Auden, to name just two Blues-inspired poets, but the form continues to receive attention and recognition from writers, and I take us now to a fictional, writerly and contemporary Los Angeles. Towards the end of Chapter 15 of Paul Beatty's novel *The Sellout* the African-American first-person narrator, known to us only by his surname, "Me", or his nickname, "Bonbon", provides a chromatic summary of the road signs in and around LA, from the "hollowed-out metallic midnight blue" of Los Angeles proper, through the sky blue of "kickback cool bedroom communities like Santa Monica, Rancho Palos Verdes, and Manhattan Beach" to the "bland brown of cheap blended malt whiskey" of Hermosa Beach, La Mirada, and Duarte and ultimately:

> The sparkling white signs denote Beverly Hills, of course. Exceedingly wide hilly streets lined with rich kids unthreatened by my appearance. Assuming that if I was there I belonged. Asking me about the tension of my tennis racquets. Schooling me on the Blues, the history of hip-hop, Rastafarianism, the Coptic Church, jazz, gospel, and the myriad of ways in which a sweet potato can be prepared. (Beatty 2015, 190–91)

The rich kids of Beverly Hills—most of them as white as their road signs—do what rich white kids do: they appropriate cultural forms and feel sure enough of themselves and their own entitlement to teach others about those forms, teaching the Blues to black kids included.

Some of my own recent "schooling" in contemporary American black music has come from two apparently unlikely, but on reflection perfectly understandable sources: on the one hand, David Byrne, who chose to end his and his band's performances on his recent *American Utopia* tour with a call and response protest song from 2015 by Janelle Monae—"Hell You Talmbout"—a song that despite its modernity and topical theme evidently owes a great deal in its form to traditional Blues. Byrne's choice is really no surprise given his political commitment and his eclectic taste in music. The other source was my twenty-something daughter, Emily, who insisted I should watch and listen to Childish Gambino's "This Is America", a song and a video that I am sure will have excited (for better and for worse) a fair number of musicologists, semiologists, dance experts and historians: it is a truly remarkable production, moving from melodic African-American folk to Trap, Soul and R&B, perhaps one of the few things missing among the references in this carousel through the history of black American music is traditional Blues. Generational factors mean that my daughter's finger is much more on the pulse of contemporary music than mine will ever be again.

Childish Gambino's song and its accompanying video touch on important contemporary issues surrounding American and African–American culture, but they are also great entertainment that while making societal and political points transport us—those of us who find them to our taste—into a state of appreciation and enjoyment. All music (all artistic expression) is, in some ways, a form of escapism, a way of metabolising, coping with, even celebrating our realities, our world that is certainly to a large extent out of kilter. The Blues, however, always kept things real in its escapism, a genuineness which perhaps explains why so many people were and still are attracted to the form and, consciously or unconsciously, are still influenced by its heritage.

But that heritage, of course, undergoes changes as it makes its way through a further diaspora—geographical, temporal and medial. The following comes from a July 1980 issue of *The Stanford Daily*, renowned student newspaper of Stanford University:

The Blues Bros. give it their all in Concord
Dan Aykroyd and John Belushi were not raised as rhythm and Blues musicians. For this reason, they have come under some fire lately. Blues purists claim that the two actors are ripping off the public in their act as Jake and Elwood Blues, two Chicago Bluesmen. There are much better, and perhaps more "real" Blues musicians who should be getting the recognition, the purists say; not these two rich white boys. And they're probably right. The Blues Brothers are an act. They're not for real. Their band, probably the best one money could buy, is just that—bought.

The purists had and still do have a valid point, but the global runaway success of the first *Blues Brothers* film, released that very year, is proof of the fact that the public are happy to be ripped off, happy to be entertained by something that is not real. The culture industry and its operators will do, consciously and unconsciously, whatever is necessary to create successes in terms of numbers of followers, in terms of numbers of cinema and concert tickets sold, recordings and t-shirts bought. Despite what the purists may feel and say, the music of Aykroyd and Belushi's creation does, of course, bear a resemblance to the origins and the word "Blues" is still very much there in the title of what has become a cult of mass culture.

Vivian and Wilhelmina Jacobs in their detailed essay on the metaphoric and symbolic values of the colour blue—in which the Blues as musical form receives only one passing mention in a footnote—provide a historical excursus of considerable depth, for the most part literary, and conclude: "We are dealing with a jumble of associations and beliefs which for us no longer possess validity, but which once permeated the opinions and judgments of mankind" (Jacobs and Jacobs 1958, 46). That "jumble of associations and beliefs" seems particularly poignant and with a relevance that goes way beyond the matter of the colour blue and into the human condition in its entirety. One particular condition, however, that does still permeate mankind in our mindsets and in our existences, to greater and lesser degrees in moments of greater and lesser duration, is melancholy—primary fount, as mentioned above, but not by any means an exclusive defining characteristic of the Blues. For over a century now, making Blues music and singing the Blues has been a tried and tested cathartic antidote to that condition.

It may seem inappropriate, perverse even, to dedicate the last words in this chapter of a book on the Blues to a quotation from a country and western song, but the last verse of George Jones's "Color of the Blues" (1958) I think makes a simple and cogent point regarding the range of the Blues' influence and legacy, and it does so succinctly and in an (almost) *aab* rhyme scheme:

> *There's a blue note in each song*
> *That I sing since you are gone*
> *Yes, blue must be the color of the Blues.*

References

Beatty, Paul. 2015. *The Sellout.* New York: Picador.

Coolen, Michael Theodore. 1982. "The Fodet: a Senegambian Origin for the Blues?" *The Black Perspective in Music* 10 (1) (Spring), 69–84.

Fleetwood, Mick. 2008. "Playlist". Accessed 25 June 2019. https://www.theguardian.com/music/2008/oct/13/mick-fleetwood-playlist.

Hamilton, Marybeth. 2001. "The Blues, the Folk, and African-American History." *Transactions of the Royal Historical Society* 11, 17–35.

Hooker, John Lee. 1996. Interviewed by Jas Obrecht. Accessed 25 June 2019. http://jasobrecht.com/john-lee-hooker-living-Blues-interviews/.

Hughes, Langston. 2014. "Songs Called the Blues." *Phylon* (1940–1956), 2 (2) (2nd Qtr, 1941), 143–145.

Jacobs, Vivian and Jacobs, Wilhelmina. 1958. "The Color Blue: Its Use as Metaphor and Symbol." *American Speech* 33 (1) (Feb.), 29–46.

Nairaland Forum, discussion of "1923 BADAGRY MERRY XMAS". 2014. Accessed 25 June 2019. https://www.nairaland.com/2061058/historical-pix-picture-christmas-celebration.

Obrecht, Jas. 1997. John Lee Hooker—Boogie All the Time. Accessed 23 November 2019. http://www.angelfire.com/mn/coasters/interv.html.

Oliver, Paul. 1969. *The Story of the Blues.* London: Pimlico.

Stanford Daily. Accessed 23 November 2019. https://stanforddailyarchive.com/cgi-bin/stanford?a=d&d=stanford19800722-01.2.25&e=en-20--1--txt-txIN.

Tallmadge, William. 1984. "Blue Notes and Blue Tonality." *The Black Perspective in Music* 12 (2) (Autumn), 155–165.

3.

The old black or the new white. Identities in postmodern lyrics: the case of the King of Desert Blues, Ali Farka Touré

Diana Sfetlana Stoica

University of Timisoara, Romania

The research presented in this chapter represents a grounded theory about the ways the key concepts of blackness and twoness are reflected in music, or, how music itself has managed to express the tendencies of identification of an African ontology. Methods of research are mixed, mostly qualitative, in a social constructivist worldview. Data analysis is carried out with reference to notions that are interpreted in a postcolonial frame, brought to the interpretation and criticism of the available, most visible, and therefore cautious, rhetoric of Ali Farka Touré's creations, as well as his artistic image.

Introduction

"It is hardly to be believed that God, who is a wise Being, should place a soul, especially a good soul, in such a black ugly body...".

Here is one of Montesquieu's statements, reported to us by Achille Mbembe, a contemporary postcolonial thinker from Cameroon (Mbembe 2001, 181). It defines the ways black identities were construed by white-western elites; evidence of these constructions is present in a multitude of writings. Introducing this chapter with the words of Montesquieu is a way of presenting a mixed qualitative analysis between codes and representations in African lyrics and music, discourse on blacks and the power of colonialist images related to them, and finally, exploring the archetypes influencing social behaviours in multiracial environments.

Investigating the foundations of the term "black" and its uses should be a central aim of any thinker or artist who questions the facts of blackness or otherness. Besides examining the essentials of this term, it would be worth asking why black discourse, in the dichotomist imaginary of the world, refers to Africans. Do Africans still identify themselves today, according to the logic of an "inferior race", or simply through the opposite concepts of "pure" and "civilized" in western pre- "human rights" rhetoric? Is there, in the creation of African people, particularly in music, a clear identification of black identities, re-contextualised in a postmodernist key?

The answers that are proposed in this chapter emerge as conclusions to a reflexive analysis of the lyrics and statements of Ali Farka Touré, renowned guitarist, Blues and soul singer of Mali, better known as the King/Godfather of the Desert Blues (1939-2006). He represents an important African exponent of the years before and after the waves of independence and change in Africa, which signify an important turn in black, negritude and race discourse. The analysis will enhance efforts to mix ideology with arts, as well as artistic and political discourse. With reference to music, not only in Africa, but especially in Africa, sounds are instruments of fusion that intend to create a frame of reality, and thus express life in all its aspects (Bebey 1975, 3).

From blackness to twoness. Shaping "othered" black music

Although black music has been "othered" (Ramsey 2003, 19) from the white point of view, a representation of the black soul remains (Bebey 1975, 16), as does blackness as a key concept in the definition of black music. In the discourse of the Other, which has dominated new political, intercultural and anthropological research in academia and media, the concept of twoness has emerged, in visual arts and music.

Twoness, as W.E.B. Du Bois recalled (Edwards 2007), refers to the division and consequent gathering of two souls, the original one and the *other-ed* one, and resulted in the process of melting of the individual soul within the souls of new civilizations or societies. This would be the case of African Americans. Twoness implies the escape from differentiation, limitation, spatiality. However, in the works of Ali Farka Touré, twoness was differently valued.[1] He could never have been *othered*, in melting pot societies like those of the United States or Europe. There are elements of his vision, or the views he sustained, that support the idea of a postcolonial perspective on *othered* blackness, correlative to twoness, and present in African music. These elements have yet to be generalized, in the context of the decolonization of artistic expressions, subsequent to the decolonization of minds.

---

[1] According to his biography, available on www.worldcircuit.com, Touré had always been fond of his homeland, his native region and of his race.

Returning to the very basis of the conceptualization of blackness, but also twoness, in music, departing from a westernized classical perception on race, it is interesting to reflect on Montesquieu's rigid assessment of music, made in his famous *The Spirit of Laws*. He thought that music could not inspire virtue but could only have "prevented the effects of a savage institution" (Montesquieu 1989, 80). This shows how music was seen as an activity, among other human activities, which educated the soul; as harmony that would assist with this process. But harmony was not recognized, even after centuries, as a component of black music, since African music was marked by "seemingly endless repetition" (Edwards 1955, 707). It may be that this endless repetition, indeed, might have offered a source of this harmony in the music, if we recall that "repetitio est mater studiorum", a notion that was to envelope the discipline of becoming of the black soul. This discipline should have stayed with the process of becoming the metamorphosis from blackness to twoness. I shall return to this after exploring 'becoming' in the lyrics of Ali Farka Touré, and after clarifying the proposed limitations on old Blacks and new Whites, or the frontiers of blackness and otherness in the discourse of music.

On the subject of music, and differences between black and white music and comparisons between black and white, it is worth highlighting the pathological implications Frantz Fanon (1952, 176) saw in relation to defending one music against another in the early fifties. For Fanon, the black was not just black, but he was black in relation to a white man (Fanon 1952, 82-83), thus their music was black in relation to white music. The fact of blackness, in its importance for the soul of blacks, continues to exist, and no people of colour could escape from this. As long as white people have created and managed the rules of the game, they have been endorsed to produce social and psychological effects, for both sides of the divide.

Although Fanon's ideas marked the beginning of a sort of emancipation from negative meanings of black and blackness in the socio-political discourse of his times, emancipation being accentuated by the fact that African countries gained independence from the West, the production of an apologetic discourse on recognition, and the rediscovery of genius in the black race (Mbembe 2001, 12) are still relevant after four decades. Does this mean that the term of blackness as controlled by post-colonial thinkers for political ends, or that the notion of black could have remained the same until our own time, in essence and visibility? Has it been re-proposed in the same logic of balance of power and knowledge, in the confrontations of state forces, or the civilized-savage dichotomy?

Concerning postcolonial discourse as a "reading back" of colonial discourse (Miles and Brown 2004, 121), proposed by Mbembe, blackness is inherently a facet of the western polarization of identity-unity and nothingness, lack or non-being (Mbembe 2001, 4). And these are all the more suggestive for Africa, in its quality of region, but also of stereotype. Thus, even if black were not used in direct reference to the colour of the skin, it would still, due to many nuances in the territory's determinism, be a feature of the African, both in Fanon's reflections and Mbembe's assumptions. Moreover, blackness was a fact of the African world and to a certain extent, even the pride of it.

Applying a reductive logic to assertions about music and the fact of blackness in the works of thinkers and artists, black music was African music. Every attempt to change it accordingly, or adapt it to other realities than those of Africa (even from abroad), would be a becoming of music, an "Othering" of it, practiced by a "new white". And this would mean a new exaltation of twoness.

Ali Farka Touré and the problematizing of blackness

What can be understood in the music of Ali Farka Touré from the point of view of a holistic hermeneutics of sounds, rhythm and lyrics, is that, by contrast with its promotion of twoness, blackness is exalted. Touré was, first of all, fond of his homeland (*Mali, Timbuktu, Niafunké*), and he sang this fondness (*Mali Dje, Talking Timbuktu, Niafunké*). He was proud to talk about black people with Correy Harris, naming them Blacks, on purpose, in Martin Scorsese's documentary about the roots of the Blues ("Feels like being home").[2]

Trying to remake the history of the Blues, Martin Scorsese caught some ideas that Touré seemed happy to share at the time. These concern reflecting a belief in Blackness, Otherness and Twoness, refracted in the theory of the culture, and finally in the music. "There are no Black Americans. There are only Blacks in America" is the statement of Farka Touré. This statement shows how in the popular belief, blackness is functional over otherness.

From this perspective, the over-pursuit of otherness in the name of natural globalization may be criticized by pointing at the specialization in, and the essence of, different identities. One way of viewing this is to remember that Blacks have never become others, especially Americans. From another perspective, Blacks have never become westernized or "new whites", as we would call them in the logic of binary imaginaries. Because the Black has not become an *Other*, Touré intrinsically denies early discourses on the possibility that virtue and beauty could be the privilege of the whites (Fanon 1952, 31), since virtue and beauty may be sought and found, at least in their music. The reference is to African music which has, in this context, both virtue and beauty, highlighted by the harmony of characteristic repetitive sounds.

---

[2] See http://Blues.gr/video/martin-scorsese-presents-the. Access 23/06/2019.

Taking into account the fact that he produced his music with wider exposure on the American continent, Touré could have been influenced by the discourse of black unity sustained by W.E.B. Du Bois, who saw the fact of blackness as a consequence of black and white hatred, and the segregation specific to American society in the first fifty years of the twentieth century: "...both whites and blacks see commonly the worst of each other." (Hayes Edwards 2007, 113). However, Touré developed, in his discourse, a reversed logic of distinctions, placing everything on the mapping of a cultural history in which Africa had a relevant role. The Blacks have left their homeland–Africa–and it looked like they were not forced to do it. They left with their culture and became African Americans, who, returning to Africa, should not have felt strangers.

By omitting historical facts, Touré offers a strange justification to white hatred, that emerges from arguments relating to adaptation and cohabitation, which both still present contemporary difficulties. Another strange feature, which may evoke ideas of an over-simplification, is the idea that Americans should be whites and not blacks, so their music should be a white one. The image of an American Black would correspond, here, to an unconceivable Other; while the African American, whose traditions are questioned in the music, would be defined as the Other, as real and conceivable in American society. This is the main struggle of conceptualization, from the point of view of western culture; the sharing with others of humanity itself, as Mbembe puts it (Mbembe 2001, 2).

Seeing these aspects from a western perspective, admitting that reaffirming or defending one's ontology is natural, discourse on blackness–besides that about the negative ends of colonialism–would mean asserting the uniqueness and originality of black folk creations. A contrast with this neat separation, and the limits of possibility of the Other to be conceived (American Black or African), may be suggested. Black music after the fifties, like jazz, gospel, rhythm, and Blues, which all take inspiration from Africa, is an Othering of the music, as Touré explains in Scorsese's documentary. Despite many distinctions between the genres, in their performance and quality, they are all grounded in techniques and frameworks that stand for African-American traditions in music (Ramsey 2003, 3).

Touré declared his acknowledgment of this evidence of the melting of music, while describing the impact John Lee Hooker's music had had on him, considering comparisons between the two kinds of music. He recognized this melting, and later constructed his own concept of Otherness in music, but only after having clarified the tropes of African music. Ethnicity, legend and history, were all left behind by Blacks after their estrangement from the African land.

Besides, Touré was talking about difference, following the clichés of the period's discourse: black emancipation, globalization, rediscovery of Africa and its proposition to the world, together with the ideologies of otherness as opposed to blackness; the endeavours of black personality and African philosophy in the public space, following the outlines expressed by Valentin Mudimbe at the end of the eighties (Mudimbe 1988, 11). Therefore, Touré should be regarded as an African looking ahead, beyond the lines of demarcation of concepts such as colony and post-colony.

Ali Farka Touré on Africa in a positive perspective

Why this preoccupation of Touré, to recall to the world the fact of blackness in music? The reading of his words and the hermeneutics of some of his lyrics, reveal his insistence to see the fact of blackness as a fact of "Africa in a positive light"; in other words, a different track than had been proposed before in social studies. Blackness, from this perspective, would not be the support of Otherness when analysed in the American context, but the reason for twoness in itself. Because African culture was not a dead culture (Hountondji 2009), or a non-culture (where culture is seen as a set of representations and expressions of reality in literature, fine arts and values in social relations), it could not become Otherness, in relation to a cultural space without borders, that music would fill.

African-American music was widely considered the Otherness of music, from the point of view of the authentic African, and also as entirely traditional and inspirational music, which Touré himself also suggested. Furthermore, it represented the articulation of a "liberation struggle" from the mind's colonization (Wa Thiong'o 1986), as well as from the hegemony, racism and social oppression found on the American continent (Ramsey 2003, 24). Finally, the Otherness of African-American music itself would become a term empty of significance. Therefore, to define African-American music, twoness would be the appropriate descriptive fact. Twoness is shaped in the discourse of Touré when talking about similitudes and differences between African music and the music of John Lee Hooker.

In the monologue of Touré, framed by Scorsese, Africans only left their ethnicity, legends, and history. Not their souls nor, consequently, their music. I shall call ethnicity, legends and history features [of the fact] of Blackness. While remaining Blacks, the African Americans Touré refers to are those who should always return to Africa, to the roots of their twoness. They had not lost their consciousness nor their knowledge, that knowledge which was capable of leading to wisdom. The meta discursive appearance of the musician Ali Farka Touré, in the public sphere of Blues and Soul, is thus linked to the general opposition to concepts such as Europe, white and American as constituting the centre of the universe, recalling Wa Thiong'o's (1986, 17) problematization.

Since it contests, in some points, the metaphor of the white mask, which guided race and identity studies in Fanon's approach, the ideology Touré expressed about black and white is not explicit. However, it delivers sustenance to a tendency in African developmental philosophy, proposing as its final goal, as Hountondji (2009, 1) observed: "an autonomous, self-reliant process of knowledge production and capitalization that enables us to answer our own questions and meet both the intellectual and the material needs of African societies".

In other words, emphasis was placed on the black, as signifying a social object; and white, as an imposed image of becoming, for that object. The self-reliance noted by Hountondji was evident in Touré's gestures, in his affinity with the music and empathy with his public. It is sufficient to see the happiness on his face while explaining the origins of the Blues, for which the documentary should be endlessly seen and appreciated.

Analysing the lyrics of Ali Farka Touré

In some of Touré's lyrics, there is also a certain sorrow of the alienated, as in "Mali Dje" (1999). Alienation from land accompanies, probably, the becoming from black to white, which is considered, by African Africanists, the danger of the century. The motif is also present in the song "Savanne", from the posthumous album featuring Toumani Diabaté, of the same title. Here alienation is both reflected by leaving a territory ("j'ai quitté mon pays"–in my translation: "I have left my country") and by dissociation from something, probably the construed Otherness ("j'ai quitté ma Louisiane"–"I have left my Louisiane"). This could be the dissociation of being an Old Black, or African, and the becoming of a new white, in a process of assimilation during which the mask, theorized by Fanon, becomes an essence.

> J'ai quitté mon pays et ma LouisianeMais dans d'autres pays, adieu SavaneJ'ai trouvé le métro n'est pas un petit boulot
> Mais je suis, je suis un NègreJ'ai quitté un ami et ma LouisianeMais dans d'autres pays, adieu Savane.Au lieu de nous donner non seulement des bombesDonnez-nous des motopompes, pour qu'on puisse quand mêmesubvenir à nos besoins naturels
> Pour trouver la vie et le savoir et la sagesse.

The sorrow for a problematized metamorphosis from black to white is highlighted by the use of the term "*Adieu*", referring to the savannah, as a global trope and also to Africa, in another colonizing one. The alienation presented in this lyrical frame, which was sung by Touré in French in opposition to neo-colonizing powers, evokes both the fact of dependence reflected by the verb "to give" (*nous donner, donnez-nous*) and the self-victimization of the dominated (Mudimbe 1988, 106). In fact, the call of the dominated Self, one of Touré's heroes, is the demand for artefacts of development–"the automatic pumps" –suggesting the need for technological participation of the West in the progress of Africa, rather than military intervention.

Self-determination and self-reliance relate to the belief that needs might be responded to if the path to knowledge and wisdom were open and free from colonial obstacles. Touré is explicitly pamphleteering, considering reflection on needs as natural, in the context of the empowerment of the dominated ("pour qu'on puisse quand meme"/ to be able at least, anyway).

At this level, self-reliance comes to contrast with the idea of the insularity of the black man, paralleled with a concern about Africa's marginality (Mudimbe 1988), which Frantz Fanon expressed. The need to come out from insularity, as Fanon pictured it, was the cause of the black man wanting to become white (Fanon 1952, 36). Considering the tendency of the developmental discourse of the 1980s, containing post-colonialist elements, the idea of self-reliance and inclusion are the foundations of the basic need for development, as reflected by Duffield (2005, 152-53):

> Development interventions create enabling choices and opportunities for such entrepreneurs to prove themselves by bettering their individual and collective self-reliance

The same logic of development may be applied to the development in music, starting with the birth of African American, in a process of mixture and evolution of traditional African sounds. It started in the twenties, as the manifestation of a specific cultural revolution that was meant to attack, among other targets, any form of irrational attitude, mystification or exploitation, as expressed by politician Sékou Touré in the late seventies (De Jong and Rowlands 2007, 219). One of the practical aspects of this cultural revolution was represented by the introduction of a certain number of African instruments in churches during the Second World War, culminating during colonial rule, which allowed African artists to be highly prepared to play and use all types of instruments at a professional level (Bebey 1975, 16), as Ali Farka Touré did.

During his thirty years of artistic activity, Ali Farka Touré pursued the idea that a cultural revolution for his region and continent was possible through opposition to the exploitation of its image. It is recognised, as Ritchie Unterberger asserts on *allmusic.com*, that Touré's success in music–he was awarded a Grammy prize for Best World Music Album in 1994 for the album

Talking Timbuktu–could have been obtained even with non-western elements in it.

In the meantime, the concept of insularity, which Farka Touré embraced and pursued in his short lyrics in English or French, was producing the exact opposite effect, since the more Farka Touré kept African traditions alive in his music (for example, by the use of traditional instruments like *njarka, nkoni, cabasa*), thereby preserving the blackness of "old blacks", the more this music was becoming international. The paradox of Ali Farka Touré' s internationality gave him the voice to assert universal messages to young people in his nation and abroad (on the African continent).

As Ry Cooder, one of his most important colleagues noted, it was not difficult for Touré to be a good musician, as he had the rhythm inside and could express it as a form of striving to achieve the blackness of the "old blacks". This feature of rhythm could be specific to a majority of Africans, as has been suggested in literature on the music (Bebey 1975, 17). However, the confidence and willingness to share the music with everybody, and not just with an elite, were not such common features (Bebey 1975, 33), so the risks of segregation, which later became auto-segregation, were also clear with reference to black music.

But the non-elitist dimension of Farka Touré's music was sustained by his belief, simply expressed through his lyrics, that connections with the territory are the secret to self-sufficiency, peace and reliance. These three ideas helped him balance his after-art life as a farmer and as a mayor. Ideas about territory and self-sufficiency, as well as important theories on the specialization of the country, which have been discussed in terms of development studies, are present in the documentary of 2001 by Marc Huraux, "Le miel n'est jamais bon dans une seule bouche" (Honey is never good in one mouth),[3] which illustrates the still contemporary dangers of the conflict between neoliberal and socialist ideologies, but also the African ontology of Ubuntu with notions of common humanity.

Given the political dimension of musical discourses, and the fact that the words of Ali Farka Touré were, and still are, difficult to understand for many listeners in black culture, Blues seemed to be a natural option for accomplishing the aim of making ideas clear (Ramsey 2003, 46). Besides, the music of Farka Touré, like other black music, was very ethnocentric (Ramsey 2003, 39). But, ethnocentricity is a concept defined under white rules. Here is

---

[3] See Film-Documentaire. Online at http://www.film-documentaire.fr/4DACTION/w_fiche_film/8098_1, accessed 23/06/2019.

another motivation for considering this smooth slipping towards a twoness that would not contest white elements in its structure. On the contrary, this twoness contains the pride of being black, sustained by Africanists and also by a priest like Blyden,[4] who exclaimed: "Be yourselves... if you surrender your personality, you have nothing left to give the world" (see Wiredu 2004, 81). As a case in point, the lyrics of the song "Ai Du", from the album *Talking Timbuktu*, featuring Ry Cooder, propose these fragments of black advice on the path of self-reliance, deriving from the acknowledgment of Self and of Others, in the Ubuntu conception of one being defined and able to exist for the other: "trust and faith in your fellow man has no equal / If you have experienced trust you will know its strength / You must know yourself before you know others".

The facts of knowledge and its convergence in power, as postmodernist Michel Foucault pointed out in the *Archeology of Knowledge*, are also represented in songs about love, that Ali Farka Touré sang only in African languages (*Songhay, Fulfulde, Tamasheq* or *Bambara*). It is at this point that Touré's choice is a complex one, but he still wishes his words to be understood. As Bebey (1975, 122) noted, African music would not exist without African languages; hence, there is a need for the idea of musicality to be seen in reference to African words, too.

African music could not be written, but has a strong focus on words and their repetition, paralleled with the repetition of sounds, and seems to emerge from the inner being of the African (Edwards 1955). In this sense, a certain monotony, as well as other limitations, were considered by western critics as fundamentals of a black inferior slave's music. That blacks could have improved it only by accepting and copying the music of whites (McGuire 1986, 111) was the thesis that Touré could not accept. He kept the repetitions to assert the thirst for knowledge of the African (*Hawa Dolo, Hawa Ne–* What is your name? Where were you born?), as well as the love theme. A habitual character of the narrations is an angel, inspiring the artist and giving life to the dimension of uprightness in his music and his mission. On closer inspection, in the lyrics of Touré, there are no elements of the pain that Mbembe would have seen in postcolonial artefacts, for instance, in his *Critique of black reason* (Mbembe 2017). Rather, there are signs of phallic domination, strategic in power relationships (Mbembe 2001, 13), for example in *Ruby* or *Manakoide*.[5] This type of domination had also been described by

---

[4] See Wiredu 2004: 79-80.
[5] See, e.g. the lyrics of Manakoide at Paroles-Musiques.com. Online at https://www.paroles-musique.com/eng/Ali_Farka_Toure-Manakoide-lyrics,p09666076, accessed 23/06/2019.

Fanon long before, who saw it as a pure racial transgression, representing a rather dramatic turning point towards violence.

Meanwhile, the domination proposed by Farka Touré in his lyrics seemed to signify gentleness, through the tenacity of sounds which inspired, in 2002, *Unfaithful*, directed by Adrian Lyne (with Diane Lane and Richard Gere), which featured western memes fully compatible with "Ai Du".

Conclusion and further discussions

It might be concluded, then, after the holistic but reductive discourse proposed in this chapter, that the tokens of Ali Farka Touré's songs are the elements suggesting the African coming out of the nothingness envisaged by Mbembe (2001, 4) in actual discourse. The coming out is assured through the love for the territory that he showed in real life, as well as in that of fiction or poetry, but also through his stubborn resistance in an international environment, representing a nation that was and continues to be highly depreciated under a western lens. The main concern of the Malian guitarist is to express, through music, his opposition to wrong assessments of Mali; by soft means, sustaining nationalism and ethnicity, which diverge from the more general discourses on the roots of the music in America, and the inspiration of Blacks.

Although named new blacks in North America, listening to Farka Touré's music, along with reflecting on his explanations, brings to mind a more important fact to note about new blacks. The musician would prefer them to be old, in the imaginary of an African dialectics, so that experience and history are regained after a long-lasting colonial period. In the meantime, there is an entrenched argument of new whites, whose identities are constructed in the context of the North American or European melting pot. The race discourse ends, however, in the territorial and cultural definitions of twoness, as opposed to the otherness and continuation of the fact of blackness.

In any of the ways it is possible to see the music of Ali Farka Touré, or however many clues we may have on the hermeneutics of his texts, it is clear that his experiences abroad occasioned in the musician a more traditional approach to race. Questioning colour in the context of insularity, spatiality and marginality, putting emphasis on the Other, is a proof of political visibility in arts, but also one of a re-proposed fact of blackness. The black and the white are still subjects of a suggestive division in music and arts. Their confusion would be temporary, at least, but would be the basis of a hypothesis on whiteness, under the mask of blackness. For this reason, the message of Ali

Farka Touré seems to be a continuation of the message Frantz Fanon prepared for his black people in order to make them react to the colonial concept.

Instead of playing with the masks, putting them on, removing them, like Fanon, Ali Farka Touré adapts his methodologies to his times, using the message to create music. That is why ideas on race, African individuality and the fact of blackness are slightly slipping backwards, from twoness, the very modern way of contextualizing otherness, to blackness, the very old fact of the black race, revalued in the logic of the global village. The music of Touré is, thus, deconstructive and simple, to the point that it can be a black or a white music in the meantime, if we would still admit any distinction.

P.S. Special thanks to Henry Marshall from the press office of Vieux Farka Touré for the given hints.

References

Bebey, Francis. 1975. *African Music. A People's Art.* Chicago: Lawrence Hill Books.

De Jong, Ferdinand, and Rowlands, Michael. 2007. *Reclaiming Heritage. Alternative Imaginaries of Memory in West Africa.* Walnut Creek: Left Coast Press.

Duffield, Mark. 2005. "Getting Savages to Fight Barbarians: Development, Security and the Colonial Present." *Conflict, Security and Development* 5 (2), 141-159.

Edwards, Hylton S. 1955. "Music in Africa." *Journal of the Royal Society of Arts* 103: 4958, 704-712.

Fanon, Frantz. 1952. *Black Skin, White Masks.* Pluto Press. Accessed 14 June 2019. http://abahlali.org/files/__Black_Skin__White_Masks__Pluto_Classics_.pdf.

Hayes Edwards, Brent (ed.). 2007. *W.E.B. Du Bois. The Souls of Black Folk.* Oxford: Oxford University Press.

Hountondji, Paulin J. 2009. "Knowledge of Africa, Knowledge by Africans: Two Perspectives on African Studies." African Centre for Advanced Studies, Benin, *RCCS Annual Review* 1, 1-11.

Mbembe, Achille. 2001. *On the Postcolony.* Berkeley, Los Angeles and London: University of California Press.

Mbembe, Achille. 2017. *The Critique of Black Reason.* Durham: Duke University Press.

McGuire, Phillip 1986. "Black Music Critics and the Classic Blues Singers". *The Black Perspective in Music* 14(2), 103-125. Online at http://www.jstor.org/stable/1214982. Accessed 22 June 2014.

Miles, Robert, and Brown, Malcolm. 2004. *Racism.* Second Edition. New York: Taylor and Francis.

Montesquieu, Charles Louis de Secondat de. 1989. "The Spirit of Laws." In *Cambridge Texts in the History of Political Thought*, edited by Anne M. Cohler, Carolyn Miller Basia, and Harold S. Stone, 1-757. Cambridge: Cambridge University Press.

Mudimbe, V.Y. 1988. *The Invention of Africa. Gnosis, Philosophy and the Order of Knowledge.* Bloomington and Indianapolis: Indiana University Press.

Ramsey, Guthrie P. 2003. *Race music. Black Cultures from Bebop to Hip-hop.* Berkeley, Los Angeles and London: University of California Press.

Wa Thiong'o, Ngugi. 1986. *Decolonizing the Mind. The Politics of Language in African Literature.* Harare: Zimbabwe Publishing House.

Wiredu, Kwasi. 2004. *A Companion to African Philosophy.* Malden and Oxford: Blackwell Publishing.

Web references

All Music. https://www.allmusic.com/. Last access 14/06/2019.

Jas Obrecht Music Archive. http://jasobrecht.com/ry-cooder-ali-farka-toure-interview/. Last access 14/06/2019.

4.

Hendrix's "Machine Gun" and the limitations of Blues performance

Daniel Lieberfeld

Duquesne University, USA

In 1967, Jimi Hendrix, asked what kind of music he was playing, replied, "Blues, man. Blues. For me that's the only music there is" (Waldrop 2012, 20). That Hendrix based his music on Blues is confirmed by those who knew him best: Kathy Etchingham, who lived with Hendrix for two years, declared, "That guy was a Bluesman. That's where his heart really lay. Anybody who tells me he would have become a jazz musician—well, balls to them… What he really liked, and what he really played at home, was Blues" (Obrecht 2018, 70). Billy Cox, Hendrix's bassist in the Band of Gypsys and perhaps his closest friend, assessed, "You can call Jimi Hendrix whatever you like, but he was a Blues master…. A hell of a Bluesman" (Obrecht 2018, 30).

Hendrix was, beyond doubt, a hell of a Bluesman. His relationship to Blues, though, was nuanced: he rejected the "Bluesman" label, with its attendant limitations on audience size and record sales. His playing synthesized a range of musical styles beyond Blues, including R&B, rock and roll, folk, avant-garde jazz, comedy records, and orchestral compositions (c.f., his studio version of "The Star Spangled Banner").

Hendrix's conception of Blues was broad, extending well beyond the standard harmonic structures, rhythms, and lyrical subject matter of the genre. Besides Blues, he noted, "I like a lot of other things too—that's why we try to do our own stuff, make something new" (Barker 2012b, 63). His eclectic tastes and awareness of the commercial and artistic limitations that straight Blues imposed gave him a dual relationship with Blues: he felt drawn to the "deep" Blues of the artists born in Mississippi between 1910 and 1920—especially Howling' Wolf, Muddy Waters, Elmore James, and John Lee Hooker. On the other hand, he stretched the formal and conceptual limits of Blues performance, foregrounding, for example, electronic sound elements to an extent previously unheard in Blues music.

To resolve the tension between keeping close to the deep Blues, but not so close as to be constraining, Hendrix rooted his music in Blues while often stretching the genre's harmonic structures, rhythms, sonic elements and lyric themes. His compositions were often Blues based, but innovative and unbounded by Blues conventions. As Cox observed, "Jimi's love of low-down Blues was evident in 'Red House.' His other Blues was kind of disguised, because he revolutionized Blues. He took it to another level" (Obrecht 2018, 74).

While writers on Hendrix often refer to him as a Blues musician, I have found no detailed, specific discussions of Hendrix's re-imagination of Blues forms or of how Hendrix's relationship to Blues compared with that of his musical contemporaries. Here, using cultural-historical and music-theoretical perspectives, I consider the Blues that Jimi Hendrix composed—the relatively rare, traditional 12-bar forms, the more frequent altered forms that Cox calls "disguised" Blues, and Hendrix's cover versions of others' Blues compositions. To illustrate Hendrix's departures from other Blues musicians, I identify elements of traditional, deep Blues in his 1969 work "Machine Gun" alongside elements of the composition that reflect Hendrix's alterations and expansions of generic Blues.[1] I also compare Hendrix's "Machine Gun" with work by more traditional Blues artists that likewise references the Vietnam war.   The methodology in these sections draws on ethnomusicology and textual analysis.

I begin by exploring how Hendrix's life circumstances and influences differed from those of other Blues artists, how he saw the Blues genre in relation to his music, and how he used "straight" and altered Blues in his compositions.[2]

---

[1] This is the version of "Machine Gun" recorded at the Fillmore East, January 1, 1970, that appears on Hendrix's *Band of Gypsys* album. The DVD *Band of Gypsys: Live at the Fillmore East* (Experience Hendrix, 1999) includes black-and-white video of the complete performance of this definitive version of "Machine Gun."

[2] The chapter's musical references are to Hendrix's official recorded output during his lifetime, tracks on the 4 LPs Hendrix released from 1967-1970 (along with the compilation LP *Smash Hits*). Aside from the half-dozen or so nearly finished recordings that appeared on the posthumous *Cry of Love* and *Rainbow Bridge* releases, posthumously released studio recordings were taken from jam sessions and compositions-in-process. Since Hendrix never intended this material's release—including what appears on the 1994 compilation *Blues*, aside from "Red House"—I mainly leave it out of the analysis. For producer Alan Douglas' role in various posthumous releases, see John McDermott.1992. *Hendrix: Setting the Record Straight.* New York: Warner. 309-323.

Blues in Hendrix's Musical Development

Hendrix's personal history is atypical of the artists who helped create electrified, urban Blues after WWII. He was born in 1942, between the earlier generation of Blues artists like Buddy Guy, Otis Rush, and Albert Collins, who were born in the mid-1930s, and the generation born in the late 1940s and early 1950s that includes Joe Louis Walker, Robert Cray, and Keb' Mo'.

Hendrix's African-American contemporaries did not often become Blues artists. More typically, the musicians among them gravitated to Soul and R&B—e.g., Smokey Robinson (b. 1940), Otis Redding and Wilson Pickett (b. 1941), and Curtis Mayfield and Aretha Franklin (b. 1942, like Hendrix). On the other hand, relatively many of Hendrix's white contemporaries did become Blues artists—including Lonnie Mack and Steve Cropper (b. 1941); Paul Butterfield, Elvin Bishop, Charlie Musselwhite, and John Hammond, Jr. (b. 1942); Mike Bloomfield, Jim Morrison, Janis Joplin, Steve Miller, and Alan Wilson, (b. 1943); and Johnny Winter (b. 1944). In Britain as well, members of Hendrix's generational cohort were at the forefront of the Blues and rock scenes: Eric Burdon (b. 1941), Paul McCartney (b. 1942), Mick Jagger and Keith Richards (b. 1943), Jeff Beck and Jimmy Page (b. 1944), and Pete Townshend, Rod Stewart, Eric Clapton, and Van Morrison (b. 1945).

Aside from Hendrix, perhaps the most notable exception to the trend of African-American musicians born in the early1940s favouring R&B over Blues was Taj Mahal (born Henry St. Claire Fredericks, Jr. in 1942), who, like Hendrix, grew up in ethnically diverse urban environments. In 1964, he formed one of the earlier racially integrated Blues bands, The Rising Sons, with Ry Cooder. Hendrix's family identity, like Taj Mahal's, was multi-ethnic, involving black, white, and Cherokee ancestry. Hendrix's father was from Vancouver, Canada. In Hendrix's classes in Seattle's Central School District were Native American, Italian, German, Jewish, Chinese, Filipino, and Japanese students—a diversity nearly unimaginable in the southern United States in the 1940s and 1950s.

Hendrix also absorbed a wider range of musical influences than did most Blues musicians. His early exposure to Blues came from the record collections of his father and of Ernestine Benson—a member of the Hendrix household who encouraged Jimi's guitar playing. In the mid-1950s, when he was 12 or 13, Hendrix heard recordings of the great Blues artists—Muddy Waters, Lightnin' Hopkins, Robert Johnson, Bessie Smith, and Howling' Wolf. "I loved my Blues," Benson recalled, "and Jimi loved that same down-home stuff" (Cross 2005, 51-52).

The early Blues influences characterized Hendrix's music. Blues guitarist Mike Bloomfield considered Hendrix the blackest guitarist I ever heard. His music was deeply rooted in pre-Blues, the oldest musical forms like field hollers and gospel melodies. From what I can garner, there was no form of black music that he hadn't listened to or studied, but he especially loved the real old black music forms, and they poured out in his playing. We often talked about Son House and the old Blues guys. But what really did it to him was early Muddy Waters and John Lee Hooker records, that early electric music where the guitar was hugely amplified and boosted by the studio to give it the effect of more presence than it really had. He knew that stuff backwards. You can hear every old John Lee Hooker and Muddy Waters thing that ever was on that one long version of "Voodoo Chile" [on *Electric Ladyland*]. (Bloomfield 1975).

At the same time, the urban, multi-cultural environment of his childhood afforded Hendrix musical diversity: his first bands played R&B and rock. He admired Chuck Berry, Eddie Cochran, and Buddy Holly, the sophisticated jazz and R&B guitarist Billy Butler and, locally, the Fabulous Wailers—who played Ventures-like proto-garage-rock around Seattle (Gossert 2012, 138).

At age 19, as an Army paratrooper, Hendrix moved to Ft. Campbell, Kentucky, near Nashville, where his musical focus became R&B and Blues. After leaving the military, he formed a band with Billy Cox but mainly made a living as a guitarist and occasional music director for an array of R&B stars touring the black clubs of the Southeast and Midwest on the "chitlin' circuit."

In an interview from early 1967, Hendrix implied that his identification with Blues deepened in this period: "When I came out [of the Army] I went down South and all the cats down there were playing Blues, and this is when I really began to get interested in the scene" (Barker 2012a, 6). His apprenticeship with first-rank R&B performers lasted nearly four years. This and Hendrix's childhood/family roots in Blues set him apart from most of his white Blues-player contemporaries.

In 1964, Hendrix moved to New York City, where his interest in cutting-edge sounds and ideas took him to Greenwich Village. He absorbed music from jazz avant-gardists Charles Mingus and Rahsaan Roland Kirk, comedy-act material, and experimental music that he would later use on recordings like "Third Stone From the Sun" and "EXP." In New York, Hendrix also became aware of new possibilities that Bob Dylan had opened for pop lyrics and vocals.

In sum, by the time he formed the Experience in 1966, Hendrix's musical direction reflected the music he had absorbed in culturally diverse American cities: rock influences in Seattle, Blues and R&B around Nashville and on the chitlin' circuit, and the experimental and folk-rock scenes of New York City. Hendrix's musical influences and interests were thus considerably wider than those of most Blues artists, black or white.

In the early and mid-1960s, Britain was more Blues-aware than was America— particularly regarding deep, Delta-style Blues—and more appreciative of guitar virtuosity. The UK music scene's orientation toward Blues and toward guitar-heroism perhaps explains why Hendrix was discovered in mid-1966 by Blues devotee Linda Keith and bassist-producer Chas Chandler, two British visitors to New York. Hendrix's chitlin'-circuit exhibitionism was also well received in England, where audiences had only had hints of such physically free showmanship during tours by Chuck Berry and T-Bone Walker. Within two years, Hendrix soared to the top of the US and UK rock scene, becoming, "outside of the Beatles, the most sought after attraction in the business" (McDermott 1992, 134).

Blues in Hendrix's Recordings and Performances

An exclusive focus on Blues was incompatible with Hendrix's expansive taste and searching artistic vision. Bloomfield, who called Hendrix "an unparalleled Blues guitarist," recalled Hendrix saying that "he found playing Blues boring" (Bloomfield 1975). Hendrix may have meant that a whole evening of playing straight-ahead Blues got boring. In England, in any case, Hendrix did not seek out backing musicians who were primarily Blues oriented, instead picking ones whose musical leanings complemented his own. Explaining why he chose bandmates Mitch Mitchell and Noel Redding—whom Hendrix described as being into, respectively, jazz and rock—he noted, "If I'd had two Blues men with me we would have gone straight into one bag, the Blues. That's not for me. This way we can do anything and develop our own music.... We'll do things our own way and make our own sound" (Swift 2012, 14). "Critics are already classifying us," he complained, asking them to "understand that we are not always in the same bag with each performance. How can you be when you are constantly reaching, improvising, experimenting? It's impossible" (Garcia 2012, 51).

Nor could the Blues genre alone easily accommodate Hendrix's extensive use of amplifier feedback as a musical element. Hendrix's sonic manipulations went far beyond what earlier Blues guitarists—who had typically learned on acoustic instruments and only switched to electric ones after establishing themselves as adult performers in urban settings—had incorporated into their music.[3]

---

[3] Hendrix played electric guitar from age 16. Even before going to England, he was using amplifier feedback to astonishing effect. Bloomfield recalled Hendrix performing in 1966 in New York: "H-bombs were going off, guided missiles were flying—I can't tell you the sounds he was getting out of his instrument. He was getting every sound I was ever to hear him get right there in that room with a Stratocaster, a Twin [amplifier], a Maestro fuzz [pedal], and that was all—he was doing it mainly through extreme volume. How he did this, I wish I understood" (Bloomfield 1975).

Hendrix had also "starved to death" playing Blues in New York and knew the market for Blues was limited (Burling 1967). One of his musical collaborators, Paul Caruso, believed Hendrix "wanted to be a rock star. He didn't want to be a struggling Blues artist drinking gin in these little clubs" (Smeaton 2013).

Nevertheless, Hendrix always included Blues in live performances and on his records. Besides his own Blues compositions, Hendrix's concerts often included covers of well-known Blues hits by earlier performers, including "Catfish Blues" (i.e., Muddy Waters' "Rollin' Stone"), Elmore James' "Bleeding Heart," Howling' Wolf's "Killing Floor" and B.B. King's version of "Rock Me Baby."[4] Hendrix kicked off the Experience's first US appearance, at the 1967 Monterrey Pop Festival, with blazingly up-tempo versions of the latter two songs. By Hendrix's last performances, he still featured Blues prominently: at the Atlanta Pop Festival in July, 1970, for example, Hendrix devoted around one-third of his 16-song performance to his original Blues compositions.[5]

Table 4.1: Hendrix's original Blues compositions and covers

JH composed 12-bar Blues	JH composed altered Blues	Blues covers
Released in JH lifetime Red House	Released in JH lifetime Stone Free; Can You See Me; Manic Depression; I Don't Live Today; If 6 Was 9; Up From the Skies; Voodoo Chile; Voodoo Chile (Slight Return); Rainy Day, Dream Away; Machine Gun	Released in JH lifetime Come On (Pts. 1 & 2) (E. King)
Unreleased in JH lifetime Lover Man; Izabella; Once I Had a Woman; various unreleased jams (e.g. "Jam 292")	Unreleased in JH lifetime Hear My Train a-Comin'; Belly Button Window; My Friend; Room Full of Mirrors; Midnight Lightning; Stepping Stone; Come Down Hard on Me Baby; etc.	Unreleased in JH lifetime Killing Floor (H. Wolf); "Catfish Blues"/Rollin' Stone (M. Waters); Rock Me Baby (B.B. King, etc.); Bleeding Heart (E. James); Hoochie Coochie Man (W. Dixon); other Blues standards at jam sessions, e.g., "The Things that I Used to Do"; "Hound Dog"; instrumental Blues, e.g., "Drivin' South"

---

[4] The sole Blues cover that Hendrix officially released was Earl King's "Come On (parts 1 and 2)."

[5] This fairly typical set included "Lover Man," "Red House," "Hear My Train a Comin'," "Room Full of Mirrors," "Stone Free," and "Voodoo Chile (Slight Return)."

In considering Hendrix's original Blues compositions, one can differentiate between those that adhere to a standard 12-bar Blues form and those that alter standard Blues forms. The sole standard 12-bar composition that Hendrix released in his lifetime is "Red House" (Table 4.1).[6]

Hendrix's other Blues are those Cox calls "disguised." These compositions qualify as Blues by virtue of having a Blues tonality, harmonic features typical of Blues (such as a change from the tonic to the sub-dominant chord in bar 5, and, often, an "AAB" lyric format typical of Blues, in which the second line repeats the first and the third line "answers" the first two). Hendrix's first composition with the Experience, "Stone Free," is a Blues with an altered structure. "Can You See Me," "Manic Depression," and "I Don't Live Today," on *Are You Experienced?*, Hendrix's debut album, is also altered Blues. On the follow-up, *Axis: Bold as Love*, altered Blues include "If 6 Was 9" and "Up from the Skies." Hendrix's original Blues on *Electric Ladyland* include "Voodoo Chile" and "Voodoo Chile (Slight Return)". While compositions such as "Manic Depression" and "If 6 was 9" are more "disguised," Hendrix himself called them "contemporary Blues," stating, for example, "We do this Blues one on [*Axis*] ... called 'If 6 Was 9.' That's what you call a great feeling of Blues" (Ruby 2012, 91).[7]

Hendrix also called his cover version of "Hey Joe" a "Blues version of a ... cowboy song" (Waldrop 2012, 20). His comment is eye-opening, in that the song's harmonic structure follows the major-key cycle of fifths, rather than a Blues form. On the other hand, "Hey Joe" has the AAB lyric form typical of the Blues and an overall tonality that can be considered Blues. While the status of "Hey Joe" as a Blues may be arguable, Hendrix's conception of the Blues genre was clearly expansive, not restrictive.

By self-consciously modernizing Blues, Hendrix was actualizing a core concept of African-American music production: taking something from the past and making it relevant to the present. In this respect, Hendrix belongs in the company of Afro-modernists like Duke Ellington, Miles Davis, and Yusef Lateef.[8]

---

[6] Hendrix also frequently performed his 12-bar-Blues compositions "Lover Man" and "Izabella." The posthumous release "Once I Had A Woman" is also a 12-bar. The filmed performance of "Hear My Train a Comin'" in London in December, 1967, on 12-string acoustic guitar indicates how Hendrix sounded playing traditional Blues.

[7] Several other Hendrix compositions that were not officially released in lifetime were altered Blues, notably, "Hear My Train a Comin'," My Friend," "Belly Button Window," "Room Full of Mirrors," "Come Down Hard on Me," "Look over Yonder" and "Stepping Stone" (Table 1).

[8] Personal communication (2019) with Dr. Kenan Foley, who inspired this chapter and generously shared his insights.

"Machine Gun" and Blues on the Vietnam War

Hendrix's performance of "Machine Gun" illustrates his foundational reliance on Blues traditions, as well as his radical departures. The performance on the *Band of Gypsys* album is among Hendrix's most ambitious works.[9] He formed the Band of Gypsys—a trio, with Cox on bass and Buddy Miles on drums and vocals—in October, 1969, after disbanding the Experience and headlining the Woodstock Festival backed by a temporary group. Interviewed about his vision for the new group, Hendrix replied, "I want to get back to the Blues, because that's what I am" (Cross 2005, 289).

"Machine Gun" is the most evidently Blues derived song on *Band of Gypsys*. For Buddy Miles, the composition's relationship to Blues was unambiguous: "'Machine Gun' is taken from a style called 'Delta Blues,'" Miles commented. "It was most definitely from the Deep South" (Smeaton 2013). The form is a one-chord Blues in the key of D minor.[10]

At New York's Fillmore East auditorium on January 1, 1970, Hendrix dedicated the recently composed "Machine Gun" "to all the soldiers fighting in Chicago and Milwaukee and New York. Oh yes, and all the soldiers fighting in Vietnam"—a dedication inclusive of anti-war protestors and demonstrators for racial justice, as well as soldiers at war.

Hendrix's father had served in the Pacific in World War II while Jimi was an infant and Hendrix and Billy Cox both served in the Army's 101st Airborne Division. Hendrix knew "he might have been stationed [in Vietnam] if he had not left the service" (Cross 2005, 215). Hendrix appears to have been anti-war, but not anti-soldier or even anti-military. He was apolitical in the sense that "he would articulate universal, rather than specific solutions… While a great number of his fans opposed the war in Vietnam, Hendrix struggled with the human toll of war, casting the politics aside" (McDermott, 1995, 132-33).

The guitar and bass begin "Machine Gun" with a melody based on the Blues scale (emphasizing the flatted third, fifth, and seventh notes of the major scale). At 0:49, drums appear with a staccato burst imitating machine-gun fire.

---

[9] "Machine Gun" is the third longest among the recordings Hendrix released in his lifetime, after "Voodoo Chile" and "1983… (A Merman I Should Turn to Be)"—both on *Electric Ladyland*. While Hendrix's performances of "Machine Gun" varied in their length, lyrics, and form, the version he officially released can be taken as representative.
[10] Hendrix had previously covered Blues that stay on the tonic chord, such as Willie Dixon's "Hoochie Coochie Man" and Muddy Waters' "Mannish Boy" and "Rollin' Stone" (the latter has a brief bridge to the subdominant and dominant, but otherwise stays on the tonic chord).

The rhythmic bursts alternate with a slow shuffle rhythm. At 1:04, Hendrix plays an introductory solo that inflects Blues with small amounts of feedback and uses microtonal bends reminiscent of Indian music to evoke Asia alongside the Mississippi Delta.[11] At 1:44, Hendrix begins singing, doubling his vocal line on guitar. The Bluesy melisma of the vocal-guitar unison imparts a feeling of barely controlled anguish.

This main section has 16 bars per verse—sung verses of 12 bars, separated by 4-bar instrumental breaks. In the verses, Miles alternates a steady backbeat with his machine-gun rhythm (the latter in odd-numbered measures). After the first three verses, Hendrix launches a second, much longer guitar solo, at 03:58, with 12 seconds of sustain on what some consider the most expressive note ever played on an electric guitar.[12]

After the extended, four-and-a-half-minute solo, Hendrix sings the fourth verse ("I ain't afraid no more…") at 7:37, accompanied by haunting, wordless background vocals by Cox and Miles. Hendrix's third solo, at 8:40, conjures bombs, rockets, and alarms against the ongoing background vocals by Miles and Cox. The machine-gun riff returns and Miles takes over the lead vocal ("Don't you shoot him down") at 9:49.

Hendrix plays a fourth solo, at 10:30, that is soft and eerie, with sparse drum accompaniment. He unleashes a final 30-second frenzy of bombs, rockets, and gunfire at 11:40 and finishes at 12:14, telling the audience, "Yeah, that's what we don't want to hear anymore."

"Machine Gun" deploys familiar elements of Blues performance: its melody derives directly from the Blues scale and Hendrix uses traditional Blues devices, such as doubling his lead vocal with the guitar. His use of electronic effects to reinforce the lyrics—for example, the gunfire sounds that follow the lyric "so let your bullets fly like rain"—recalls the use of bottleneck-slide glissandos to accompany the lyric line "Can't you hear the wind howl?" in Delta Bluesman Robert Johnson's "Come on in My Kitchen." For musicologist Francis Bebey (1975, 115), African music seeks to "translate lived experience into living sound". "Machine Gun" extends this tradition.

---

[11] Ry Cooder, noting the pervasiveness of microtonal nuances in Muddy Waters' guitar playing, assesses him as fundamentally "Oriental in his approach" (Obrecht 2000, 105).

[12] For Phish guitarist Trey Anastasio, "Not only is 'Machine Gun' my favorite guitar solo of all time, but it also includes … the greatest single note ever played on electric guitar: the high screaming note Jimi plays right at the beginning of his solo. That hanging note is the deepest, most intense note I've ever heard" (Guitar World 2002: 190-91. See also Ratliff 201, 154). Miles Davis, asked what he heard in Hendrix's music, pungently responded, "It's that goddamned motherfucking 'Machine Gun'" (Cross 2005, 286).

The song's lyrics, though not in AAB form, repeat the first line of most verses in a Blues-like manner. The lyric content is also Bluesy in that it describes a lone protagonist trying to persevere through a bad situation. The Blues is a culture and an attitude, as well as a song form and a musical genre. It enacts perseverance and resilience in the face of the precarious life of itinerant African-American musicians in a white-supremacist society. The assertive self-affirmation, defiance, and one-upmanship ("I ain't afraid no more... Your cheap talk don't cause me pain") exemplifies this aspect of Blues culture.[13]

However, "Machine Gun" pushes far beyond traditional Blues. For musician and critic Vernon Reid, "Machine Gun" is "like a movie about war without the visuals. It had everything—the lyrics, the humanism of it, the drama of it, the violence of it, the eeriness of it, [and] the unpredictability of it" (Milkowski 2001). The sonic environment, the multiple sections within the extended performance, and the narrative perspectives in Hendrix's lyrics, all contribute to the song's multidimensional, quasi-cinematic quality.

Hendrix sings the first four verses from a first-person perspective seemingly addressed to the machine gun itself, or what it represents—death and the war machine. That perspective shifts when Buddy Miles narrates the final verse in the third person ("He's been shot down to the ground... He ain't going nowhere").[14]

The lyrics are "finger pointing," somewhat in the manner of Dylan's "Masters of War": Hendrix blames "evil men" for making the fighters on the battlefield kill one another, "even though we're only families apart," and warns that the violence will come back to hurt those responsible. "Machine Gun" may be the only Blues to imagine the Vietnam War from the perspective of an American, or perhaps Vietnamese, battlefield soldier—the protagonist has no national identity.

---

[13] As Hendrix commented in a 1968 interview, "Do you remember how Muddy Waters used to get into 'Hoochie Coochie Man'? Like what they called the black Blues then, it was bringing the black person up higher ... encouragement ... just like you have Ulysses and all the mythological-type things" (Gossert 2012, 139).

[14] This shift resembles the final chapter of Erich Maria Remarque's World War I novel, *All Quiet on the Western Front*, in which the narrative perspective changes from first person to third person to describe the protagonist's death. While several Blues songs conjure a dying or desperate protagonist, few, if any, end with an image of a dead one. The last line of Johnson's "Crossroads" ("I believe I'm sinkin' down"), for example, conveys the protagonist's desperation, but not his death. Hendrix, in a previous song, "Wait Until Tomorrow," does have the protagonist narrate his own death.

With his instrument, Hendrix paints a sonic portrait of modern warfare and killing machinery: tracer bullets, bombs, jets and helicopters, radio communications, and wounded and dying soldiers—while maintaining the music's tonality. Other Blues artists created wailing amplified sounds, but no comparable sonic intensity and certainly no such explosive, eerie, anguished evocation of war.

The structure of "Machine Gun" may also be linked to African-American sermonic traditions: in the manner of a preacher, Hendrix announces the general topic to the audience, sets out the lyric and musical themes that recur through the piece and goes through several rounds of improvised departures from, and restatements of, the theme—each improvisation progressively more spontaneous and far-ranging. But where an African-American church service might typically end with singers and musicians combining for a joyful climax, there is, in Hendrix's performance, a kind of recession, disappearance and, finally, silence following the last sound barrage.

At least 24 Blues recordings from the mid-1960s to early 1970s reference the Vietnam war. Several use the war to highlight the lack of civil rights for African-Americans (e.g., J.B. Lenoir's "Everybody Crying about Vietnam" and Champion Jack Dupree's "Vietnam Blues"). In other Blues, the war is ancillary to traditional Blues themes—for example, the singer is in love with a woman whose husband is serving in Vietnam (Lightnin' Hopkins' "Please Settle in Vietnam").[15] These Vietnam-Blues recordings are musically generic.

"Machine Gun" is different. It imagines the soldier's experience on the battlefield and universalizes that experience. The word "Vietnam" does not appear in the song—only Hendrix's spoken introduction mentions it. Hendrix's is a fully realized work of art specific to the time that inspired it, yet evoking transcendent themes, such as resilience in face of fear.

The commonplace portrayal of Hendrix as having simply dressed up the Blues with psychedelic trappings is misleading: as a composer and performer, Hendrix was an innovator with a core foundation in the aesthetics of African derived music. His use of the Blues indicates one possibility for transcending the limitations of Blues performance and one way of making Blues relevant to contemporary audiences. Hendrix's presumptively unique qualities—childhood connections to the Blues; apprenticeship with members of the founding generation of rock and R&B; musical virtuosity; compositional and lyrical mastery; and openness to innovation and the avant-garde—indicate that his

---

[15] A list of Blues songs that mention Vietnam can be found at
https://rateyourmusic.com/list/JBrummer/vietnam-war-the-Blues.

particular solution to the limitations of Blues performance is likely non-replicable. Yet Hendrix's example also shows that the possibilities of Blues performance are unlimited. He challenges musicians to discover other pathways to keeping this profound, powerful music creative and vital.

References

Barker, Steve. 2012a. "Jimi Hendrix talks to Steve Barker." In *Hendrix on Hendrix: Interviews and Encounters with Jimi Hendrix,* edited by Steven Roby, 5-10. Chicago: Chicago Review Press.

Barker, Steve. 2012b. "Jimi Hendrix talks to Steve Barker." In *Hendrix on Hendrix: Interviews and Encounters with Jimi Hendrix,* edited by Steven Roby, 61-70. Chicago: Chicago Review Press.

Bebey, Francis. 1975. *African Music: a People's Art.* Chicago: Lawrence Hill.

Bloomfield, Michael. 1975. "Michael Bloomfield Reminisces." *Guitar Player,* September. Accessed 21 February 2019. http://crosstowntorrents.org/archive/index.php/t-961.html.

Burling, Klas. 1967. Hendrix interview, 25 May. Accessed 21 February 2019. http://www.earlyhendrix.com/timeline-menu.

Cross, Charles. 2005. *Room Full of Mirrors: a Biography of Jimi Hendrix.* Paris: Hachette.

Garcia, Bob. 2012. "Our Experience with Jimi." *Open City,* 24-30 August 1967. In *Hendrix on Hendrix: Interviews and Encounters with Jimi Hendrix,* edited by Steven Roby, 49-54. Chicago: Chicago Review Press.

Gossert, Gus. 2012. "Interview with Gus Gossert." 1968. In *Hendrix on Hendrix: Interviews and Encounters with Jimi Hendrix,* edited by Steven Roby, 137-140. Chicago: Chicago Review Press.

Guitar World. 2002. Guitar World Presents the 100 Greatest Guitarists of All Time. Milwaukee: Hal Leonard Corp.

McDermott, John. 1992. *Hendrix: Setting the Record Straight.* New York: Warner Books.

Milkowski, Bill. 2001. "Jimi Hendrix: Modern Jazz Axis." *Jazz Times,* 1 July. Accessed 21 February 2019. https://jazztimes.com/features/jimi-hendrix-modern-jazz-axis/.

Obrecht, Jas, ed. 2000. *Rollin' and Tumblin': the Postwar Blues Guitarists.* San Francisco: Miller Freeman Books.

Obrecht, Jas. 2018. *Stone Free: Jimi Hendrix in London, September 1966–June 1967.* Chapel Hill: University of North Carolina Press.

Ratliff, Ben. 2017. *Every Song Ever: Twenty Ways to Listen in an Age of Musical Plenty.* New York: Picador.

Ruby, Jay. 2012. "Interview with Jimi Hendrix." *Jazz and Pop,* July 1968. In *Hendrix on Hendrix: Interviews and Encounters with Jimi Hendrix,* edited by Steven Roby, 87-96. Chicago: Chicago Review Press.

Smeaton, Bob. 2013. *Hear My Train A Comin'.* PBS American Masters. DVD.

Swift, Kevin. 2012. "Hendrix the Gen Article." *Beat Instrumental*, 1 March 1967. In *Hendrix on Hendrix: Interviews and Encounters with Jimi Hendrix*, edited by Steven Roby, 13-16. Chicago: Chicago Review Press.

"Vietnam War: The Blues." Accessed 21 February 2019. https://rateyourmusic.com/list/JBrummer/vietnam-war-the-Blues/.

Waldrop, Jan. 2012. "Jimi Hendrix Shows his Teeth." In *Hendrix on Hendrix: Interviews and Encounters with Jimi Hendrix*, edited by Steven Roby, 17-22. Chicago: Chicago Review Press

5.

The protean character of the Blues

Uwe Zagratzki

University of Szczecin, Poland

Reflections on the evolution of the Blues

Blues at its heart refers to the basic instincts of Wo/Man, to the ontological equipment, as it were, like love, hate, fear, greed, envy and such like and the emotions caused by it. Revealing passions, triggering and expressing them defines the liberating power of the Blues, hence it has an anthropological dimension.

But Wo/Man also live in social contexts like class, race, gender and consequently are exposed to poverty, wealth, power, oppression, racism. Hence Blues also has a social dimension. Each of us knows examples when Blues lyrics articulate the daily worries and tribulations of black men and women, the singer's as well as the audience's. Raymond Williams has coined the term "alternative" for these modern cultural formations to mark a type of external relations in cultural formations: "alternative, as in the cases of the provision of alternative facilities for the production, exhibition or publication of certain kinds of work, where it is believed that existing institutions exclude or tend to exclude these". Another useful cultural category for the purpose of this study is "specializing, as in the cases of sustaining or promoting work in a particular medium or branch of an art, and in some circumstances a particular style" (Williams 1981, 70). Early Blues matches these patterns. Hence in line with a materialistic tradition of cultural studies, this article a) aims at contextualising the alternative Blues culture under changing social and cultural conditions and at analysing the entailing aesthetic continuities and discontinuities of the music thereof and b) applies Walter Benjamin's media theory, in particular, his notion of the "aura", to fathom the continued alternative non-conformity of the Blues in the context of post-modernism.

From the start, after the American Civil War, the Blues, both as music style and as a cultural event, interwove both aspects. Fish fries in the countryside turned into communal affairs when in the era of the Early Country Blues a male solo artist sang about the lot of a down-and-out black sharecropper, abandoned lovers or love in vain thus reflecting upon the shared experience of male and female listeners sitting in the audience. He could be sure of verbal responses to his calls as the Blues is dialogic, but merely naming the anxieties did not prevent the listeners from dancing: triggering bottled-up passions in mind and body thereby purging and curing bad emotions. Early Blues being male and working-class moulded African song material into a post-slavery discourse of formally emancipated African-American sharecroppers to which belonged physical excitement and emotional depth. The performative act and the "energizing intersubjectivity" (Baker Jr. 1998, 5) released through it reclaimed an artistic, thus limited, control over social lives and also within limits restored multiple chaos whose primary cause was massive socio-economic changes at that particular moment of American history.

Another moment came with the Classic Blues era dominated by powerful black female voices. Instead of addressing the white landowners' economic supremacy as had been the case with the Bluesmen of the previous era the object of discontent changed and black and white patriarchy came under attack–the agenda of conflicting encounters shifted from class to gender. Black women spoke up against all-male aggressiveness and unjustified chauvinism against which they set a straightforward black jargon, sexual outspokenness and reflections about a reversal of gender-roles.

In line with reclaiming alternative or symbolic power over defining their values and traditions black workers migrating from the Southern countryside to Northern industrial city ghettos from the 1930s to the 1950s chose down home Blues to be their chief medium of cultural re-appropriation after years of musical socialisation in Southern radio Blues programmes and juke joints.

> In speaking about urban city Blues of the 1930s and 1950s we speak about an aggressive means of communication inside black city communities. Amplified guitar-and bass-oriented sound and unceasing energy delivered 'messages' which would have otherwise been lost or silenced and which were best clad in heavy rhythms, loud vocals and vernacular lyrics. (Zagratzki 2017, 234).

What we find is resilience in the face of commercialisation through amplified voices as a means of putting across alternative definitions of white strategies of othering. Ongoing urban city Blues voices retained meaningful articulations of black identities within black communities, on the one hand; on the other, they put their cultural notions across the colour line. Vocality–since the origin of the Blues its most manifest feature–in a new guise thus deconstructs white supremacy in the field of music exerted by record companies as a vital instrument of a white power-based culture industry and infrastructure (e.g. TV). Muddy Waters' "I'm a Man" makes a strong point of black male self-confidence on the grounds of sexual bravado and in resistance to a Southern Jim Crow racism which discriminated against black man on the grounds of denying him his mature personality by calling him "boy":

> I'm a full grown man
> I'm a man
> I'm a natural born lover's man
> I'm a rollin' stone
> I'm a man
> I'm a hoochie coochie man
> [...]
> You know I'm made to move you honey.

City aggressiveness required loud voices and hard-hitting lyrics to be heard, the more, if the lyrical-I represents a victimized urban black ready to take up a struggle for survival. Again Muddy Waters song " I'm ready" is a case in point:

> I got an ax and a pistol on a graveyard framed
> That shoots tomstone bullets, that's wearing balls and chains
> I'm drinking TNT. I'm smoking dynamite.
> I hope some screwball start a fight.
> Cause I'm ready, ready as anybody can be.

From Northern American cities the Blues migrated to Europe, mainly to Britain, in the early 1960s where it met head-on with a white working-class sub-culture. Rejecting the lifestyles and value systems of a petrified post-World War II establishment and enjoying a newly-won affluence and spending power, the teenagers' cultural and – bound up with it – musical experiments resulted in shaping a new *Sound der Revolte* ["sound of the revolt"] (Siegfried 2008). Bluesrock, grounded in the Blues and amalgamated with a speedier rock, came to be the adequate means of expressing the post-war generation's rebelliousness. This cultural transfer–in Bitterli's terms a "Kulturberührung", friendly, temporal, coincidental contacts (Bitterli 1992, 17-27)–was grounded in a white stereotype of the 'noble black savage' who sang his protest against the same cultural and political opponent the white kids felt to be in opposition to–the white, male middle class. By mere emulation of African-American urban Blues and what was thought to be the–re-discovered – underlying "rebellious matrix" of black cultural resistance and its idiom British Bluesrock bands created their own sub-cultural identity. The first LP record released by the Rolling Stones (*The Rolling Stones* 1964) may serve as a suitable example, but the same can be said about The Yardbirds, Cream or John Mayall and the Bluesbreakers. This could only work for the white kids' ends as race and generation conflicts were made to match and then merged into one Blues idiom: "black non-conformism was the model of the 'white negroes' revolt" (Zagratzki 2017, 241) An essential characteristic of the re-construction was a 'positive' racism through inventing, at least, romanticising a spirit of resilience which assisted in projecting the white youngsters' needs on the blacks' struggle and which entailed a new identity resulting from identification and solidarity. Othering the black Blues artist for the sake of a white anti-establishment provocation was at heart as imperialist as bourgeois racism of the past had been.

A more radical step into politics occurred in West Germany. Here in the 1960s Blues became incorporated into militant left struggles. As black militancy was considered to take the lead in the battle of marginalised groups against capitalist repression worldwide and West German militants saw themselves to be part of this struggle, again this reconstruction allowed for the Blues, which had always in the understanding of the left militants articulated white oppression and black hope to become "the shared medium of revolutionary change and utopian freedom" (Zagratzki 2017, 242).

To sum up: despite–or because of–ongoing re-negotiations of meaning, which shine through best in controlled improvisations where innovative time- and culture-related requirements are introduced within the limits of the musical standard, the evolution of the Blues throughout features strong elements of stamina and resilience, even resistance, which, according to Raymond Williams, meet the definition of what he came to identify as an "alternative" cultural formation.

What is left of this in the context of post-modernism? We should critically re-phrase the position of the Blues in a globalising world and, for a keen recognition of its alternative, sub-cultural character look at daily encounters with it, disregarding, for a moment, the commercial side as part of an established Blues circuit.

Traces of the Blues in everyday discourses

The most frequent moment when each and every one encounters the Blues, is when we are 'having it' in phrases like "Brexit Blues" or "Autumn Blues". The general idea is of a low mood, a melancholy, sadness, even of a depression. Consulting dictionaries confirms this notion of being in a bad state of mind. *A Dictionary of English Synonyms* (1978) lists up under the entry: "Melancholy, dejection, depression, despondency, hypochondria, dumps, megrims, vapours, low spirits, blue-devils, the dismals" (68). These definitions relate to both noun and adjective ("sad and without hope"). For the latter, we also find informal phrases "concerned with sex": "some of his jokes were a bit blue" (*Langenscheidt-Longman Dictionary of Contemporary English* 1995, 129).

When it comes to the music proper we find "a slow sad style of music that came from the southern US" (129). On a more neutral note is *Collins Advanced Dictionary* (2009, 158): "The Blues is a type of music which was developed by African American musicians in the southern United States. It is characterized by a slow tempo and a strong rhythm." The cliché about the Blues as being sad and melancholic originated in the 1950s and 1960s when white audiences discovered the Blues. White ears pretended to hear layers in the songs which were neither supported by African-American perceptions of the Blues as cathartic nor by the happy-go-lucky hokum Blues. Yet the misnomer still survives to date.

Less expected encounters occur in niches where the Blues is alive and kicking, like commercial ads. Leading international clothing companies use the Blues in their ads for a distinguished promotion of their commodities. John Lee Hooker and Gary Moore come to mind here. The same with TV and film productions where for various reasons the Blues is mainly utilised for heightening mawkish scenes, whereas on YouTube the assumed erotic asset of a Blues melody serves to stress the contents of a video clip, in particular on the occasion of commercials promoting lingerie. A similar connection but in reverse order is re-produced in a series called "Relaxing Blues" in which visuals showing scantily-dressed women support the Blues line. Combining both eroticism and driving energy a video clip of the Rolling Stones' latest release "Blue and Lonesome" features a young sexy woman driving a wild Mustang car to the tune of "Ride'Em On Down". In sum, as with white attitudes to the Blues biased listenings–erotic, aggressive, melancholic–direct the way to the exploitation of the genre for promoting goods (with the exception of the Stones' video clip) originally disconnected to the music–e.g. lingerie, clothing, cars–and contemporaneously spread it to audiences who for whatever reason may remain at a distance to the Blues.

Shopping malls are another space of unexpected encounters with the Blues. Entering a huge shopping mall in the centre of Warsaw, Poland, the present writer was welcomed over the loudspeakers by B.B. King's warm voice and Lucille's gripping answers.

It has become a fashion recently to place pianos at big train stations like London's St. Pancras or international airports to be played by anyone ready to follow the inviting "Play me. I'm yours"-sign. Tracing these spontaneous public get-togethers on YouTube one is quickly aware of the amount of Boogie Woogie and Blues tunes played free of charge for the pleasure of pedestrians, shoppers and travellers who seemingly relish the entertaining suspension of the big city hustle and bustle offered by pianists Dr K aka Brendan Kavanagh or Henri Herbert. Whereas at these moments the Blues ad hoc reclaims public spaces and by this act re-negotiates the meaning of the "original"-here transmuting commercial shopping malls, airports or train stations imaginatively into spontaneous fun spaces denying or, at least, interrupting the continuous flow of profit maximisation and urban hectic life–at other moments it sells itself for much money and yet has a similar effect on the surroundings as is the case with Blues cruises for the better-off.

Any listing of unexpected encounters with the Blues would be incomplete, if we did not mention hundreds of unofficial sessions and rehearsals which are not meant to reach the public eye/ear or those events which are meant to raise the attention of an audience which is not considered to be a target group in the first place. Like a charity ("FR Altenhilfe") organized by one of Germany's leading national dailies (*Frankfurter Rundschau*) in order to raise funds for pensioners. For the first time in the 2018 event the "Matchbox Bluesband", one of Germany's long-standing Blues bands was invited to perform in front of senior citizens. However, in 2018 one can argue a German generation has reached old age which is familiar with the Blues (like the writer) and therefore a knowledgeable audience.

Blues–alternative art form resisting 'aura'

What does this say about the Blues as an alternative culture and alternative work of art? We proceeded on the assumption that for some time black (and later white) non-conformity, not to say rebelliousness, found an articulate medium in the Blues. Have these features survived in the present? Does "semiotic guerrilla warfare" (Umberto Eco in Hebdige 1979, 105) live on in the "underground" of the dominant culture and (by its very existence) uphold a subtle notion of the non-conforming resisting character of the Blues? Do we still sense the spirit of rebellion when listening to, e.g. a B.B. King tune or Lightnin' Hopkins or Joe Bonamassa? Do we hear the voice of the black (and white) oppressed? Has black cultural memory been retained in the Blues to date or has it been adopted by modern Rap and Hip Hop? Can it still be useful in identity formation? Does it still talk about the harsh and gloomy underside of capitalism?

Or has a dominant culture's discourse streamlined or even bought up the rebellious sting? Certainly one can argue that outside the specific historical context of a Southern juke joint or a Chicago black ghetto of the past post-modern Blues (urban and country) has lost its point of social reference and along with it its controlling function so that nostalgic vestiges of non-conformity are what have been left. It seems the Blues has crossed over from the institutionalised spaces of a black sub-culture as stereotyped by fish-fries, country dances, juke joints, later urban clubs to multiple, heterogeneous discourses of fashion, consumption, melancholy and sex in a post-modern world. With time it shifted shape from being a central tool of alternative articulations originating within a living practice of a sub-culture into being a commodity of mainstream aesthetics and consumption. Alternative non-conformity may linger, though – for those who have the glossary to interpret.

And here we approach a tentative answer through Walter Benjamin's media theory and along with it a required glossary of "rebellion". In his seminal essay "Das Kunstwerk im Zeitalter seiner technischen Reproduzierbarkeit" (1938) the German Marxist philosopher put forth a concise definition of the Greek notion of "aura":

> What, then, is the aura? A strange tissue of space and time: the unique apparition of a distance, however near it may be. To follow with the eye – while resting on a summer afternoon – a mountain range on the horizon or a branch that casts its shadow on the beholder is to breathe the aura of those mountains, of that branch. (Benjamin 1938, in Jennings 2008, 23).

Detlev Schöttker elucidates:

> Die Aura, in der Natur wie in der Kunst, ist geprägt durch ihr Hier und Jetzt, ihre Unnahbarkeit, Echtheit, Einmaligkeit. Es ist die Aura, die die Werke zu historischen Zeugen macht und ihnen Autorität verleiht...Mit der Reproduzierbarkeit hebt sich sowohl die Einmaligkeit auf, als auch deren Ferne, ein Kunstwerk wird zu jeder Zeit an jedem Ort betrachtbar und besitzbar. Damit verliert es seine historische Zeugenschaft und letztlich seine Autorität. (Schöttker 2007, 211) [Aura in nature and arts is defined by its here and now, its unapproachableness, its genuineness, its uniqueness. Only the aura turns works (of art) into historical witnesses and bestows authority on them...Reproducibility annuls its uniqueness as much as its remoteness, [in consequence] a piece of art can be observed and possessed any time and at any place. Hence it ceases being a historical witness and eventually loses its authority. (My translation, UZ)].

In short, the sensation of a moment is not reproducible, since an identical historic(al) moment never recurs again.

In essence Benjamin's definition of "aura" characterises the specificity of a work of art, its uniqueness and "authenticity", its unapproachableness, its restriction to a locality and its embeddedness in history, all of it concisely encapsulated in Benjamin´s above description of "the unique apparition of a distance, however near it may be" (Jennings 2008, 23). Benjamin based his deliberations on visual arts, particularly on the burgeoning art of film in the 1930s. As the particularities of a visual work of art differ from those of an acoustic one Benjamin's "aura" is not adaptable to music (which he was aware of), yet still, his reflections are useful in the given context. Wolfram Ette has pointed to this phenomenon in his essay "Benjamins Reproduktionsaufsatz und die Musik" (Ette 2013). He argues that particularly music has changed the aesthetic habits of reception/perception most drastically in as much as our daily aesthetic routines have come to be defined by "technically reproducible music". Especially for youth cultures but also common recipients music is an identity marker (Ette 2013, 144). The reason for the dominance of technically reproducible music is, according to Ette, its permissiveness and flexibility which allows for multitasking while listening. (Ette 2013, 145). He translates Benjamin's

Rezeption in der Zerstreuung (diversion) (Benjamin 1936, in Schweppenhäuser 1996, 41) into *zerstreute Wahrnehmung* (diverted perception) (Ette 2013, 145) to distinguish from contemplation (*Sammlung)* (Benjamin 1936, 40) initiated by traditional aura as it positively picks on specific elements from the work of art, selects perception and by way of montage combines anew and by that disclaims a mimetic reflection of the integrated whole:

> Die Komplexitätsreduktion, die der zerstreut Rezipierende vollzieht, ordnet das, womit er etwas anfangen kann, auf sich hin, arrangiert es mit dem Bezug auf seine eigene empirische Existenz – eben jene empirische Existenz, die im kontemplativen Hören tendenziell ausgelöscht wird. (Ette 2013, 146). [The reduction of complexity accomplished by the diverted recipient orders what pertains to him, arranges it in relation to his own empirical existence – the empirical existence which contemplative listening is prone to eradicate. My translation, U.Z.]

And he further elucidates: "Genau aus diesem Grund sind wir beim zerstreuten Hören in gewisser Hinsicht Produzenten: Produzenten nämlich unserer eigenen, sich im Kunstwerk reflektierenden Lebenswirklichkeit" (Ette 2013, 146) [This is why in some respects we become producers in the act of diverted listening: producers of our own living reality reflected in the work of art. My translation, U.Z.]

Popular music–of which the Blues is a part–by its essence is a case in point. Without technical reproduction, its existence would be impossible as the history of the Blues has shown: originating in an oral and performative tradition it survived via field recordings, but concurrently lost its "aura" articulated in the "here and now" of the performance in the process of hybridization. Another evidence of diverted reception of Blues shows up in modifying the complexity of a text through reductive memorising and montage of memorised lines, finally resulting in "diverted productivity" (Ette 2013, 146). The recipient's appropriation of a Blues song disclaims the integrated whole of the piece–its aura–hence enables him to re-model it in relation to the recipient´s ends and needs expressed by singing, covering, cross-over or dancing, that is body talk. Orality–in contrast to visual arts– provides "a wider range of emotions on a more immediate level of sensations...sound is fleeting and one must react immediately or lose the perceptual experience entirely." (Sidran 1971, 2). Via Benjamin's notion of "aura" we have come to underscore Bonanomi's and Dandy's findings as to authenticity as well as Claviez's rejection of the same concept on the reclamation of time as contingent.[1]

---

[1] See Part Three *"Authenticity and identity in contemporary Blues studies."*

I started from Williams' assumption of alternative cultural formations struggling for existence outside established institutions–here the early black Blues forming alternative institutions within white power structures before its technical reproducibility–and its evolution towards incorporation into the white mainstream and the concurrent denial of this assimilation. Benjamin's media theory, but even more Benjamin's implied recognition that music lacks unique aura (see Ette 2013, 148) allows for the *underground* character of the Blues in the sense that its de-constructiveness and flexibility empowers the recipients to relate it back to their individual existence. Blues thus contributes to appropriating (or authoring) their respective cultural practices also in the age of technical reproducibility. Diverted perception works through ever-remodelled orality and performativity and thus is–according to Benjamin–political in reference to the listener as well as the art (Ette 2013, 148).

Let me conclude on an ambivalent note. Both readings of the Blues–dominant and alternative–hold a pinch of truth as they both depend "on different decodings of the signifiers" related to the distinctions of cultural formations: "...defining Blues as commodity and Blues as social expression are by no means mutually exclusive." (Lawson 2010, 27).[2] Blues is protean and thus appears to approve of multiple readings.

References

Baker Jr., Houston. 1998. *Blues, Ideology and African American Literature. A Vernacular Theory.* Chicago: Chicago University Press.

Bitterli, Urs. 1992. *Alte Welt – neue Welt.* München: Deutscher Taschenbuch Verlag.

Collins Advanced Dictionary. 2009. John Sinclair, ed. Glasgow: Heinle.

Dictionary of English Synonyms and Synonymous Expressions. 1978. Richard Soule, ed. revised by Alfred Dwight Sheffield. London: Frederick Warne.

Ette, Wolfram. 2013. "Benjamins Reproduktionsaufsatz und die Musik." In *Klang und Musik bei Walter Benjamin,* edited by Tobias Robert Klein, 142-148. München: Wilhelm Fink Verlag.

Hebdige, Dick. 1979. *New Accents. Subculture: The Meaning of Style.* London: Methuen & Co.

Jennings, Michael W., Brigid Doherty, Thomas Y. Levin, eds. 2008. *The Work of Art in the Age of its Technological Reproducibility – Walter Benjamin.* Cambridge, Mass., London: The Belknap Press of Harvard University Press.

---

[2] Recent examples of the lasting commitment of the Blues to social and political issues are, chosen at random, two titles from the album "Ain't Givin' Up" by the top German band Blues Company released in January 2019: "Guns" tackles school shootings, whereas "The News" talks about frustrating experience in times of fake news and lies.

Langenscheidt-Longman Dictionary of Contemporary English. Third ed. 1995.
   Randolph Quirk, ed. Harlow, München: Langenscheidt-Longman Group.

Lawson, R.A. 2010. *Jim Crow's Counterculture. The Blues and Black
   Southerners 1890-1945.* Baton Rouge: Louisiana State University Press.

Schöttker, Detlev. 2007. *Walter Benjamin. Das Kunstwerk im Zeitalter seiner
   technischen Reproduzierbarkeit. Kommentar.* Frankfurt am Main: Suhrkamp.

Schweppenhäuser, Hermann, Rolf Tiedemann, eds. 1996. *Walter Benjamin.
   Das Kunstwerk im Zeitalter seiner technischen Reproduzierbarkeit.* Frankfurt
   am Main: Suhrkamp.

Sidran, Ben. 1971. *Black Talk.* New York: Da Capo Paperback.

Siegfried, Detlef. 2008. *Sound der Revolte. Studien zur Kulturrevolution um
   1968.* Weinheim. München: Juventa Verlag.

Williams, Raymond. 1981. *Culture.* Glasgow: Fontana Paperbacks.

Zagratzki, Uwe. 2017. " From Early Country Blues to Rap." In *Chaos in the
   Contact Zone,* edited by Stephanie Wodianka, Christoph Behrens, 221-245.
   Bielefeld: transcript Verlag.

Part Two:
**Blues on the page:
perspectives from literary criticism**

6.

"Singing your mean old Backlash Blues": Blues, history, and racial inequality today

Chiara Patrizi

University of Roma Tre, Italy

Introduction: the Blues of Langston Hughes

This chapter discusses Langston Hughes's "The Backlash Blues" starting from a brief analysis of the socio-cultural context of the 1960s and a close reading of the poem and its music version by Nina Simone. It shows how the poem still represents an example of the political role of the artist, and how it reveals the vitality of the Blues as a form of social expression. Reference is made to various scholarly traditions, such as African-American and Blues literature (DuBois; Jones; Tracy; Williams), socio-political research (Alexander; Bonilla-Silva; Davis), as well as works by literary authors (Baldwin; Ward).

"The Backlash Blues" is said to be the last poem Langston Hughes sent his editor for what became his final collection, *The Panther and the Lash*, posthumously published in 1967. The collection as a whole has often been considered a transition work in Hughes's production, showing the hints of a possible growing interest in more overtly socio-political themes, expressed through what have been defined as "protest Blues poems" (Tracy 2001, 216).

The second half of the 1960s marked a traumatic transition period for the Civil Rights Movement too—and for the African-American community in general. Indeed, even though the Movement had achieved some important victories (the Civil Rights Act of 1964, the Voting Rights Act of 1965, among others), the fracture between those who believed in non-violent activism and those ready to achieve their long-deserved rights "by any means necessary" (Malcolm X 1964), such as the Black Panther Party, was getting everyday bigger, until the day of Martin Luther King's murder. Hughes's engagement in political discourse and action is well-known, and he did not fail to address the most problematic aspects of such events—albeit at the very end of his career and life.

I will examine Langston Hughes's poem and compare its two versions, in which Blues and social protest are expressed in two slightly different ways. Through this comparison, the aim is to show how the Blues ethos and aesthetic are able to provide the proper environment where Black artists can examine and deal with historical and social issues—too many of which were unresolved in Hughes's times and sadly remain so even today.

In "The Backlash Blues", by means of a twelve-bar Blues structure with AAB lyric pattern,[1] the poet enumerates the racial frustration and the everyday discriminations and mistreatments African Americans kept suffering in a "brand-new" desegregated America. The very concept of "backlash" is useful to understand how black people's identity seems not to be allowed to exist on its own, but only as opposed and inferior to that of the "dominant group" (the white people). The poem calls attention to how black people were still not entitled to full-scale citizenship, while they were still required to fight for their country when necessary, as in the case of the Vietnam War.

These are the same issues raised by Dr. Martin Luther King in the speech he delivered in 1967 at Manhattan Riverside's Church, during which he firmly criticized the "cruel irony of watching Negro and white boys [...] as they kill and die together for a nation that has been unable to seat them together in the same schools." When in Vietnam, these boys shared the "brutal solidarity" of killing and burning the villages of a poor people but, King continues, "we realize that they would hardly live on the same block in Chicago" (King 1967).

Similarly, when Hughes addresses his words to "Mister Backlash," the personification of American white society, he makes himself the spokesman of the dissatisfaction of the entire African-American community. From the very beginning, the question is "who do you think I am?" (Hughes 2002, 142) and that "I" clearly implies a "we" that the black audience well understands, following the communal tradition of the Blues (Williams 1999, 446). Here, the first-person perspective does not imply a subjective/personal story, but rather the persona is representative of the community's shared history, social situation, and feelings. In the first stanza, Hughes worries the line by dropping the first "Mister Backlash" and adding the imperative "Tell me," so that the question becomes more pressing and, as it appears in the fourth line without "just," it conveys a significance that carries with it centuries of black history. It is as if Hughes were reminding both his black and white audience that, from the very

---

[1] A structure that has become one of the "trademarks" of Hughes's writing since the late 1920s. See Tracy, *Langston Hughes and the Blues*: 144–45.

beginning, white people have forced on African Americans an identity specifically intended to overpower them.

As Michelle Alexander's 2010 ground-breaking work *The New Jim Crow* points out, "[s]lavery defined what it meant to be black (a slave), and Jim Crow defined what it meant to be black (a second-class citizen)" (Alexander 2010, 197), and the tone of the question in the poem may imply that the time has come when black people are not willing anymore to let white America define their identity in terms of subordination and humiliation. A "white backlash" was nothing new for those African Americans who had to face the everyday repercussions of a society in large part still pro-segregation; however, in the poem, this time something may be different: "the world is big," (Hughes 2002, 142) Hughes warns in the fourth stanza with a touch of irony, and there are many so-called "people of color" in such a world, maybe more than whites.

In *Langston Hughes and the Blues*, Steven C. Tracy notes that the final stanza is almost identical to the first one, but even the small differences are substantial: in writing "I'm gonna leave you, Mister Backlash, / Singing your mean old backlash Blues" (Hughes 2002, 142), Hughes portrays an active response on the part of the speaker, who is getting ready to finally overturn the situation, and so the coda suggests that the final "backlash Blues" may be the white man's (Tracy 2001, 216). This is another feature typical of the Blues which Sherley Williams (1999, 446) clarifies as follows: "The internal strategy of the Blues is action, rather than contemplation, for the song itself is the creation of reflection. And while not all Blues actions achieve the desired result, the impulse to action is inherent in any Blues which functions out of a collective purpose." The collective purpose here is towards a claim for one's right to full-scale citizenship, to be achieved through an active revolt against the control applied by white society. Hence the poet is performing the same task of staging an environment "in which analysis can take place," that Williams sees as a distinctive trait of the Blues performer (Williams 1999, 447), a process made possible thanks to his sharp irony and strong eloquence.

What can such an analysis achieve in terms not only of artistic expression but especially of racial and social empowerment? A possible answer can be found in the words of another great artist and activist of our times, Nina Simone. In 1968, when New York public television interviewed the singer on what freedom meant to her, she thought about it a bit and then declared: "I'll tell you what freedom is to me: no fear!" (Simone 1970)—and one can imagine Langston Hughes agreeing with such a statement. He surely shows no fear in the straightforwardness of "The Backlash Blues." Beware, white people—the poem admonishes—pretty soon you may not be the only ones to crack the lash against someone else: the time will come when black people will come together and you will not be able to keep your privileges so easily anymore.

From music to poetry and back again

The Backlash Blues" was also the last gift that Langston Hughes left his dear friend Nina before dying, a gift she honoured by bringing the poem back to music and transforming it into a Chicago-style urban Blues, recorded as "Backlash Blues" on her 1967 album *Nina Sings the Blues*. As De Angelis (this volume) has noted, there are significant variations between the first version of the poem (interpreted by Nina Simone) and the poem which Hughes revised for publication months later,[2] possibly in order to reconnect with the old Blues tradition, both as culture and as literature.

Both the poem and the song use a twelve-bar chord progression, but the lyric pattern is different, so that the result is a more modern Blues composition, in accordance with Simone's style. I mentioned before that the poem employs an AAB scheme, but the different stanzas are not as much "closed unit[s] without run-over lines or run-over thoughts" (Williams 1999, 448) as they are in other poems by Hughes: in this case, the ending response of each stanza remains somehow slightly suspended, thus creating an emotional tension. The poet is preparing listeners for the conclusion which is being built up slowly line after line, and more explicitly clarified in the coda ("I'm gonna leave you, Mister Backlash, / Singing your mean old backlash Blues"). Interestingly, in the first music version, the final response is brought to the audience's attention from the very beginning. Here, the traditional repeating lines are absent and two stanzas are merged into one, so that Nina Simone sings four lines in each four-bar segment, whereas the poem will have just two lines in four measures and restore the AAB scheme. Thus the two lyric structures differ significantly:

Mister Backlash, Mister Backlash, just who do you think I am? You raise my taxes, freeze my wages, send my son to Vietnam. You give me second-class houses, second-class schools. Do you think that all colored folks are just second-class fools? (Simone and Hughes, "Backlash Blues")	Mister Backlash, Mister Backlash, Just who do you think I am? Tell me, Mister Backlash, Who do you think I am? (Hughes, "The Backlash Blues")

---

[2] See De Angelis, "Going back home: the politics of the Blues in Langston Hughes's 'The Backlash Blues'" in this collection.

The lyric structure of the song gives the entire stanza a more pressing tone[3] which justifies and indeed requires the inclusion of that specific response. The variation in the lyric composition allows Nina Simone (and Langston Hughes) to state her (and their) firm purpose to immediately overturn the current state of play, as early as the end of the first verse:

Mr. Backlash, —— I'm gonna leave you with the backlash Blues. (Simone and Hughes, "Backlash Blues")	You raise my taxes, freeze my wages, Send my son to Vietnam. (Hughes, "The Backlash Blues")

The singer does not wait until the end of the song to tell white people that she is going to leave them with the backlash Blues and therefore, through her voice, Hughes's words take the shape of an outspoken political manifesto (Kernodle 2008, 312).

The second verse contains a significant variation in tone and mood, too: the recognizable irony in the poem's description of the world, which is first just "big," then "big and round," then again a "great big world," and finally "big and bright and round," is almost non-existent in the first music version, and is rather a looming warning to all the white backlashers. There will be time during the guitar solo to reflect on the previous statements and wonder what is going to happen next, in the concluding verse. Here, the first four measures of the final verse are cut off, so that the singing starts somehow abruptly at the fifth measure and the song proceeds towards its climax in the ending lines, which incorporates the coda of the poem, "*you're the one / will have the Blues*" (Hughes 2002), and adds to it a fierce "not me—Just wait and see!" (Simone and Hughes 1967).

Nina Simone's studio rendition already contains certain nuances that mirror the artist's strong commitment to the African-American civil rights' struggle. However, it is the live version recorded at the Westbury Music Fair on 7 April 1968 (three days after the assassination of Dr. Martin Luther King Jr.) which unleashes the poem's energy with unprecedented effectiveness. The concert that night was dedicated to King's memory and the band performed the touching "Why? The King of Love is Dead," that the bassist Gene Taylor had just written in the hours following the assassination. In her autobiography, *I Put a Spell on You*, Simone remembers the performance as "one of my very best, focused by the love and quiet despair we all felt at our loss" (Simone and

---

[3] Note also the choice of a direct question in "Do you think that all colored folks are just second class fools?" which becomes indirect in the final version of the poem.

Cleary 2003, 115) and indeed the entire concert is certainly a masterpiece of her career.

The song is almost unrecognizable to the listener of such a powerful and much more incisive rearrangement: the harmonica is gone, and a pronounced Blues stomp led by Simone's imperious piano emphasizes her charismatic singing even more. After the instrumental improvisation, the metrical structure turns into a sixteen-bar progression, and it is at that point that she adds, as she was used to do during her performances, a passionate utterance that opens the way to the song's triumphant ending. She shares with the audience a late conversation she had with Hughes, during which

> he said "Nina, keep on working 'til they open up the door,
> one of these days when you made it and the doors are open wide,
> make sure you tell 'em exactly where it's at so they'll have no place to hide."
> (Simone 1968)

Nina Simone believed that "an artist's duty, as far as I'm concerned, is to reflect times," which is what she always did and what she does here too, by declaring herself to be the repository of Hughes's political and artistic intent (Gaines 2013, 251), and she surely sees it as her duty, in such a moment, to honour the poet's legacy. Any trace of underlying meanings is gone from the piece, to be replaced by a ferocious straightforwardness, almost a call to arms to all black people:

> So Mr. Backlash, Mr. Backlash, hear me now, somehow someway,
> I'm gonna leave you with the Blues.
> (Simone 1968)

"How does it feel to be a problem?" was the "unasked question" in DuBois's *The Souls of Black Folk* (2008, 9), a question to which the singer seems to answer that it feels even worse when you are finally aware that the problem has never been you, that the rage you feel is legitimate, and that a revolution should start because of a centuries-old injustice that has not even started fading yet. As Hughes had foreseen, it was the beginning of a new era of social protest, in which non-violent practices seemed to be not so effective anymore. For "[t]he thing that died along with Martin in Memphis that day," Nina Simone remembers, "was non-violence, we all knew that. It was a time for bitterness—almost funny if it hadn't been so sad" (Simone and Cleary 2003, 114). The shared sadness and bitterness permeate the performance while Simone's voice involves the audience in that communal experience that characterizes the essence of the Blues and urges them to action: one year after his death, Hughes's words are kept alive in their natural environment, and they still sound relevant and appropriate to describe the ongoing racial issues in America today—which is quite something for a poet and a musical genre that have too often been considered "too simple" (Tracy 2004, 3) and dated to outlive their times.

Of course, Langston Hughes's art and the Blues have more than metrical structures in common, not least the fact of operating within African-American folklore (Tracy 2001, 12–13), an environment in which both storytelling and music play a fundamental role. Both derive their force from what can be defined as a profound understanding of the social importance of art in general—as LeRoi Jones/Amiri Baraka enthusiastically announced when he realized that "the music was explaining the history as the history was explaining the music. And that both were expressions and reflections of the people!" (Jones 2002, ix–x). This principle is represented in Blues ethos by the artists' awareness of their role of bearers of the truth: they are the instruments through which communal values are re-examined, heightened, preserved with an active purpose (Williams 1999, 446–447). With his art, Hughes certainly aimed at performing the same role: he wanted to express the dignity of the common people and to speak for their rights and socio-political claims (Tracy 2004, 9). Such a will had been unmistakably declared already in 1926, in "The Negro Artist and the Racial Mountain," in which the then young and promising voice of the Harlem Renaissance celebrates the glory of African-American folklore and music, and praises its "low-down folks," who are not embarrassed by who they are and therefore represent the future of the black community. Hughes wants to be part of that future, too: he is proud of being identified with that community, for "[a]n artist must be free to choose what he does, certainly, but he must also never be afraid to do what he must choose" (Hughes 2002, 35).

Throughout his long career, Hughes had always been faithful to that early commitment and his final work makes no exception: *The Panther and the Lash* is a collection of politically militant poems which encourage and support young artists and activists by focusing on key moments of the recent history of African Americans. At the same time, the poet himself is making an important effort to be true to the present social and political situation without losing the link with the past, that of the Black community and his own (Smethurst 2004, 164–67). It is in the light of this effort that a poem like "The Backlash Blues" must be investigated, for it manages to apply the Blues form to the language of late 1960s racial struggles, thus preserving that cultural continuum in Black culture which is deeply rooted in its African heritage. The content of the poem brings readers back to DuBois's (2008, 11) description of the "American world—a world which yields [the Negro] no true self-consciousness, but only lets him see himself through the revelation of the other world." Still, in 1967, the white man seems to believe he can trick the black man into his trap. This time, however, the speaker in Hughes's poem has finally achieved his longed-for self-consciousness: with his Blues, he resolutely refuses a second-class identity and announces that he is ready to fight back for his rights.

What happens to a dream deferred?

Regrettably, fifty years and a black president later, not much has changed. Hughes portrayed a society in which black people's identity was defined only by being placed in negative comparison to that of white people and, even though some important victories on civil rights have surely been achieved, the age of colour-blindness has not brought about the end of racism. As many scholars have noted (Alexander 2010; Bonilla-Silva 2006; Davis 2012), it can be said that what has changed during the last decades is the *code*, the language through which discrimination is perpetrated, and the strategies that the establishment uses to enable society to be always divided between oppressors and oppressed. Therefore, asking oneself "what does it mean to be black?"[4] today is not obsolete, since the time has not come yet in which the answer does not depend on white society's perception.

In 1963, James Baldwin addressed these issues in a passionate letter he wrote to his nephew, warning the boy that "[y]ou can only be destroyed by believing that you really are what the white world calls a nigger," and condemned the kind of existence that the white world had planned for black people. "This innocent country" expected African Americans to live and die in a ghetto without asking for anything more: "You were born where you were born and faced the future that you faced because you were black and for no other reason. The limits of your ambition were, thus, expected to be set forever." Not surprisingly, Baldwin's words could refer to the current century, too, as he concludes that: "You were born into a society which spelled out with brutal clarity, and in as many ways as possible, that you were a worthless human being. You were not expected to aspire to excellence: you were expected to make peace with mediocrity" (Baldwin1995, 4–7).

Similarly, Hughes's Blues expressed both the frustration of being a second-class citizen and the will to overturn that condition. But that "mean old backlash" practice has not died after the Civil Rights Era: on the contrary, with the creation of the mass incarceration system it has even perfected itself by spreading the idea that to be black today means to be a criminal (Alexander 2010, 197). A criminal is not seen as a "decent" and valuable member of society, therefore to be labelled as such has profound effects on every aspect of a person's life, especially from the cultural viewpoint of American

---

[4] A question that is very much related to the history of Blues culture, too.

individualism. It fosters a new kind of prejudice towards black people, the belief that, if this is what they get, then they probably deserve it, as individuals: it means that they do not try sufficiently hard to overcome the obstacles that life has placed in front of them. This made it possible to pass so-called "colour-blind" laws that specifically target black (and non-white) communities without overtly declaring it.[5] Moreover, this socio-political strategy has created an environment in which even solidarity within the communities has become less frequent than before (who would risk being associated with a criminal?), and it took years of blatant police violence and "colour-blind" racial inequality to see the birth of movements like the now-famous Black Lives Matter.

The history of African Americans is burdened with slavery and racism, injustice, grief, and too often hopelessness. Aware of that, Langston Hughes always worked to promote what we today define as "empowerment" among his community, and to foster an active reflection on freedom and black identity that must be rooted in history. Recently, Angela Davis has observed how the lack of historical memory in the United States has had dangerous consequences on the perception of current reality: in fact, if "we have discarded anachronistic notions of race that are grounded in pseudoscientific classifications of humanity that are hierarchical by their very nature, if we have discarded these notions of race, we cannot discard the work that race has done to shape our histories" (Davis 2012, 187). History, then, must be used to shape our self-consciousness, and to choose the kind of individuals and citizens we want to become. More than fifty years later, the call is the same made by Baldwin (1965), when he urged all American people to accept their own history, because clearly "it is a terrible thing for an entire people to surrender to the notion that one-ninth of its population is beneath them." The injustice of the past cannot be cancelled, Baldwin knows too well, but facing one's troubled history can finally lead to "forge a new identity." This can happen only when all Americans understand that they need each other, black or white, in order to build a future for their country. But until white America acknowledges that "I am one of the people who built this country [...] there's scarcely any hope for the 'American Dream,' because the people who are

---

[5] Consider, for instance, how Alexander analyses the origins and political scheme behind the War on Drugs, the three-strikes and stop-and-frisk laws, the felony disenfranchisement, the growing privatization of healthcare and education, etc.). See Alexander 2010 for a detailed analysis of the social implications behind recent and current U.S. internal politics (5-6, 60-96, 185–87, 192–93).

denied participation in it, by their very presence, will wreck it. And if that happens, it is a very grave moment for the West."

It is indeed a very grave moment for the entire society when to be non-white (not only African American) still implies a life in fear in your own country. Therefore, if we agree with Nina Simone that freedom means essentially "no fear," we must acknowledge that true freedom is far from having been achieved. Being forced to live in fear in a place that is supposed to be home entails a huge sense of disconnection between the individual and their country–which makes it painfully difficult to match the imposed identity (i.e. the black citizen as the criminal) with the identity felt and perceived by the person, and this is too often reminiscent of DuBois's "double-consciousness." In such troublesome situations, far from being dead, the Blues offers a way of facing existence that is, as I have mentioned, both rooted in history and focused on action. The very concept of "worrying the line" implies a creative effort to "styliz[e] a particular existential condition into significance" (Connor 2012, 146), thus providing instruments and techniques through which one can look at the world and "innovate" it (as with the tropes of repetition and improvisation/innovation in Blues music). These cultural "working tools" of the Blues have remained valuable and effective throughout the centuries, from slavery times to nowadays.

For this reason, I wish to conclude by mentioning the 2016 essay and poetry collection *The Fire This Time*, which takes on Baldwin's legacy (the title explicitly alludes to his work, *The Fire Next Time*) and that of a social and cultural tradition rooted in the Blues ethos, thus undertaking the demanding task of "wrestl[ing] with the spectres of race and history in America, and how those spectres are haunting us now" (Ward 2016, 14). The collection follows the path started by those artists, thinkers, and activists who showed how the present is inevitably tied to the past and how consequently such a past weighs on the future. It is true that reality may appear desperate sometimes; still, these authors fight together the fear and sense of displacement implied in a negative black identity—an identity that they all strongly refuse. As the Blues used to do, these writers wish to provide people with the instruments and setting through which they understand who they are, as human beings and as citizens, and know that they are worth a place in the world that no one else should impose on them. Ultimately, when Jesmyn Ward affirms that "this work helps me to believe that this is worthwhile work, and that our troubling the water is worthy" (Ward 2016, 5), she is taking on a conception of history and hope and a sense of community that are inherent to the Blues ethos and tradition. This history speaks to all America, and it allows Ward to meditate on the social role of narration—and, therefore, of literature—especially in tough political times:

all these essays give me hope. I believe there is power in words, power in asserting our existence, our experience, our lives, through words. That sharing our stories confirms our humanity. That it creates community, both within our own community and beyond it. (Ward 2016, 16)

Just like Hughes and Baldwin troubled the water before in order to make America face its history, today's young activists and artists call their nation to the same effort, which is considered everyday more compelling and imperative.

Today, Blues is kept alive as a music genre also because it is capable of addressing social and political issues in current U.S. society. It is even more alive as the cultural expression of the African-American community, since it encompasses its attitudes about the world, even when these are not expressed through music but using other forms of art and narrative.

References

Alexander, Michelle. 2010. *The New Jim Crow: Mass Incarceration in the Age of Colorblindness.* New York: The New Press.

Baldwin, James. *The Fire Next Time.* (1963) 1995. New York: The Dial Press. Reprint, New York: Modern Library.

Baldwin, James. 1965. "Has the American Dream Been Achieved at the Expense of the American Negro?" (public debate with William F. Buckley). The Cambridge Union Society. Accessed 25 June 2019. https://www.youtube.com/watch?v=WPz7kTnEWKE&t=2454s.

Bonilla-Silva, Eduardo. 2006. *Racism without Racists: Color-Blind Racism and the Persistence of Racial Inequality in the United States.* Lanham, MD: Rowman and Littlefield.

Connor, Kimberly R. 2012. "Worrying the Line: Blues as Story, Song, and Prayer." In *Blues–Philosophy for Everyone: Thinking Deep About Feeling Low,* edited by Jesse R. Steinberg and Abrol Fairweather, 142–152. Oxford: Wiley-Blackwell.

Davis, Angela Y. 2012. *The Meaning of Freedom: and Other Difficult Dialogues.* San Francisco: City Lights Books.

Du Bois, W.E.B. (1903) 2008. *The Souls of Black Folk.* Chicago: A.C. McClurg and Co. Reprint, Project Gutenberg EBook.

Gaines, Malik. 2013. "The Quadruple Consciousness of Nina Simone." *Women and Performance: a Journal of Feminist Theory* 23 (2), 248–267.

Hughes, Langston. (1967) 2002. "The Backlash Blues." In *The Collected Work of Langston Hughes.* Vol. 3: *The Poems, 1951–1967,* edited by Arnold Rampersad, 142–143. Columbia and London: University of Missouri Press.

Hughes, Langston. 2002. "The Negro Artist and the Racial Mountain." In *The Collected Work of Langston Hughes.* Vol. 9: *Essays on Art, Race, Politics, and World Affairs,* edited by Christopher C. De Santis, 31–36. Columbia and London: University of Missouri Press.

Jones, LeRoi. (1963) 2002. *Blues People: Negro Music in White America.* New York: William Morrow. Reprint, New York: Harper Perennial.

Kernodle, Tammy L. 2008. "'I Wish I Knew How It Would Feel to Be Free': Nina Simone and the Redefining of the Freedom Song in the 1960s." *Journal of the Society for American Music* 2 (3), 295–317.

King, Dr. Martin Luther. 1967. "Beyond Vietnam: A Time to Break Silence" (speech). *Riverside Church, New York City.* Accessed 25 June 2019. https://www.youtube.com/watch?v=Esh1amdajKA.

Malcolm X. 1964. Speech at the Founding Rally of the Organization of Afro-American Unity. Accessed 25 June 2019. https://www.youtube.com/watch?v=WBS416EZsKM.

Simone, Nina. 1968. "Backlash Blues." *'Nuff Said!* RCA Records, compact disc.

Simone, Nina. 1970. "Freedom" TV special "Nina: A Historical Perspective," directed by Peter Rodis. YouTube video. Accessed 25 June 2019. https://www.youtube.com/watch?v=Si5uW6cnyG4.

Simone, Nina, and Stephen Cleary. (1992) 2003. *I Put a Spell on You: The Autobiography of Nina Simone.* New York: Pantheon.

Simone, Nina, and Langston Hughes. 1967. "Backlash Blues." Nina Simone *Sings the Blues.* RCA Records, compact disc.

Smethurst, James. 2004. "The Adventures of a Social Poet: Langston Hughes from the Popular Front to Black Power." In *A Historical Guide to Langston Hughes,* edited by Steven C. Tracy, 141–168. Oxford: Oxford University Press.

Tracy, Steven C. (1988) 2001. *Langston Hughes and the Blues.* Champaign: University of Illinois Press.

Tracy, Steven C. 2004. "Introduction: Hughes in Our Time." In *A Historical Guide to Langston Hughes,* edited by Steven C. Tracy, 3–22. Oxford: Oxford University Press.

Ward, Jesmyn. 2016. "Introduction." In *The Fire This Time: a New Generation Speaks About Race,* edited by Jesmyn Ward, 3–11. New York: Scribner.

Williams, Sherley A. 1999. "The Blues Roots of Contemporary Afro-American Poetry." In *Write Me a Few of Your Lines,* edited by Steven C. Tracy, 445–455. Amherst: University of Massachusetts Press.

Further Reading

Dickinson, Donald C. 1967. "Working with Langston Hughes." *Negro American Literature Forum* 1 (2), 13–15.

Johnson, Patricia A. and Walter C. Farrell, Jr. 1979. "How Langston Hughes Used the Blues." *MELUS* 6 (1), 55–63.

Tracy, Steven C. 1981. "To the Tune of Those Weary Blues: the Influence of the Blues Tradition in Langston Hughes's Blues Poems." *MELUS* 8 (3), 73–98.

Waldron, Edward E. 1971. "The Blues Poetry of Langston Hughes." *Negro American Literature Forum* 5 (4), 140–149.

7.

Going back home:
the politics of the blues in Langston
Hughes's "The Backlash Blues"

Valerio Massimo De Angelis

University of Macerata, Italy

One of Langston Hughes's last poems (maybe the very last one) brought him back to his origins, both poetical and political. This "intensely musical" author, whom, as Arnold Rampersad recalls (Rampersad 2007, ix), composer Elie Siegmeister defined (with some exaggeration, perhaps) the most musical poet of the twentieth century, started his career by making the Blues both the form and the subject matter of many of his poems (his very first poetry collection, published in 1926, took the title from what is still today Hughes's most famous poem, "The Weary Blues"). Hughes ended his career by striking the same note with "The Backlash Blues," first published in *The Crisis* in June 1967 and then, later in the same year, in the collection *The Panther and the Lash*, but originally intended for Nina Simone's album *Nina Sings the Blues*, recorded in January. The two texts are not exactly the same (and the title of the song is "Backlash Blues," without "The"), because Hughes revised the poem after the issuing of the album, and

> converted the original text into a more standard AAB 12-bar Blues format by repeating the first lines of the five stanzas. He also changed the coda, eliminating the last lines that follow the warning that Mister Backlash will have the Blues, "Not me – / Wait and see!"[1] (Tkweme 2008, 508)

To further complicate the back-and-forth movement between the poem and the song(s), "when Simone recorded the song again in April 1968, she too

---

[1] On the specific ways Hughes and Simone used the blues poetic structure in "The Backlash Blues" see Chiara Patrizi's "'Singing Your Mean Old Backlash Blues': Blues, History, and Racial Inequality Today," in this volume.

substantially changed the text, by adding an entirely new final verse which brought the two artists' personal stories and relationship into the dialogue" (Tkweme 2008, 508). The relevance of this Blues in Nina Simone's musical career is testified by the fact that when she died (on April 21, 2003), a "one-page tribute in the *New Internationalist* ('Sounds of Dissent,' 2003) recounted her life and career. Some of the lyrics from three of her songs were included to summarize her revolutionary impact on the world: 'Mississippi Goddam,' 'Images,' and 'Backlash Blues'" (Bratcher 2007, 47).

This essay aims at highlighting how the use of the metaphor of the "backlash" allows Hughes to make a subtly complex metapoetical and also metamusical reflection on the (social and cultural, and even historical) meaning of the Blues in 1960s America. This makes it "signify" (I am of course referring to the practice of "signifying" in African American culture, as Gates (1988) describes it) much more than appears on the surface. The dialogue between Hughes's poem and Simone's recordings also shows the "dynamic" relevance of this/these text/s and of the Blues form/culture at large in the context of the American 1960s, especially in the aftermath of Martin Luther King's murder.[2]

The original poem is indeed built upon that interplay between the Blues form and the rhetoric of political engagement which was at the very heart of Langston Hughes's early career, especially in the 1930s,[3] and which had been somehow abandoned by the poet after World War II, especially after his investigation and interrogation by the McCarthy Committee for his former Communist allegiances. In some sense, the title of the poem, which refers to the "backlash" of white dominant culture trying to resist the Civil Rights movement, also "signifies" its reverse, the backlash whites are about to experience and the hopefully near at hand "disenfranchisement" of racism. But it may also be interpreted as a covert allusion to the need of both the poet himself and of the African American community in general to go back to their origins, rooted in that aesthetics of the Blues which critics like Gates and Houston A. Baker, Jr. (1984) see as the "matrix" of "Black" culture.[4] This is the text of the poem:

---

[2] On the cultural and also political function of the blues and related musical forms in the years of the Civil Rights movement up to the late Sixties, see especially Guralnick 1999, Roy 2010, Adelt 2011, Rabaka 2016.

[3] Stefania Piccinato stresses that in the 1930 phase of Hughes's poetry was "marked by a different lyrical and political commitment, earnestly digging deeper in precise and well-defined directions"; Piccinato 1979b, 121; translation mine).

[4] On Hughes's fascination with the origins of African American culture, and especially with its most "primitive" (and all the more subversive for it) features as translated into

Mister Backlash, Mister Backlash,
Just who do you think I am?
Tell me, Mister Backlash,
Who do you think I am?
You raise my taxes, freeze my wages,
Send my son to Vietnam.

You give me second-class houses,
Give me second-class schools,
Second-class houses
And second-class schools.
You must think us colored folks
Are second-class fools.

When I try to find a job
To earn a little cash,
Try to find myself a job
To earn a little cash,
All you got to offer
Is a white backlash.

But the world is big,
The world is big and round,
Great big world, Mister Backlash,
Big and bright and round –
And it's full of folks like me who are
Black, Yellow, Beige, and Brown.

Mister Backlash, Mister Backlash,
What do you think I got to lose?
Tell me, Mister Backlash,
What you think I got to lose?
I'm gonna leave you, Mister Backlash,
Singing your mean old backlash Blues.

---

black music, see Chinitz 2008. But of course Hughes also used black vernacular music to deconstruct all easy identifications of (especially poor) African Americans as non-sophisticated "primitives," negotiating "the problems presented by popular-culture and high-culture representations of the black poor by embedding their stories and their voices in a wide variety of 'authentic' black forms, especially the blues" (Smethurst 2007, 122). It goes almost without saying that these "negotiations" have as a primary target the dismantling of those "ethnocentric aesthetic assumptions" theorized by Modernism which, according to Paul Gilroy, "have consigned these musical creations [early blues and jazz] to a notion of the primitive that was intrinsic to the consolidation of scientific racism" (Gilroy 1993, 76).

You're the one,
Yes, you're the one
Will have the Blues.
(Hughes 1995, 552)

One could also add that, in a sort of *mise en abyme*, this strategy of reverting to an already mythicized past (that of the Harlem Renaissance and of the triumph of the Blues) repeats and redoubles that search for equally mythical roots which was central both to the "New Negro" movement (with its emphasis on the need to resurrect a legendary African tradition, much more "usable" to the ends of self-affirmation than the much less distant past of slavery)[5] and to Hughes himself, whose very first poem, "The Negro Speaks of Rivers" (1921), draws a wide-ranging historical horizon reaching back to the (black) origins of human civilization. Besides, Hughes's "looking backwards" fits into the widespread "Blues revival" of the 1960s, with the re-discovery of many Blues artists from the 1920s and 1930s who had somewhat disappeared from the landscape of American popular music after the appropriation and "bleaching" of black musical forms by white rock 'n' roll singers and musicians.

The very first source of inspiration for the poem was the famous, and overtly "political," "Poor Man's Blues," originally recorded by Bessie Smith in 1928– thus doubly confirming Steven Tracy's statement that,

> though some commentators have suggested that black vernacular music is frequently not political in nature or interest, Hughes's work is politically pointed and relevant, often as a result of his employment of the black vernacular music tradition (Tracy 2004, 109).

because Smith's is both a monument of "black vernacular music tradition," and "politically pointed and relevant." But while "Poor Man's Blues" does not directly address the African American predicament, focusing instead on class differences and the denunciation of the sacrifice the "poor men" had made (in World War I) to defend that same economic and political system that exploited and excluded them, Hughes's poem links social and pacifist

---

[5] Michael Feith has motivated the celebration of ancient Egyptian and Ethiopian civilization by at least some of the leaders of the Harlem Renaissance stressing the fact that those empires both belonged to East Africa, "whereas the overwhelming majority of the slaves imported to the United States came from West Africa. The reappropriation of these two empires by the Harlem Renaissance appears therefore as a product of contemporary Pan-Africanism … Another important motivation for this abrogation of distances lies in the impetus toward a politics of pride" (Feith 2004, 281).

discourse[6] to the vindication of the rights of coloured people, and therefore re-connects with that "identification of racial struggle with class struggle and political engagement" (Piccinato 1979a, 141; translation mine) which had characterized post-Depression African American culture. And, Tracy adds, in "The Backlash Blues" "Hughes raises questions about the identity that white society has imposed on the black man and the method by which the system attempts to guarantee the failure of the black man in that society" (Tracy 2001, 216).

On the other hand, in their foregrounding political protest, both "Poor Man's Blues" and "The Backlash Blues" may seem to go against the grain of most Blues tradition, that according to critical consensus up to the 1960s almost never explicitly calls for direct social action.[7] In some sense, by going back to his own roots as a Blues poet and by selecting as his main source of inspiration Bessie Smith's Blues, in "The Backlash Blues" Hughes seems to be trying to unearth and update a "political" tradition that until well into the 1950s had remained at least partially buried, hidden both by the various strategies of indirectness African American forms of expression had systematically deployed in order not to attract the blame and censorship of white culture,[8] and by the inability of (mostly white) musical scholars to

---

[6] The attack on the Vietnam War made the poem reach a wider audience than the African American one, particularly in the song versions recorded and performed by Nina Simone: "Writer Morgan Monceaux, remembering his tour of duty when a friend from home sent him a Nina Simone recording, says, 'I played it over and over again. The anger and passion matched exactly my feelings that America was going crazy in Vietnam'" (Loudermilk 2013, 125).

[7] As a matter of course, the political dimension of the blues has always been *there*, even if in oblique and indirect ways. As the many authors (the best-known Alessandro Portelli) of a seminal Italian book on African American culture stress in their introduction to the volume, a "typical false problem, at least as regards the way it has been set up, is that of the political contents of the Blues. On the one hand, in pointing out the fact that the Blues never explicitly deals with politics, attempts have been made to demonstrate that Blacks were lacking any willingness to oppose. On the other, correctly noticing that the Blues faithfully mirrors a real situation which is full of tensions that cannot but be political, it has been stated that the Blues is always and totally political. The latter conclusion needs at least a qualification. The political dimension of the Blues must not be sought in its explicit contents, but rather in its formal autonomy, which always and vigorously affirms the diversity and cultural autonomy (preliminary to political autonomy) of Black people" (Portelli et al. 1979, 41-42; translation mine).

[8] Of course, as Erik Nielson states, "by remaining as elusive as possible, the spirituals, blues, and jazz have all demonstrated their opposition to cultural negation. Yet that elusiveness suggests an ongoing dynamic from which black art does not escape

detect the political subtext (sometimes not even "sub," but clearly visible) of a wide range of Blues songs. A notable example is that of Samuel Charters, whose *The Country Blues*, published in 1959, was the very first "serious" book-length study of the Blues. This says a lot about the undervaluation of Blues music until well after World War II, and even the earliest comprehensive survey of African American rural folk music, *The Negro and His Songs* (1925) by Howard W. Odum and Guy B. Johnson, mainly dealt with the most archaic musical expressions, dedicating little or no space to Blues. Charters instead located the Blues at the very centre of the tradition of American folk music,[9] but at the same time stated that only rarely did the Blues touch political issues. Charters nonetheless opened the way to a new Blues scholarship that began to investigate the importance of social protest in many Blues songs, and this somehow triggered a response in Blues musicians, who started to be much more bluntly "political"–of course, this was also due to the influence of both the Civil Rights movement and youth counterculture.

But "non-political" Blues had a political dimension too. By turning upside down the imagery of romantic, sophisticated sentimentality that dominated Tin Pan Alley and popular music in general, many Blues songs exploited the rhetoric of forlorn love and hopeless melancholy to indirectly "signify" the alienation of the black individual, excluded as s/he was from the (white) American dream of progress and happiness. In more than a few instances Blues songs even proudly exhibited the new self-awareness of an African American community that had managed to break free from at least some of the many shackles imposed by white society: Angela Davis (1999) has stressed for example how Blues queens like Bessie Smith or Ma Rainey often sang the unprecedented opportunity, for black women, to travel throughout the country and to choose their own sexual partners (not even necessarily male). Besides, as Allan Moore has remarked, "both women's enfranchisement and the first classic Blues

---

untouched by the 'white shadows' that Hughes laments. Instead, it bears the mark of those shadows" (Nielson 2012, 173). One of the possible reasons for Hughes's adoption once again, at the end of his career, of a radically outspoken political stance, may well be the desire to exorcize those shadow-like ghosts which heavily conditioned his post-World War II poetry, and that made their presence visible precisely through their visible absence, as any ghost or shadow must do. The image of the "white shadows" is taken from the 1931 poem "House in the World," where Hughes juxtaposes the hopeful search for a house not haunted by those shadows to the angrily sad recognition that "*There is no such house, / Dark brothers, / No such house / At all*" (ll. 5-8).

[9] Until then Blues had been considered as being somewhat a more or less marginal addition to that tradition, like in the famous folksongs collection edited by John and Alan Lomax in 1941, *Our Singing Country*.

recording date from 1920" (Moore 2002, 4). The "backlash" Hughes describes is therefore not only the reverse reaction that had to ultimately doom power structures of white superiority white power structures, but also the recovery of an already existing tradition of "lashing back" that especially female Blues singers had established in the past: when in "Mistreating Daddy" Bessie Smith compared herself to "the butcher right down the street," threatening her man, if he insisted in interfering with her business, to cut him "all to pieces like I would a piece of meat," she could also be insinuating a "signifying" analogy between the "daddy" mistreating her and the white man oppressing black people, who might be able and ready to strike back in retaliation.

"The Backlash Blues" can therefore also be interpreted also as a complex meta-commentary by Hughes on the politics of the Blues, and once again this means a "going back" to the origins of his poetry, and more specifically to "The Weary Blues" (1925), which "stages both the genesis of poetical creation inspired by Blues and, opening up a new meta-level, the procedures of reception and interpretation of the text-inside-the-text Hughes inserts in his poem" (De Angelis 2017, 147; translation mine). This can be inferred by comparing the poem and the song by Nina Simone in the two different versions mentioned above, the second one recorded on April 7, 1968, three days after Martin Luther King's assassination. The poem ends with the (really revolutionary) dislocation of the Blues from the "black" to the "white" sphere: what has always been considered as quintessential to the experience of African Americans "backlashes" to the white "Mister Backlash," who is left singing his own "mean old backlash Blues," because from now on it will be his turn to "have the Blues." This reversal turns upside down what Hughes had denounced in the 1930s, in a number of poems and especially in "White Man" (1936), as "the exploitation of black musicians, such as Louis Armstrong, by the White Man" (Young 2007, 138). The exploitation of black music now backfires, and dislocates Mr Backlash/the White Man in the same destitute position he had economically and culturally profited from when Blues and jazz had been represented and marketed simply as the primitive forms of musical expression of a "backward" people.

Besides systematically playing with the practice of "signifying," so that words like "backlash" and "Blues" acquire different, sometimes even opposite, meanings at each occurrence, and at each implicit suggestion of further allusions, the final lines also stage a sort of re-actualization of the other "matrix" of African American cultural expression – the slave narrative. Being as it is a story of self-deliverance and ultimately of a flight from the space of slavery, dominated by the power of the white master, the slave narrative of the past is here the "matrix" for the parallel story of the (not so) free African American who, having nothing left to lose, decides to leave his (American) master alone, because "The world is big and round," and "full of folks like me who are / Black, Yellow, Beige, and Brown."[10] The new narrative of liberation tells the story of the "flight" from America, towards a much wider and multi-ethnic world that at that time seemed to offer the promise of a new "coloured" Renaissance (and in his last years Hughes was actively involved in the Pan-African movement).

Blues scholarship has now and then highlighted the "escapist" features of especially early Blues,[11] but James Baldwin himself[12] once stressed that "he who finds no way to rest cannot long survive the battle" (Baldwin 1972, 126), thus suggesting that escapism can have a positive power as a strategy that does not necessarily end up in passivity and surrender, but on the contrary in a re-fueling through parallel and "slanted" ways of not only resilience but also resistance. I appropriate this view, precisely because "escaping" can be turned into its "signifying" opposite–a recollection of that strategy of *actually* running away which average "escapism" would like to make us forget together with everything linked to the experience of slavery. Anyway, what remains to Mister Backlash, in the poem, is his old Blues, implying that whites have always had their own Blues,[13] but maybe have never been able to express them except through the "mean" mistreatment of blacks. As a matter of fact, on the historical level this "backlash" of the "white backlash" has never literally occurred, not even after the eight years of the Obama administration,[14] and

---

[10] By the way, one of Duke Ellington's most sophisticated jazz suites was titled *Black, Brown and Beige* (it was recorded live during a famous concert at the Carnegie Hall in New York City, in January 23, 1943), since it ambitiously (and successfully) tried to represent the whole experience of the African diasporas. Hughes added another "ethnic colour," yellow, so as to make the poem even more universally (or maybe we should better say cosmopolitically) meaningful.

[11] See for example Lawson 2010, on the shift from pre-Great Depression "black escapism" to the growing ethics of hard work and social commitment gradually taking hold in the Thirties and after World War II.

[12] With "Sonny's Blues" James Baldwin had already written in 1965 a sort of meditation on the metaphorical analogy of the blues with dope as a way out of the African American quandary, "the only light we've got in all this darkness" (Baldwin 1998, 947). And Ralph Ellison too remarked how "the art–the blues, the spirituals, the jazz, the dance–was what we had in place of freedom" (Ellison 1972, 255).

[13] Something Frederick Douglass already hinted at in his *Narrative*, when he pointed out how slavery de-humanized not only the slave but also the master.

[14] As W. Jason Miller has pointed out in his analysis of the strange triangulation linking Langston Hughes, Martin Luther King and Barack Obama (with the latter two quoting but not naming the former), even before becoming President, Obama was so confident in the almost complete fulfillment of Martin Luther King's dream that in his acceptance

we are now witnessing a revival of the white backlash, countered as it can by movements such as Black Lives Matter.

In the 1967 recording, Nina Simone used the original version of the poem: this version features two last lines eliminated from the poem published in *The Panther and the Lash*, which reinforce the "passing" of the Blues from Black to White: "*Not me – / Wait and see!*" In the 1968 recording, in the album *'Nuff Said*, Nina Simone adds a totally new stanza, in which she invokes the late Hughes as, in W.S. Tkweme's words, "a recently departed ancestor whose charge to her from beyond the grave was to continue to challenge white supremacy politically, intellectually, and culturally" (Tkweme 2008, 509), and implicitly as a sort of twin brother to the *just* departed Martin Luther King:

> When Langston Hughes died, when he died he told me many months before
> He said Nina keep on working till they open up the door
> One of these days when you've made it and the doors are open wide
> Make sure you tell 'em exactly where it's at so they'll have no place to hide
> So Mr. Backlash, Mr. Backlash, hear me now, I'm warning you, yeah
> Somehow someway, yeah, I'm gonna leave you with the Blues.

By doing so, Nina Simone introduced a further turn of the screw, because her backlash is also that of Hughes (and King) "backlashing" from beyond the grave and through Nina Simone's voice that white supremacy which had closed the doors to her own career as a promising classical piano player. Leaving Mister Backlash with the Blues for her means also that black musicians must be able (and allowed) to go beyond the limits of any fixed "ethnic" protocol of self-expression, and at the same time that the Blues itself is something that vastly exceeds the enclosed world of black music. Simone

---

speech, after having been nominated Presidential candidate at the 2008 Democratic Convention, he implicitly set Hughes's vision of the African American predicament as a sort of pessimistic counter-narrative to King's trust in the future, because the people gathered in Washington D.C. in August 28, 1963, could, and luckily did not, have heard, instead of King's hopeful words, "words of anger and discord, they could have been told to succumb to the fears and frustrations of so many dreams deferred" (qtd. in Miller 2013, 456). Obama is of course indirectly quoting *Montage of a Dream Deferred*, Hughes's 1951 collection which contains the famous metaphor of dreams deferred as raisins in the sun (in the "Harlem" poem), doomed to festering, stinking and maybe finally exploding: "What happens to a dream deferred? // Does it dry up / like a raisin in the sun? / Or fester like a sore – / And then run? / Does it stink like rotten meat? / Or crust and sugar over – / like a syrupy sweet? // Maybe it just sags / like a heavy load. // *Or does it explode?*"). In some sense, Hughes's bleak 1951 forecast (at the height of his "distancing" from overt political commitment, one should note) has eventually proved more correct than either King's or Obama's (or even his own, in "The Backlash Blues").

made another addition and commentary to the song in the live performance at the Newport Jazz Festival on July 1, 1968, ten days after Hughes's death (he had passed on June 22):

> "Langston used to sit on the Newport festival board," Nina told the audience when she introduced "Backlash Blues." "He was here when it began, you know, and he wrote this tune . . . and gave it to me to put some music to. It was his final slap in the face of the white backlash of his country," she went on. "So we're going to do his tune, and of course he's gone from us, but not really. He's out there somewhere." (Cohodas 2010, 200)

Simone was therefore not only reinventing, in her performance(s), the poetical/political identity of the "queens" of the classic Blues era, when, perhaps "because the Blues was seen as 'race music' and catered to a black audience, black women were better able to articulate themselves as individuals and as part of a racial group in that art form" (Christian 1985, 122). Just like Hughes had re-enacted and renewed in the poem his former commitment to the "political aesthetics" of the Blues, she was also explicitly and programmatically renewing, by paying homage to the late poet, the tradition of political engagement translated into the Blues which Hughes had so poignantly embodied. Through the various versions of "The Backlash Blues"–a Blues "in progress," if there ever was one–Hughes and Simone managed to build up an extremely complex and dynamic relationship with the origins of the Blues *and* with its political meaningfulness: by "going back home," they made that "home" go forward into the future, and showed that, in its being the matrix of African American culture, the Blues was still *there*, providing a major source of social awareness and artistic creativity.

One final note. There are at least three famous African American songs titled "Going Back Home."[15] Two of them are actually titled "I'm Going Back Home," and one is from Nina Simone (again), recorded in the same 1967 of "Backlash Blues" (in the *High Priestess of Soul* album), but it is not a Blues – it is rather a very rhythm-'n'-bluesy gospel, about the nostalgia for the peaceful life in the countryside, as opposed to the too fast and stressful pace of living in the city. Another is the 1930 recording by Memphis Minnie and Kansas Joe McCoy, with the added vocals by Joe Johnson, telling the straight story of the sorrowful breaking apart of a love relation. But in 1934 Kansas Joe McCoy recorded "Going Back Home," a totally different and much more ambiguously ominous Blues about a Ulysses-like impossible *nostos*, and ending with the not-so-ambiguous threat of the final stanza: "But you will never forget the day I knock upon your

---

[15] By the way, "go," "back" and "home," as Jean Charles Khalifa has shown in his essay in this volume, are three of the most recurrent words in blues lyrics.

door." This line suddenly introduces a "you" never mentioned before in the song– and one must of course ask who this "you" may be: perhaps that white man who is the real but untold cause of the unerring wandering of the poetic self, and who is about to experience an unexpected backlash? And maybe this is what "The Backlash Blues" is all about – going back home, from the 1960s, to when not only Harlem was in vogue, and African American culture was spectacularly staging its renaissance, but above all to when black music and poetry had become powerfully political forms of expression, as they had to be once again, "backlashing" forward to the present.

References

Adelt, Ulrich. 2011. *Blues Music in the Sixties: A Story in Black and White*. New Brunswick, NJ: Rutgers University Press.

Baker, Houston A., Jr. 1984. *Blues, Ideology, and Afro-American Literature: A Vernacular Theory*. Chicago: University of Chicago Press.

Baldwin, James. (1965) 1998. "Sonny's Blues." In *Early Novels and Stories*, 831-864. New York: Library of America.

Baldwin, James. 1972. *No Name in the Street*, New York: The Dial Press.

Bratcher, Melanie E. 2007. *Words and Songs of Bessie Smith, Billie Holiday, and Nina Simone: Sound Motion, Blues Spirit, and African Memory*. London. Routledge.

Charters, Samuel. 1959. *The Country Blues*. New York: Rinehart.

Chinitz, David. 2008. "Rejuvenation through Joy: Langston Hughes, Primitivism, and Jazz." In *Langston Hughes*, edited by Harold Bloom, 61-77. New York: Infobase.

Christian, Barbara. 1985. *Black Feminist Criticism: Perspectives on Black Women Writers*. New York: Pergamon Press.

Cohodas, Nadine. 2010. *Princess Noire: the Tumultuous Reign of Nina Simone*. Chapel Hill: University of North Carolina Press.

Davis, Angela Y. 1999. *Blues Legacies and Black Feminism: Gertrude "Ma" Rainey, Bessie Smith, and Billie Holiday*. New York: Vintage.

De Angelis, Valerio Massimo. 2017. "That's What the / Blues Singers Say: La meta-poetica del blues di Langston Hughes. In *Una bussola per l'Infosfera: Con Ishmael Reed tra Musica e Letteratura*, edited by N. Paladin and G. Rimondi, 147-162. Milano: Agenzia X.

Ellison, Ralph. 1972. *Shadow and Act*. New York: Vintage.

Feith, Michael. 2004. "The Syncopated African: Constructions of Origins in the Harlem Renaissance (Literature, Music, Visual Arts)." In *The Harlem Renaissance*, edited by Harold Bloom, 275-294. Broomall, PA: Chelsea House.

Gates, Henry Louis, Jr. 1988. *The Signifying Monkey: A Theory of Afro-American Literary Criticism*. Oxford: Oxford University Press.

Gilroy, Paul. 1993. *The Black Atlantic: Modernity and Double Consciousness*. London and New York: Verso.

Guralnick, Peter. 1999. *Sweet Soul Music: Rhythm and Blues and the Southern Dream of Freedom*. Boston: Back Bay Books.

Hughes, Langston. 1995. *The Collected Poems of Langston Hughes*, edited by Arnold Rampersad. New York: Vintage Classics.

Lawson, R. A. 2010. *Jim Crow's Counterculture: the Blues and Black Southerners, 1890-1945*. Baton Rouge: Louisiana State University Press.

Lomax, John A. and Lomax, Alan (eds.) 1941. *Our Singing Country: a Second Volume of American Ballads and Folk Songs*. New York: Macmillan.

Loudermilk, A. 2013. "Nina Simone and the Civil Rights Movement: Protest at Her Piano, Audience at Her Feet." *Journal of International Women's Studies* 14 (3): 121-136.

Miller, W. Jason. 2013. "'Don't Turn Back': Langston Hughes, Barack Obama, and Martin Luther King, Jr." *African American Review* 46 (2-3): 425-438.

Moore, Allan. 2002. "Surveying the Field: Our Knowledge of Blues and Gospel Music." In *The Cambridge Companion to Blues and Gospel Music*, edited by Allan Moore, 1-12. Cambridge: Cambridge University Press.

Nielson, Erik. 2012. "A 'High Tension' in Langston Hughes's Musical Verse." *Melus* 37 (4): 165-185.

Odum, Howard Washington, and Guy Benton Johnson. 1925. *The Negro and His Songs: A Study of Typical Negro Songs in the South*. Chapel Hill: University of North Carolina Press.

Piccinato, Stefania. 1979a. "*Negro Renaissance* e *New Negro Movement*: Il Nuovo Intellettuale Afro-Americano." In Portelli 1979, 125-144.

Piccinato, Stefania 1979b. *Testo e Contesto nella Poesia di Langton Hughes*. Rome: Bulzoni.

Portelli, Alessandro et al. 1979. "Dalla Resistenza alla Rivolta: Forme e Funzioni della Cultura Popolare Afro-Americana." In *Saggi sulla Cultura Afro-Americana*, edited by Alessandro Portelli, 9-59. Rome: Bulzoni.

Rabaka, Reiland. 2016. *Civil Rights Music: The Soundtracks of the Civil Rights Movement*. Lanham, MD: Lexington Books.

Rampersad, Arnold. 2007. "Introduction." In *Montage of a Dream: the Art and Life of Langston Hughes*, edited by John E. Tidwell and Cheryl R. Ragar, ix-xii. Cambridge: Cambridge University Press.

Roy, William G. 2010. *Reds, Whites, and Blues: Social Movements, Folk Music, and Race in the United States*. Princeton NJ: Princeton University Press.

Smethurst, James. 2007. "Lyric Stars: Countee Cullen and Langston Hughes." In *The Cambridge Companion to the Harlem Renaissance*, edited by George Hutchinson, 112-125. Cambridge: Cambridge University Press.

Tkweme, W.S. 2008. "Blues in Stereo: the Texts of Langston Hughes in Jazz Music." *African American Review* 42 (3/4): 503-512.

Tracy, Steven C. 2001. *Langston Hughes and the Blues*. Urbana and Chicago: University of Illinois Press.

Tracy, Steven C. 2004. "Langston Hughes and Afro-American Vernacular Music." In *A Historical Guide to Langston Hughes*, edited by Steven C. Tracy, 85-118. New York: Oxford University Press.

Young, Robert. 2007. "Langston Hughes's Red Poetics and the Practice of 'Disalienation.'" In *Montage of a Dream: the Art and Life of Langston Hughes*, edited by John E. Tidwell and Cheryl R. Ragar, 135-146. Cambridge: Cambridge University Press.

8.

A Bluesy sound: from Weary Blues to "Nigger-Reecan Blues"

Irene Polimante

University of Macerata, Italy

Introduction

The following paper introduces a brief comparison between two poets who are distant in time but close in the search for an "aesthetic compromise" between different genres: poetry and music, Blues to be precise. Whether their literary effort echoes back to the old rivalry between poetry and song[1]—as one aspect of the more complex juxtaposition between orality and literacy— Hughes and Perdomo's attempt to blur the boundaries of poetry and Blues casts light on contemporary practices of hybridization, performativity and intermediality in poetry.[2]

The history of the Blues has always been closely linked to the African-American tradition as an expression of the trials and tribulations "of the Negro's *conscious* appearance on the American scene" (Jones 1963, xii). This musical genre, together with work songs, gospels, spirituals, jazz, etc., belongs to a culture which has long privileged orality over literacy (Crown 2003, 224-25), while its literature has been created "within the framework of multiple relationships and the tension between the white literary and the black oral traditions" (Williams 1977, 542). This tension fosters a relation of mutual inspiration and influence between Blues and poetry, while unfolding thorny issues, such as: the distinction between verbal and musical genres[3]; the powerful combination of the literary "narcissistic complex" with the folk

---

[1] Cf. Jacques Derrida 1976, Giorgio Agamben 1999.
[2] Cf. Freda Chapple and Chiel Kattenbelt 2006, Amy M. Robbins 2014, and Thomas F. DeFrantz and Anita Gonzalez 2014.
[3] Cf. Kit Robinson. 1985. "Song," In *Writing/Talks: Poetics of the New*, edited by Bob Perelman, 48-62. Carbondale and Edwardsville: Southern Illinois University Press.

"form of things unknown" (Henderson 1982, 25); and the opposition of "high vs low" culture, with the consequent emphasis on the "cultural cross-breeding in literature and the musical arts" which, in the 1920s, began to move African-American culture, music, and vernacular forms closer to popular mainstream (Tracy 2004, 95). Moreover, the couple "Blues-poetry" opens an array of methodological problems that, in terms of the ancient dichotomy between literacy and orality, primarily affects poetry because of its ambivalent nature, which hangs in the balance between literature and sound,[4] especially in the form of song.[5] In *Sing to Me Now*, Jahan Ramazani highlights how this old question is absolutely crucial to understanding twenty-first-century American poetry, since poetry's "entanglement with song reveals not only attention but also tension, not only cross-genre longing and idealization but also rivalry and friction" (Ramazani 2011, 720-21). And this antagonism, according to Ramazani, is also present in the works of poets like Kevin Young, Patricia Smith, Harryette Mullen, Tracie Morris, and Terrance Hayes. These artists not only continue to be inspired by African-American music genres, like Blues, jazz, and hip hop, but they also entwine their poetry with song, creating what Cathy Park Hong characterized as the "vital collision," the "mash up" (Ramazani 2011, 720). In other words, the old interplay of poetry with song has become part of "a broader discourse that poetry engages with other media" (Ramazani 2011, 719). This "inter-discursive collage," as Ramazani defines it, primarily informs the controversial relationship between poetry and song, insofar as, during the process of poetry's metabolization of the extra-poetic discourse, poetry itself is unravelled by song (Ramazani 2011, 722). This is possible due to the fact that music has a "dissociative" quality that produces a "disintegrative effect on words" during the vocal performance (Ramazani 2011, 723). Therefore, "the music appropriates the poem by contending with it, phonetically, dramatically, and semantically" (Ramazani 2011, 723). Moreover, such a contention is further sharpened by another important difference between song and poetry. Song, unlike poetry, combines three media: words, music, and voice (Ramazani 2011, 725). For this reason, "in comparison to sung verse, literary verse seems deficient in melody and harmony, the physicality of the embodied voice, and the thick social and performative context" (Ramazani 2011, 725). In Ramazani's terms, even performance poetry cannot satisfy these requirements, since poetry lacks the materiality that Roland Barthes finds in the singing voice: "the grain". In fact, Ramazani concludes, the Barthian grain of the voice—or, "the body in the

---

[4] Cf. Bernstein et al 2009, Perloff and Dworkin 2009.
[5] Cf. Gregory Nagy (1996).

voice as it sings" (Barthes 1977, 188)—not only, completely disappears from the printed poem, but it is "of lesser significance in poetry recitations and readings than in song" (Ramazani 2011, 725). However, despite Ramazani's critical analysis, the whole history of African-American culture and literature seems to prove the contrary, showing a felicitous and prosperous union between music and poetry.

In *Black and Blues Configurations*, Walton Muyumba traces the development of African-American contemporary poetry from the early twentieth century to the beginning of the new millennium, identifying two artistic landmarks that, "over the past several decades [...] have introduced an array of new techniques and styles to Anglophone poetics," which are still deeply influencing the poetic practice of the XXI century (Muyumba 2014, 1073). The first is Langston Hughes's poetry, which serves as a model "to express black experience through the absorption of Blues-idiom music and African-American vernacular speech into modern lyrical forms" (Muyumba 2014, 1050). The second reference is to the bebop revolution which, during the 1940s, shook African-American music, arts, and aesthetics. The black musicians who developed it "presented ways of taking up various modernist traditions (visual art, dance, literary arts, and music), revising and reorienting their elements improvisationally" (Muyumba 2014, 1050-1051). The innovations brought by the bebop movement influenced the following generations of African-American poets "who emerged in the 1950s and 1960s as the literary avant-garde not only referenced black music in their works but also shaped their poems through bebop" (Muyumba 2014, 1051). These two artistic benchmarks symbolically represent a crucial literary turn, that, in musical terms, Muyumba describes as a shift from the innovations of Bessie Smith, Ma Rainey, Louis Armstrong, Nat King Cole, and Duke Ellington, to new poetics, which are more "attuned" to Thelonious Monk's, Dizzy Gillespie's, and Charlie Parker's inventions (Muyumba 2014, 1051). The key elements of such historical bridging are two poets: Langston Hughes and Melvin Tolson. In fact, Muyumba outlines how their allusive improvisational sensibility, the adoption of a Blues-idiom musicality, coupled with a combination of both formal and experimental techniques have left a legacy that affects poetry to this day—starting from the surrealist bebop poems by Bob Kaufman, passing through the recovery of the African-American oral tradition by Baraka's Black Arts Movement, and culminating with the Dark Room Collective, that in the late 1990s refused specific political ideologies or aesthetic agendas (Muyumba 2014, 1073). Describing such a heterogeneous *milieu*, Muyumba comments:

> It's possible to read this lineage without thinking about groupings—modernists versus postmodernists, the BAM [Black Arts Movement] versus the post-BAM— because these artists all use the Blues idiom as a touchstone. And when a poet invokes that idiom, she's also explaining that her aesthetic approach necessitates invention, improvisation, and innovation. (Muyumba 2014, 1073)

Blues, indeed, encodes both an appeal to tradition and a push for innovation, that have inspired many poets "to incorporate the essence of the Blues into works outside the reference of music" (Waldron 1971, 140). One of the most successful poets in this endeavour has been Langston Hughes, whose musical sensibility has captured "the mood, the feel, and the spirit" of this genre (Waldron 1971, 140).

Langston Hughes's *The Weary Blues*

From the very beginning of his career, Hughes sought ways "to deliver voice and music into the visual medium of print" in the attempt to make sound visible in his poetry (Wheeler 2008, 62). In *Poetry of Mourning*, Ramazani comments that Hughes's endeavour to intersect the visual with the aural is immediately evident in the poet's first anthology *The Weary Blues* (1926). The volume, in fact, works "an intricate mediation on the simultaneous distance and proximity between Hughes's Blues poetry and Blues song" (Ramazani 1994, 144). Such a duality is especially represented in the Blues poem "The Weary Blues". As Ramazani posits, the title itself figures the poem's ambiguous relation to the Blues, since "it is either a metonymic borrowing from 'The Weary Blues' quoted in the poem (making the work about a weary Blues) or a synecdochic equation of the entire poem with a 'Weary Blues' (in which case the poem is a weary Blues)" (Ramazani 1994, 144). As a matter of fact, such an ambiguity is the main feature of Hughes's "lucky poem" (Hughes 1963, 92), which represents the poet's effort to write a Blues poem, that concerns "a working man who [sings] the Blues all night and then [goes] to bed and [sleeps] like a rock" (Hughes 1963, 215), while including the verse of the first Blues song that Hughes had ever heard when he was a kid in Kansas (Hughes 1963, 215). In this way, the title opens to "a discursive gap" that informs a complex frame device to discriminate, not only Blues from poetry, but the literary from the folk tradition (Ramazani 1994, 144). Hughes, indeed, builds the poem through a series of literary, linguistic, visual, and aural contrasts, which serves him a double purpose. He can mingle the poetic language with the sung verse and, at the same time, provide a meta-reading of the creation of a Blues form from a poetic perspective. As Ramazani states, Hughes is able to "indulge a Blues lament while gaining a reflective distance on it" (Ramazani 1994, 144). In doing so, Hughes may involve the reader in the creative Blues process (Waldron 1971, 148), by representing in the poem two distinct artistic practices that do usually not happen simultaneously: the composition and performance of both Blues and poetry.

The second stanza of the poem clearly shows how the frame device sets up a visual contrast, which makes it possible for the reader to immediately distinguish the work of the two main poetic voices—the poet and the Blues man—thanks to their specific stylistic patterns.

In a deep song voice with a melancholy tone
I heard that Negro sing, that old piano moan—
"Ain't got nobody in all this world,
ain't got nobody but ma self.
I's gwine to quit ma frownin'
and put ma troubles on the shelf".
Thump, thump, thump, went his foot on the floor.
He played a few chords then he sang some more
"I got the Weary Blues
and I can't be satisfied.
Got the Weary Blues
and can't be satisfied—
I ain't happy no mo'
and I wish that I had died".
And far into the night he crooned that tune.

(Hughes in Piccinato 1971, 62-65)

The overall framework is built on a series of oppositions: poem-song; written text-oral performance; professional literacy-folklore tradition; and high-low culture. This last contrast is heightened by the use of two different linguistic varieties: the poet's middle-English, with its long "pentameter lines, inter spliced with irregular part-line (Ramazani 1994, 145); and the Bluesman's African-American vernacular English (Ramazani 1994, 145), with its shorter and more regular verses[6]. All these contrasts between poetic and sung text create a tension that has to be experienced both visually and aurally. Taking this tension as a starting point, the poet starts investigating The Weary Blues' inner orality. In order to do so, Hughes composes his poem using Blues conventions, such as the "call-and-response" between singer and audience, which is reproduced by the repetition of the interjections "O Blues!" and "Sweet Blues!". The "line repetition" of the same sentence—"he did a lazy sway..." and, immediately after, "he did a lazy sway..."—or the repetition of the same sentence with a variation of one or few words—"I heard a Negro play" in the first stanza becomes "I heard that Negro sing" in the second; or, again, "that poor piano moan" in the first stanza turns into "that old piano moan." In the last stanza, Hughes closes the poem with a classic Blues-triple-rhyme: "bed/head/dead" (Ramazani 1994, 145).

---

[6] For an analysis of the Blues' influence on Hughes's Blues poems, see David Clintz. 1996. "Literacy and Authenticity: The Blues Poems of Langston Hughes." *Callaloo* 19 (1), 177-192. For a detailed recount on the Blues that inspired this poem, with an excursus on the history and characteristic of early Blues, see Steven C. Tracy. 1981. "To the Tune of Those Weary Blues: The Influence of the Blues Tradition in Langston Hughes's Blues Poems." *Melus* 8 (3), 73-98.

This interpolation of the musical code in the poetic frame also influences the language. The difference between the language of poet and singer diminishes when the standard diction modulates into the colloquial by "eliding the f in 'tune o' those Weary Blues' and discreetly incorporating African-American idiom (made that poor piano moan, a musical fool) and syncopation (Droning a drowsy syncopated tune)" (Ramazani 1994, 145). However, the syncopated effect is also created by the frequent use of alliterations and internal rhymes; the changes in pace when the poet switches from English to vernacular, and vice versa; and by the onomatopoeic sound of the word "thump", repeated three times in the same line. The linguistic and stylistic combination of poetic elements with those of the Blues reveals the strong relationship between poet and singer, who are also symbols of the two different inner voices of Hughes.[7] He construes the poem as a setting to express both his literary and musical skills, creating a work of art, where two different genres, poetry and song, may coexist without losing their own specific features.

The climax of such syncretism among author, poet, and singer is reached during live performance. In 1958, Hughes performed "The Weary Blues" to accompaniment with the Doug Parker Jazz Band on the CBUT program "The 7 O'clock Show".[8] After the host, Bob Quintrell, introduces the "reading," the camera moves to the band, that opens the piece with twenty-four seconds of Blues riff. While the band plays, the camera widens the view field to include the poet on the left of the frame. Once the music ends, Hughes makes his own Bluesy poetic intro, too:

> Sun's a settin'. This is what I'm gonna sing.
> Sun's a settin'. This is what I'm gonna sing:
> I feel de *bluuues*[9] are comin',
> I wonder what de bluuues will bring.[10]

Hughes reproduces the pace, rhythm, and intonation of the previous Blues riff, by "playing" his voice as an instrument. He shortens the pronunciation of the first part of the two initial lines—"Sun's a settin'"—while lengthening and stressing the sound of the word "Blues". Like a director, Hughes gives the attack

---

[7] On Hughes's meta-poetry, with a detailed analysis of the complex interrelation between the syntactic structure and the two poetic persona of the poet and the singer, see Valerio Massimo De Angelis. 2017 "'That's What the/Blues Singers Say': La meta-poetica del Blues di Langston Hughes." In *Una bussola per l'infosfera: con Ishmael Reed tra musica e letteratura*, edited by Giorio Rimondi, Nicola Paladin, 147-162. Milano: Agenzia.

[8] "The Weary Blues." *YouTube*. Video File. February 11, 2019. https://www.youtube.com/watch?v=uM7HSOwJw20&t=3s, last access 11/06/2019.

[9] I have adopted this transcription to give a visual image of the long sound.

[10] "The Weary Blues." *YouTube*. Video File. February 11, 2019. https://www.youtube.com/watch?v=uM7HSOwJw20&t=3s, last access 11/06/2019.

to the band with the first "Blues"; and when he concludes, wondering what the Blues would have brought, the camera cuts away to the trumpet player for a short solo. The whole performance goes on with the constant interplay between poet and musicians. The music does not work as a mere background to the poem, but participates in its development, with an ongoing dialogue between instruments and voice. Moreover, using eye-level placement, the camera takes a medium/medium-close shot of the poet, keeping the whole band in the immediate background. This is the prevalent frame adopted for almost the entire performance, permitting the simultaneous presence of both poet and jazz band on camera. Due to such a stratagem, the wide array of complex contrasts that informs the whole poem is made visible, by displaying a set of visual and musical correlatives. For example, during the performance, Hughes embodies the dual personae of poet and singer while, at the same time, his physical presence testifies to his authorship. Again, the opposing couple poem-song is exhibited and resolved in the concomitant performances of Hughes and the jazz band. Furthermore, the two performances unveil another kind of contrast; the racial difference between the white musicians at the back and the black poet in the front. The contrast works perfectly as the poem's correlative, within the elegant and extremely formal framework of the TV show. The visual opposition between black and white, in fact, parallels a similar tension in the poem, where the poet expresses his grief for the African- American segregated condition, by projecting his feelings onto the poetic persona of the singer. The result of such a displacement is a series of parallelisms: the singer with his piano; the piano with the melancholic tune; and the Blues' melancholy with the musician/poet's racial inheritance.

Langston Hughes's legacy

This strong coalescence of poetry, song, and performance lies at the basis of Hughes's artistic heritage, that many writers and poets have tried to take up, as well as to emulate. The political and artistic efforts of the first African-American "avant-garde"[11] are well-known. From the late 1950s-early 1960s, under the leading figure of Amiri Baraka, they pointed to the deep connections between African-American music and literature.[12] The intertwining of Blues idiom and poetic forms, thus, became part of a wider project for the creation of a counter-cultural aesthetic critique, establishing a new set of black cultural theories to

---

[11] For a detailed description of the main differences between the two principle schools of thought in the Black Arts Movement, see Charles Rowell. 2004. "The Editor's Note." *Callaloo* 27 (4), vii-ix.

[12] On the aesthetic reframing of the study of African-American culture as also a pillar of the Black Arts Movement, see Amiri Baraka (aka LeRoi Jones). 1963. *Blues People: Negro Music in White America* . New York: Morrow, and 1998. *Black Music*. New York: Da Capo.

apply to the investigation of any form of black art (Muyumba 2014, 1055), in response to, and fulfilment of, white critics' "vernaculars and practices" (Baraka 1998, 20). At the end of the twentieth century, poets both inside and outside the Black Arts movement—like Toi Derricotte, Rita Dove, Yusef Komunyakaa, and Cornelius Eady—gave an impulse to a more complex and multifaceted poetic practice (Muyumba 2014, 1066). They included Blues idioms inside their creative processes as one strategy to negotiate a balance between "their artistic goals and the operation of race in the production, dissemination, and reception of their writing" (Shockley 2011, 9). At the beginning of the twenty-first century, with the re-insurgence of popular forms of poetry, like spoken word poems, performance poems and slam poems, it seemed it was time for a celebration of the "hip-hop poetica" (Covac 2007, 222). Even today, poets like Patricia Smith, Tracie Morris, Kevin Young, Allison Joseph, and Terrance Hayes produce poems that are in-between in terms of song-structure, featuring word play, wide use of "juxtaposition and (over)layering of styles and genres" (Covac 2007, 226-227). Despite its success, however, the satirical confrontational dynamic of hip-hop, with its "systemic rupture of line and time" (Covac 2007, 225), has not supplanted the "Blues poetica" that, along with spirituals, jazz, and rap, participates in the communal narration of the African-American experience. In the poetic scene of the twenty-first century, the most important example of artistic fusion of Blues rhythms and forms with poetic aesthetic is Kevin Young's poetry. His Blues Poems (2003) is the first collection of poems and lyrics devoted exclusively to the Blues (Young 2003, 11). Covering a span of time that goes from World War II to the early twenty-first century, Young celebrates an important part of the African-American tradition, by showing how old and new voices reinvent the relationship between Blues and poetry.[13]

Willie Perdomo's "Nigger-Reecan Blues"

Among the new poetic voices that Kevin Young enlists in Hughes's contemporary legacy is the poet and spoken word performer Willie Perdomo, who, in the early 1990s, gained notoriety in the Nuyorican Poets Café slam scene thanks to poems which addressed the polyphonic reality of New York City. The starting point of Perdomo's poetics is a personal exploration of the different languages and vernaculars which are spoken in the neighbourhood where he used to live: *el barrio* (Spanish Harlem) (Gräbner and Casas 2011, 76). Using a broad array of "urban, multicultural, post-hip hop vernaculars" (Noel 2011, 864), Perdomo plays with different accents and pronunciations of English words to represent the sonic portrait, or better, the soundscape of a "vernacular city, enriched by the languages

---

[13] Blues, as topic, form, and source of inspiration will be at the center of other works by Kevin Young, like *Jelly Roll: A Blues* (2003); *Black Maria* (2005); *For the Confederate Dead* (2007); *Dear Darkness: Poems* (2008); and *Blue Laws* (2016).

and cultures of migration and diaspora" (Noel 2011, 864). Indeed, the language, primary medium of communication, also becomes the main expressive form through which a national as well as a local, urban identity is expressed. And in "Nigger-Reecan Blues", Perdomo works on the differences in rhythms and sounds between English and Spanish: two languages which constitute and represent the complex and multiple identity of the poet himself, who, in the unsuccessful attempt to define his "Afro-Latinidad," expresses such an impossibility in the form of a Blues poem. "Nigger-Reecan Blues" first appeared in Algarín and Holman's anthology *Aloud*[14] in 1994. It was published again in the 1996 collection *Where a Nickel Costs a Dime*[15] and, in the same year, Perdomo recorded the poem for the Mouth Almighty Records' project *Flippin' the Script: Rap Meets Poetry*. However, the major visibility for both poet and poem arrived with Perdomo's participation in Russell Simmons's TV show *Def Poetry Jam*, which was broadcast by HBO from 2002 to 2007. Perdomo develops "Nigger-Reecan Blues" as a dialogue between multiple poetic persona that interact with the poet himself, Willie. The initial line posits a controversial question: "Hey, Willie. What are you, man?", that opens the field to a series of other questions and answers, which shows the many "complexities of situating a Nuyorican identity that is Puerto Rican but also racially black" (Noel 2014, 128).

> -But who said you was a Porta Reecan?
> -Tu eres Puerto Riqueno, brother.
> -Maybe Indian like Gandhi Indian.
> -I thought you was a Black man.
> -Is one of your parents white?
> -You sure you ain't a mix of something like
> -Portuguese and Chinese?
> -Naaaahhh...You ain't no Porta Reecan.
> -I keep telling you: The boy is a Black man with an accent.
> [...]
> You soy Boricua! You soy Africano! I ain't lyin'. Pero
> mi pelo es
> kinky y kurly y mi skin no es negra pero it can pass...
> -Hey, yo. I don't care what you say – you Black.
> I ain't Black! [...]
>
> (Perdomo in Algarín & Holman 1994, 111-12)

---

[14] Only in this anthology appears the dedication to Piri Thomas, the Puerto Rican writer and essayist, who first addressed the complex identity problem of being both Puerto Rican and African American in his autobiographical work *Down These Mean Streets*. 1968. New York: New American Library.

[15] The title is named after a line of Langston Hughes's poem *Prime*, published under the section "Words on Fire." 2002. In *The Collected Works of Langston Hughes: The Poems: 1951-1967*. Vol. 3, edited by Arnold Rampersad. Columbia and London: University of Missouri Press.

The dialogue is built on a series of affirmations and refutations that ironically play with the stereotypes related to those physical features that should identify the poet's ethnicity. Thus, since his hair is "kinky y kurly" Perdomo is defined as "Black," despite the light colour of his skin, coupled with the use of Spanish language next to English. La Fountain-Stokes explains that the whole system of affirmation/refutation and differentiation of ethnic labels has to do with the workings of race (La Fountain-Stokes 2014, 248). In the Caribbean, he posits, "a light-skinned person like Perdomo in fact would usually not be identified as black, but rather mulato or trigueño, an intermediate racial category that oscillates between black and white according to the particular social context" (La Fountain-Stokes 2014, 248). However, such dynamics of racial "classification are eclipsed in the United States by the dominant views" (La Fountain-Stokes 2014, 248), where white is the neutral colour compared to all the others. The result is an unresolvable difference that the poet embraces and even emphasizes.

Perdomo, in fact, intensifies all these racial differences using language as a field of clash and encounter between his two identities, African-American and Nuyorican. Through the abundant use of code-mixing, cacophony, repetition, alliteration, and rhythm, the poet switches from English to Spanish and vice versa, crossing over African-American Vernacular English—"ain't," "Cuz," "bro"—and the Spanish pronunciations of English words—"Porta Reecan," "yo," "la madam blankeeta de madesson avenue". In so doing, Perdomo is not simply representing his own condition, but he is opening the discourse in order to represent linguistic and identity dynamics that are common inside the community of Spanish Harlem.

This is particularly evident during Perdomo's performance of the poem,[16] when the whole set of accents, tones, and sounds displays its full expressive potential. In a sequence of mid and medium shots, with very few close-ups, the poet reads the 1996 version of the poem. Little attention is given to what happens on stage, because all the action takes place in Perdomo's mouth. The poet, in fact, using his body and voice to reproduce the various poetic personae, experiments with different, often dissident or marginalized identities. Moreover, in this playing with multiple roles—author, performer, character and persona— while the "poet's presence at the site of enunciation emphasizes the poet's position as an author" (Gräbner and Casas 2011, 11), the speaking voice does not always coincide with that of Perdomo. The poet focuses, precisely, on the divergence between who speaks and what is said, to create irony as well as to

---

[16] "Nigger-Reecan Blues". *YouTube*. Video File. February 11, 2019, https://www.youtube.com/watch?v=Mvo0g3dHAHw, last access 11/06/2019.

highlight the controversial condition of those who, like Perdomo himself, have to coexist with an "unresolved difference" (Noel 2014, 128), a hybrid identity.

> I'm a Spic! I'm a Nigger!
> Spic! Spic! Just like a nigger!
> Neglected, rejected, oppressed and dispossessed,
> From banana boats to tenements
> Street gangs to regiments
> Spic, spic, spic. I ain't no different than a nigger!
>
>   (Perdomo 1996, 20-21)

With the repetition of the derogatory terms for a Spanish speaking person (Spic) and for an African-American person (Nigger), Perdomo acknowledges "the power of discriminatory labels and outside constraints," which participate in an oppressive system that marks Puerto Rican and African-American identities as inferior (La Fountain-Stokes 2014, 249). The futility of the struggle is given by the fact that both Puerto Ricans and African Americans are victims of the same oppressive system they often help maintain. What is left is this poem, a "nigger-reecan Blues" that, following the Blues tradition, describes old feelings and states of being in new ways. And if, as Langston Hughes used to say, "the Blues are 'laughing to keep from crying'" (Young 2003, 12), Perdomo's irony is perfectly in tune with that story of insistence and resistance that the Blues plays and tells.

Conclusions

The complexities of such a problematic relationship between music and poetry, especially in relation to the African-American tradition, would require an extensive discussion of the matter that cannot be condensed in this abridged presentation. The purpose of the paper, in effect, has been introductory. Considering the above-mentioned historical and literary framework, the analyses of Hughes's and Perdomo's poems, in both their performative and written forms, emphasize a common tendency in a large part of contemporary American poetry: the challenge to form. In this light, Hughes and Perdomo become symbols of a literary tendency that, from the second half of the twentieth century to our own time, has seen many other poets implement different strategies to achieve the immobility and "aphonia" of the written word. Where Hughes plays with the Blues form in order to create poems, like "The Weary Blues," that can "sound" on the page as well as on stage, in a perfect ensemble with the jazz band, Perdomo relies upon the power of the spoken word. In "Nigger-Reecan Blues," the Blues motif is re-elaborated and interpreted through a hip-hop syncopated rhythm, while the performance of a simulated dialogue creates space for all the different voices in Perdomo's neighbourhood to be spoken, heard, and enhanced. Performance, thus, turns the poem into a poetic speech that directly addresses the audience. Although not all the African-American poems can be classified as using the spoken word, the rise in popularity of this poetic form, together with hip-hop and slam poetry, has re-empowered the old debate on the relationship between poetry and orality, with a strong emphasis on music. Whereas "the power of music that poetry lacks is the ability to persuade without argument" (Williams 2001, 38), what links these two art forms "is their emphasis on performance" (Grassian 2009, 134). As the two poets here presented testify, a poem can perform in numerous ways, according to a wide range of possibilities, which go from the performance of the written text to the poet's performance in a television studio.

References

Algarín, Miguel, and Bob Holman, eds. 1994. *Aloud: Voices from the Nuyorican Poets Café.* New York: Henry Holt.
Barthes, Roland. 1977. "The Grain of the Voice." In *Image Music Text*, edited by Stephen Heath, 179-189. London: Fontana Press.
Covac, Kevin. 2007. "Toward a Hip-Hop Poetica." In *Spoken Word Revolution Redux*, edited by Mark Eleveld, 222-228. Naperville: Sourcebooks MediaFusion.
Crown, Kathleen. 2003. "Choice Voice Noise: Soundings in Innovative African-American Poetry." In *Assembling Alternatives: Reading Postmodern Poetries Transnationally*, edited by Romana Huk, 219-245. Middletown CT: Wesleyan University Press.
Gräbner, Cornelia, and Arturo Casas, eds. 2011. *Performing Poetry: Body, Place and Rhythm in the Poetry Performance.* Amsterdam and New York: Rodopi.
Grassian, Daniel. 2009. *Writing the Future of Black America: Literature of the Hip Hop Generation.* Columbia, South Carolina: University of South Carolina Press.
Henderson, Stephen E. 1982. "The Blues as Black Poetry." *Callaloo* (16) (October), 22-30.
Jones, LeeRoi. 1963. *Blues People: Negro Music in White America.* New York: William Morrow and Co.
Jones, LeeRoi. 1998. *Black Music.* New York: Da Capo.
Hughes, Langston. "The Weary Blues." YouTube. Video File. Accessed 15 June 2019. https://www.youtube.com/watch?v=uM7HSOwJw20&t=3s.
Hughes, Langston. 1963. *The Big Sea: an Autobiography.* New York: Hill and Wang.
Hughes, Langston. 1971. "The Weary Blues.." In *Langston Hughes: anch'io sono America (antologia poetica)*, edited by Stefania Piccinato, 622-665. Milano: Accademia-Sansoni Editori.
La Fountain-Stokes, Lawrence. 2014. "Speaking Black Latino/a/ness: Race, Performance, and Poetry in Tato Laviera, Willie Perdomo and Josefina Báez." In *The AmeRícan Poet: Essays on the Work of Tato Laviera*, edited by Stephanie Alvarez and William Luis, 240-257. New York: Hunter.

Matthews, Sebastian and Stanley Plumly, eds. 2001. *William Matthews. The Poetry Blues: Essays and Interviews*. Ann Arbor, Michigan: The University of Michigan Press.

Muyumba, Walton. 2014. "Black and Blues Configurations: Contemporary African American Poetics." In *The Cambridge History of American Poetry*, edited by Stephen Burt, 1048-1078. Cambridge: Cambridge University Press.

Noel, Tomás Urayoán. 2011. "Bodies that Antimatter: Locating U.S latino/a Poetry, 2000-2009." *Contemporary Literature* 52 (4) (Winter), 852-882.

Noel, Tomás Urayoán. 2014. *In Visible Movement: Nuyorican Poetry from the Sixties to Slam*. Iowa: University of Iowa Press.

Perdomo, Willie. 1996. *Where a Nickel Costs a Dime*. New York: W.W. Norton.

Perdomo, Willie. 2019. "Nigger-Reecan Blues". *YouTube*. Video File. Access 11 June, 2019. https://www.youtube.com/watch?v=Mvo0g3dHAHw.

Ramazani, Jahan. 1994. *Poetry of Mourning: the Modern Elegy from Hardy to Heaney*. Chicago and London: University of Chicago Press.

Ramazani, Jahan. 2011. "'Sing to Me Now': Contemporary American Poetry and Song." *Contemporary Literature* 52 (4) (Winter), 716-755.

Rampersad, Arnold. 2002 [1986]. *The Life of Langston Hughes, vol. 1: 1902-1941*. Oxford and New York: Oxford University Press.

Shockley, Evie. 2011. *Renegade Poetics: Black Aesthetics and Formal Innovation in African American Poetry*. Iowa City: University of Iowa Press.

Tracy, Steven C. 2004. "Langston Hughes and Afro-American Vernacular Music." In *A Historical Guide to Langston Hughes*, edited by Steven C. Tracy, 85-118. New York: Oxford University Press.

Waldron, Edward E. 1971. "The Blues Poetry of Langston Hughes." *Negro American Literature Forum* 5 (4) (Winter), 140-149. Oxford and New York: Oxford University Press.

Wheeler, Lesley. 2008. *Voicing American Poetry: Sound and Performance from the 1920s to the Present*. Ithaca and London: Cornell University Press.

Williams, Sherley A. 1977. "The Blues Roots of Contemporary Afro-American Poetry." *The Massachusetts Review* 18 (3) (Autumn), 542-554.

Young, Kevin. 2003. *Blues Poems*. New York: Alfred A. Knopf.

Further Reading

Agamben, Giorgio. 1999. *The End of the Poem. Studies in Poetics*. Stanford, California: Stanford UniversityPress.

Bernstein, Charles, Marjorie Perloff, and Craig Dworkin, eds. 2009. *Close Listening: Poetry and the Performed Word*. New York and Oxford: Oxford University Press.

Chapple, Freda, and Chiel Kattenbelt, eds. 2006. *Intermediality in Theatre and Performance*. Amsterdam: Rodopi.

Derrida, Jacques. 1976. *Of Grammatology*. Baltimore: Maryland: John Hopkins University Press.

DeFrantz, Thomas F., and Anita Gonzalez, eds. 2014. *Black Performance Theory*. Durham: Duke University Press.

Nagy, Gregory. 1996. *Poetry and Performance: Homer and Beyond.* Cambridge: Harvard University Press.

Perloff, Marjorie, and Craig Dworkin. 2009. *The Sound of Poetry/The Poetry of Sound.* Chicago and London: University of Chicago Press.

Robbins, Any Moorman. 2014. *American Hybrid Poetics: Gender, Mass Culture, and Form.* New Brunswick, New Jersey: Rutgers University Press.

9.

"The Weary Blues" by Langston Hughes: catharsis and the healing power of poetry and music

Adriano Elia

University of Roma Tre, Italy

The influence of music—notably Blues and Jazz—on many of Langston Hughes's poems has long attracted the attention of scholars, who have examined in different ways the interaction of poetry and music in Hughes's output. Within this critical framework, it is appropriate to consider on the one hand the reasons why music has been so crucial as a source of inspiration for Hughes, and on the other the extent to which its influence has affected and enriched his poetical contribution.

One of the first works of Blues performance in literature, Hughes's "The Weary Blues" (1925) is a poem resonating both thematically and stylistically with the Blues. Presented by an anonymous narrator describing a pianist singing a Blues number in a Harlem club on Lenox Avenue, the poem—and the gloomy Blues song it evokes—nurture a cathartic purification of the emotional condition of sadness and loneliness. Simultaneously both a melancholic method of grievance and a therapy for sorrow, the very act of writing and singing the Blues releases the anguish felt by the poet and the pianist, and becomes an antidote to the discomfort expressed by the poem and the song.

This chapter investigates the issues of catharsis and the healing power of poetry and music as revealed in "The Weary Blues". Hughes supposedly wrote the first draft in around 1922, while he was working on a boat on the Hudson River. He struggled for a while to devise a satisfactory ending, but eventually "The Weary Blues" became a turning point in his career. In 1925 it won a poetry contest run by the magazine *Opportunity*, and this prize contributed to Hughes's growing reputation as one of the stars of the Harlem Renaissance.

As is known, part of this poem is not original, as actual Blues lyrics are embedded in it. Apparently, the young Langston first heard the Blues from an orchestra of blind musicians in Kansas City.[1] Hughes remembered the refrain of one of those songs and used it years later in this poem, where he claims instead to have heard the song in a Harlem cabaret. Whatever the actual origin of the Blues song may be, his objective was that of turning into poetry his musical influences in order to celebrate the daily life of those whom he defined as "low-down folks". As he put it: "I tried to write poems like the songs they sang on Seventh Street", a street in Washington DC where black working-class people lived.[2]

Perhaps the main reason why Hughes decided to write Blues poems was that he wanted to give more dignity to this popular form of art. Rampersad (2002, 66) has suggested that, in some ways, writing "The Weary Blues" was for Hughes an operation similar to the one carried out by the classically trained black musician Scott Joplin, who had worked to notate ragtime in order to preserve its beauty as art. By the same token, Hughes made a connection between formal poetry and the lowly Blues "in order that its brilliance might be recognized by the world [...] in so honouring the Blues, he had done something unprecedented in literature."

Hughes thus attempted to universalize the message of the Blues, to expand what Ralph Ellison (2002, 66) would later define as an "autobiographical chronicle of personal catastrophe expressed lyrically." The personal becomes universal in Hughes's poetry—"The Weary Blues" gives us an effective account of the sufferings not only of an individual, but of a whole people.

Lingering briefly on the main stylistic features of the poem, poetic techniques such as alliteration, assonance, onomatopoeia, repetition and syncopation, among others, generate a certain musicality of the verses. Quite significant is the presence among the lines of "ebony and ivory"—an old trope that was given immense popularity by the 1982 number-one single by Paul McCartney and Stevie Wonder—by which the narrator contrasts the Bluesman's black skin with

---

[1] In the autobiography *The Big Sea* (1993 [1940], 215), Hughes actually claimed that the poem "included the first Blues verse I'd ever heard way back in Lawrence, Kansas, when I was a kid", but in a 1964 interview he said he had heard it in Kansas City instead. As his biographer Rampersad (2002 [1986], 16) noted, "the effect on him was one of piercing sadness, as if his deepest loneliness had been harmonized."

[2] Hughes 1994, 92; Hughes 1993 [1940], 209. Regarding the connection between Hughes's poetry and the Blues, see, among others, Tracy 1981, 73–98; Chinitz 1996, 177–92; Bonner 1990, 15–28; Huang 2011, 9–44. For a detailed discussion of this poem see De Angelis 2017, 147–62.

the white keys of the piano: "With his ebony hands on each ivory key / He made that poor piano moan with melody" (lines 9–10).[3] Moreover, by invoking the spirit of Blues ("O Blues!", lines 11 and 16; "Sweet Blues!", line 14), Hughes captured in poetry the orality of the call-and-response format used in black churches and among Southern field labourers.

Indeed, Hughes maintained that he did not need to use a complex or refined form in order to describe effectively the everyday life of African Americans: "Certainly the Shakespearian sonnet would be no mould in which to express life on Beale Street or Lenox Avenue [...] I am not interested in doing tricks with rhymes. I am interested in reproducing the human soul if I can" (Bloom 1999, 17). However, although "The Weary Blues" remains a simple and straightforward poem form-wise, at the same time it employs one of the main strategies that modernist poetry, notably T.S. Eliot's *The Waste Land* (1922), is based upon, i.e., intertextuality. In fact, "The Weary Blues" incorporates two fragments of a song performed by a Bluesman:[4]

> Ain't got nobody in all this world,
> Ain't got nobody but ma self.
> I's gwine to quit ma frownin'
> And put ma troubles on the shelf.

The first fragment unveils both the Bluesman's isolation as well as his willingness to overcome it: by putting his "troubles on the shelf", he seems determined to fight against his loneliness. In the second fragment, which follows the typical AAB Blues poetic pattern characterized by first line, repeat line and response line—even though each line is split into halves—the Bluesman loses instead any motivation to overcome his emotional condition of unhappiness:

> I got the Weary Blues
> And I can't be satisfied.
> Got the Weary Blues
> And can't be satisfied—
> I ain't happy no mo'
> And I wish that I had died.

---

[3] The trope's first occurrence can be traced back as early as 1849: "black and white are seen strung along the great table, like the keys of a piano, and, like the aforesaid instrument, the black keys make fully as much noise as the white; all mingle for a while in the utmost harmony and good feeling". See C.F. Sturgis 1980 [1849], quoted in Breedon 1980, 262.

[4] Lines 19–22 and 25–30 respectively.

With regard to content, it must be recognized that Hughes himself seemed to diminish the metaphorical significance of the poem. In his autobiography *The Big Sea*, he described it simply as "a poem about a working man who sang the Blues all night and then went to bed and slept like a rock" (Hughes 1993, 215). Nevertheless, its message is not as simple as the often unassuming Hughes would lead us to believe. By using these fragments different in tone, he managed to condense opposing motifs involved in and suggested by the Blues, which we may define respectively as the *Blues catharsis* and the *Blues suicide* motifs. It is indeed the shift from the determination to fight the feeling of misery to the sense of defeat leading the Bluesman to long for death that gives us a clear idea of the complexity of the Blues and of this poem in exposing such contradictory mindsets.

Sugimori and Rabas (2014, 79–80) noted that the Blues suicide motif, revealed by the self-destructiveness of the protagonist in the latter fragment, is apparent not only in the "The Weary Blues", but also in further early poems such as, among others, "Bad Luck Card" (1926) and "Bad Man" (1927). However, on several occasions, the Blues suicide motif was disrupted in some ways by the use of irony. For example, in the 1943 poem "Too Blue"—which hints at "The Weary Blues"—the protagonist is too "blue" even to commit suicide:

> I got those sad old weary Blues.
> I don't know where to turn.
> I don't know where to go.
> [...]
> I wonder if
> *One* bullet would do?
> [...]
> But I ain't got
> Neither bullet nor gun—
> And I'm too blue
> To look for one.

Irony and laughter are certainly crucial issues in Blues songs, and along with sadness, they generate a tension aimed at overcoming pain through tragicomedy. Hughes himself acknowledged the importance of this almost philosophical strategy and made a distinction between the spirituals and the Blues, the latter being "more dolorous than the spirituals because its sorrow is untampered by tears but intensified by an existentialistic laughter." (Ikonne 1999, 31). For this reason, he admired the "low-down folks" with their "incongruous humour that so often, as in the Blues, becomes ironic laughter mixed with tears" Hughes (1994, 92–93). Hughes (1941, 143, 144) correctly maintained that, despite being "folk-songs born out of heartache [...] there's almost always something humorous about them—even if it's the kind of humour that laughs to keep from crying." As one of the characters offers in Hughes's play *Don't You Want To Be Free?* (1938), the Blues are "sad funny songs—too sad to be funny and too funny to be sad." Three years later, in the essay "Songs Called the Blues", Hughes (1941, 144) stressed the complexity of the Blues as a multifaceted artistic phenomenon:

> There are the family Blues, when a man and woman have quarreled, and the quarrel can't be patched up. There's the loveless Blues, when you haven't even got anybody to quarrel with. And there's the left-lonesome Blues, when the one you care for's gone away. Then there's also the broke-and-hungry Blues, a stranger in a strange town. And the desperate going-to-the-river Blues.

With regard to the Blues catharsis motif, the emotional purification produced by the Blues is an issue that predictably has long received attention, at least since 1934, when Melville Herskovits, influenced by the then relatively new Freudian insights, underlined that a "therapeutic value of bringing a repressed thought into the open" was achieved in Blues songs; or when Blues scholar Paul Oliver (1960) made a similar point, suggesting that for the Bluesman "[s]inging his condition brings relief to his heart and order to his disturbed thought"; or Harold Courlander's reflections in 1963, when he argued that a Blues song "serves as balm or antidote [...] the finer the singing or creative effort, the more effective is the song as a catharsis."[5] Later, critics such as Roopen Majithia (2012, 84) and Ben and Owen Flanagan (2011, 75–76) noted that it was indeed the prerogative to bring about the Aristotelian catharsis that has given and still gives the Blues a universal power to appeal to and bring together people of different backgrounds.

As is known, the term derives from the ancient Greek κάθαρσις, a medical term meaning "purgation" or "purification". Aristotle used it in his *Poetics* (384–322 B.C.) to indicate the relieving of emotional tensions on a spectator through certain kinds of art, notably tragedy or music, in order to arouse "pity and fear", and in so doing generate the purification of these emotions (Aristotle 1961, 1449). By experiencing fear in a controlled situation and through sympathetic identification with the tragic protagonist, the spectator's anxieties are directed elsewhere and his/her insight and outlook are enhanced. This way, tragedy produces a healthful and humanizing effect on the spectator or reader.[6]

However, as Ben and Owen Flanagan (2011, 79, 83) claimed, the Blues triggers a far broader range of emotions than just pity and fear, universal themes such as

---

[5] Herskovits 1966 [1934], 137; Oliver 1963 [1960], 81; Courlander 1963, 124, quoted in Ottenheimer 1979, 75, very useful for a discussion of catharsis associated with the Blues.
[6] https://www.britannica.com/art/catharsis-criticism.

solitude, nostalgia, jealousy, suffering, anxiety, existential struggle, presence or absence of God, among others. Functioning as a medium through which the performer provides emotional release in the audience by evoking these feelings, the Blues generates sympathy in the spectators, even relief when the misfortune being dealt with is alien to them. As mentioned above, in the Blues catharsis the effect of the purification shifts from the spectator back to the actual purveyor: as well as relieving, it also releases strong emotions through art (in this case poetry and music) that help us understand and dominate the evoked emotional states. Useful in this regard is the distinction made by Charles Keil between the urban Blues singer, who has to make the cathartic experience available to the audience in a sort of purifying ritual, and the rural Blues singer, who generally achieves an individualized catharsis: "The sight and sound of a common problem being acted out, talked out and worked out on stage promote catharsis, and the fact that all present are participating in the solution gives solidarity."[7]

All these insights inspired by Aristotle's *Poetics* seem to be quite fitting as a reading model for "The Weary Blues", a poem about failure that, in an ironical twist, has become so successful. Here, the Blues plays a double role: it embodies not only the sorrow, but also its therapy. For example, exclamatory phrases such as "O Blues!" and "Sweet Blues!" (lines 11, 14, 16) are used as an acknowledgement of the comfort given by the Blues to soothe the pain. The following lines also suggest that the experience of the Blues, however painful, may also be rewarding, because the actual singing of the Blues is an effective means of overcoming the Blues itself:

> Sweet Blues!
> Coming from a black man's soul.
> O Blues!
> In a deep song voice with a melancholy tone
> I heard that Negro sing, that old piano moan—

The Harlem pianist releases his emotional burden, transforming it into musical expression. He receives consolation after his tribulations from singing his song. The narrator describes the musician's emotional condition as he performs; he makes "that poor piano moan with melody." The piano thus becomes his soul mate: "that old piano moan[s]" just as he is doing. This lamentation is turned into a cathartic release: singing and playing the Blues is the best way to discharge sorrow and melancholy.[8]

---

[7] Keil 1966, 76, 137, quoted in Ottenheimer 1979, 75–76.
[8] Hughes's poem "Evenin' Air Blues" (1927) tellingly reveals this feeling: "But if you was to ask me / How de Blues they come to be, / Says if you was to ask me / How de Blues they come to be / You wouldn't need to ask me: / Just look at me and see!".

The Blues therefore embodies both sadness and its cure. But what exactly makes the Blues cathartic? In order to find a tentative answer to this question, it is worth trying to connect music, poetry and psychoanalysis. In the essay meaningfully titled "The Artistic Transformation of Trauma, Loss, and Adversity in the Blues", Steinberg, Pynoos and Abramovitz (2011, 56–57) investigated the ways which Blues performers have used to transform and transcend trauma, loss and the painful experiences they were involved in.[9] A typical technique is that of putting the experience into words in order to simultaneously find a new perspective on the trauma as well as share it with others for emotional support. In psychiatry, this operation is termed "re-experiencing" through "retelling", which is something that actually takes place by using the traditional Blues AAB format, with the second line repeating the issue presented in the first one. Naming a painful experience is a strategy aimed at both diminishing as well as communicating it in order to gain understanding and comfort from other people. The Blues thus prompts a dialogue between performers and audience that is beneficial for both parts. With regard to this, Robert and Benjamin Stolorow (2013, 5) argued that "in the unifying experience of the Blues, songwriter, performers, and listeners are joined in a visceral-linguistic conversation in which universally traumatizing aspects of human existence can be communally held and borne."

Another method Bluesmen occasionally employ to release strong emotions is showing detachment and imperturbability. In the case of Hughes, in the autobiography *The Big Sea*, he recalled his childhood days in Lawrence, Kansas. His grandmother would tell him stories about "people who wanted to make the Negroes free" (Hughes 1993, 17). In these stories, nobody ever cried, and the young Langston seemed to absorb this message fully—he didn't shed a tear even when she died because she had involuntarily taught him the pointlessness of crying about anything. Such imperturbability proved essential for Hughes as a means to keep safe his true self. This is apparent in a historical video broadcast on the Canadian program "The 7 O'Clock Show" in 1958, where Hughes recites "The Weary Blues" accompanied by the jazz of the Doug Parker Band.[10] Although the poem and the embedded Blues song are about the emotional condition of sadness and loneliness, Hughes's detached delivery somehow disrupts the content. His gravitas was probably intended as a reaction to decades of minstrel shows, where African Americans were always portrayed as stereotypical caricatures.[11] Such stoicism is also detectable in

---

[9] See also Scorsese (2003).

[10] Hughes 1958.

[11] Elia 2019.

this poem: as Steven C. Tracy (1981, 90) argued, the poet "is not a performer but an analytical, detached voice striving to identify with the 'Sweet Blues! / Coming back from a black man's soul!'".

At the end of the poem, the narrator describes the actions of the Bluesman following his performance. The Bluesman goes to bed while still feeling the Blues aroused by his song:

> The singer stopped playing and went to bed
> While the Weary Blues echoed through his head.
> He slept like a rock or a man that's dead.

This is a perfectly appropriate ending—no wonder Hughes had to make a considerable effort to devise it. Even James Baldwin, while not liking all of the poem, defined it "remarkable".[12] Along with the common interpretation comparing it to death, sleep can also be seen in a more positive light as a route to a state of purification, confidence and absence of sorrow. This is probably the message that Hughes wanted to deliver with this poem—the longing for sleep could be seen as a way to alleviate suffering by stopping willing, following a tradition inspired by Buddhism, Stoicism and, in more recent times, the philosophy of Arthur Schopenhauer, who claimed that will, craving and desire were the main causes of anguish.[13]

Several critics wondered why the Blues, despite being a typically African-American expression, has such a universal appeal, emotionally involving people from a wide range of cultural backgrounds.[14] It is peculiar that a piece of music conveying feelings of suffering and failure has become so enjoyable and successful. As hinted above, perhaps it is exactly the catharsis brought about by the Blues that makes it still so enthralling and topical. Such purification is pleasant as it relieves both the audience and the performer from something unpleasant and painful, leading them to a healthy psychological state. The therapeutic power of the Blues and the universality of the themes dealt with in Blues lyrics—love, loss, alienation, injustice, sorrow, among others—are essential elements to the allure of the Blues.[15] Paul Oliver (1972, 6) illustrated very effectively the different aspects and the complexity of the Blues both as sorrow as well as its therapy. The Blues is

---

[12] Baldwin 1959, in Bloom 1999, 42: "I do not like all of 'The Weary Blues,' which copies, rather than exploits, the cadence of the Blues, but it comes to a remarkable end."
[13] Drake 2011, 70.
[14] Besides Majithia and B. and O. Flanagan, see R.D. Stolorow, B.A. Stolorow 2013, 5.
[15] Majithia 2012, 89–90.

both a state of mind and a music which gives voice to it [...] the wail of the forsaken, the cry of independence, the passion of the lusty, the anger of the frustrated and the laughter of the fatalist. It's the agony of indecision, the despair of the jobless, the anguish of the bereaved and the dry wit of the cynic. As such the Blues is the personal emotion of the individual finding through music a vehicle for self-expression.

There is a direct connection between Blues, catharsis, sadness and beauty. In many ways, sadness is not just depressing, but it may cultivate beauty and, as David C. Drake (2011, 69) rightly argued, when this happens sadness becomes nourishing and therapeutic: "emotional purging is a major part of what draws people to Blues music, and it is precisely the experience of sadness as beauty that facilitates this purging." Hughes (1941, 145) himself attempted to look into this mystery, and his words from the above-mentioned essay "Songs Called the Blues" are still topical and give us some more interesting clues:

> the Blues have something that goes beyond race or sectional limits, that appeals to the ear and heart of people everywhere – otherwise, how could it be that in a Tokyo restaurant one night I heard a Louis Armstrong record of the St. Louis Blues played over and over for a crowd of Japanese diners there? You don't have to understand the words to know the meaning of the Blues, or to feel their sadness, or to hope their hopes.

Ultimately, these reflections cogently illustrate the reasons why the Blues is a form that remains attractive and celebrated all over the world. It is the enduring shift between desperation and laughter through self-catharsis and audience catharsis that makes the Blues performance so familiar and effective. The Blues is a healer, to quote John Lee Hooker, and, despite its massive commercialization, in today's difficult times it may still function as a shelter from the emotional pain that is inherent to the human condition.

References

Aristotle. 1961. *Poetics*. New York: Hill and Wang.

Baldwin, James. 1959. "James Baldwin on 'Selected Poems'." In *Langston Hughes*, edited by Harold Bloom, 41-42. Broomall, PA: Chelsea House Publishers.

Bloom, Harold,. ed. 1999. *Langston Hughes. Comprehensive Research and Study Guide*. Broomall, PA: Chelsea House Publishers.

Courlander, Harold. 1963. *Negro Folk Music, U.S.A.*. New York: Columbia University Press.

Drake, David C. 2011. "Sadness as Beauty–Why it Feels So Good to Feel So Blue." In *Blues–Philosophy for Everyone: Thinking Deep About Feeling Low*, edited by Jesse R. Steinberg and Abrol Fairweather, 66–74. Malden, MA: Wiley-Blackwell.

Elia, Adriano. 2019. "Langston Hughes' 'The Weary Blues'." *Blog 606*, February 12 2019. Accessed 25/06/2019. https://sixoh6.com/2019/02/12/bhm-celebration-of-art-poetry-langston-hughes-the-weary-Blues/.

Ellison, Ralph. 2002 [1955]. *Living with Music: Jazz Writings*, edited and with an Introduction by Robert G. O'Meally. New York: Random House.

Flanagan, Ben, and Owen Flanagan. 2011. "Anguished Art–Coming Through the Dark to the Light the Hard Way." In *Blues–Philosophy for Everyone: Thinking Deep About Feeling Low*, edited by Jesse R. Steinberg and Abrol Fairweather, 75–83. Malden, MA: Wiley-Blackwell.

Herskovits, Melville. 1966 [1934]. "Freudian Mechanisms in (Primitive) Negro Psychology." In *The New World Negro: Selected Papers in AfroAmerican Studies*, edited by F. Herskovits, 135-145. Bloomington: Indiana University Press.

Hughes, Langston. 1941. "Songs Called the Blues." *Phylon* (1940-1956) 2 (2) (2nd Qtr.), 143–145.

Hughes, Langston. 1958. "'The Weary Blues' on CBUT". Accessed 25/06/2019. https://www.youtube.com/watch?v=uM7HSOwJw20.

Hughes, Langston. 1993 [1940]. *The Big Sea*. New York: Hill and Wang.

Hughes, Langston. 1994 [1926]. "The Negro Artist and the Racial Mountain." In *The Portable Harlem Renaissance Reader*, edited by David Levering Lewis, 91–95. New York: Viking.

Hughes, Langston. 2015 [1926]. *The Weary Blues*, New York: Alfred A. Knopf.

Ikonne, Chidi. 1999. "Chidi Ikonne on the Narrative Style of 'The Weary Blues." In *Langston Hughes. Comprehensive Research and Study Guide*, edited by Harold Bloom, 29-31. Broomall, PA: Chelsea House Publishers.

Keil, Charles. 1966. *Urban Blues*. Chicago: University of Chicago Press.

Majithia, Roopen. 2012. "Blues and Catharsis". In *Blues–Philosophy for Everyone: Thinking Deep About Feeling Low*, edited by Jesse R. Steinberg and Abrol Fairweather, 84–95. Malden, MA: Wiley-Blackwell.

Oliver, Paul. 1963. *The Meaning of the Blues*. New York: Collier.

Oliver, Paul. 1972 [1969]. *The Story of the Blues*. London: Penguin Books.

Ottenheimer, Harriet J. 1979. "Catharsis, Communication, and Evocation: Alternative Views of the Sociopsychological Functions of Blues Singing." *Ethnomusicology* 23(1) (Jan.), 75–86.

Rampersad, Arnold. 2002 [1986]. *The Life of Langston Hughes*. Vol. 1: *1902-1941*. Oxford and New York: Oxford University Press.

Steinberg, Alan M., Robert S. Pynoos and Robert Abramovitz. 2011. "The Artistic Transformation of Trauma, Loss, and Adversity in the Blues". In *Blues–Philosophy for Everyone: Thinking Deep About Feeling Low*, edited by Jesse R. Steinberg and Abrol Fairweather, 51-65. Malden, MA: Wiley-Blackwell.

Steinberg, Jesse R. and Abrol Fairweather, eds. 2011. *Blues–Philosophy for Everyone: Thinking Deep About Feeling Low*. Malden, MA: Wiley-Blackwell.

Stolorow, Robert D., and Benjamin A. Stolorow. 2013. "Blues and Emotional Trauma." *Clinical Social Work Journal* 41 (1), 5–10.

Sturgis, Rev C. F. 1980 [1849]. "Duties of Christian Masters to their Slaves." In *Advice Among Masters: the Ideal in Slave Management in the Old South*, edited by James O. Breedon, 262. Westport, CT: Greenwood Press.

Sugimori, Masami, and Kevin Rabas. 2014. "Resisting the Suicidal Blue(s): Text, Voice, and Music in Langston Hughes, Leonard Feather and Charles Mingus's *Weary Blues*." *Re-Markings* 13 (1), 78–85.

Tracy, Steven C. 1981. "To the Tune of Those Weary Blues: The Influence of the Blues Tradition in Langston Hughes's Blues Poems." *MELUS* 8 (3), 73–98.

Further Reading

Bonner, Patricia. 1990. "Cryin' the Jazzy Blues and Livin' Blue Jazz: Analyzing the Blues and Jazz Poetry of Langston Hughes". *West Georgia College Review* 20, 15–28.

Chinitz, David. 1996. "Literacy and Authenticity: the Blues Poems of Langston Hughes." *Callaloo* 19 (1), 177–192.

De Angelis, Valerio Massimo. 2017. "'That's What the / Blues Singers Say': La meta-poetica del Blues di Langston Hughes." In *Una bussola per l'infosfera: Con Ishmael Reed tra musica e letteratura*, edited by N. Paladin and G. Rimondi, 147–162. Milano: Agenzia X.

Eliot, Thomas Stearns. 2002 [1922]. *The Waste Land and Other Poems*. London: Faber and Faber.

Huang, Hao. 2011. "Enter the Blues: Jazz Poems by Langston Hughes and Sterling Brown." *Hungarian Journal of English and American Studies* XVII (1), 9–44.

Patterson, Anita. 2000. "Jazz, Realism, and the Modernist Lyric: the Poetry of Langston Hughes." *MLQ: Modern Language Quarterly* 61 (4), 651–682.

Scorsese, Martin. 2003. *Martin Scorsese Presents the Blues–A Musical Journey*. https://www.youtube.com/watch?v=e_mmNV-W74g. Accessed 25 June 2019.

Part Three:
Authenticity and identity in contemporary Blues studies

10.

Dead or alive:
Blues and the question of authenticity

Thomas Claviez

University of Bern, Switzerland

Towards a semiotics of authenticity

In what follows, I would like to address one notorious concept whose dogged reappearance in discussions about the Blues is not only a nuisance, but one that also has important and dangerous implications, as I will try to show: that of "authenticity." As I realized when I taught a seminar on the Blues in Spring 2018, this notion crops up in connection with virtually every aspect or facet of the Blues, be that the well-known triumvirate race, class and gender, but also with regard to questions about Blues aesthetics, Blues literature, the "origin" of the Blues (immensely important for any considerations on authenticity,) and what have you.[1] Can white boys play the Blues? Or, for that matter, white girls? What happens once the culture industry gets its dirty hands on it? What happens if it becomes electrified, popular, successful? Hardly once, however–and this holds true not exclusively for debates about the Blues, but also for other contexts in which this concept is invoked–are the implications of the concept of authenticity critically and sufficiently reflected upon.

Strangely enough, although its heuristic value has been severely challenged under the onslaught of poststructuralist and deconstructive criticism, authenticity's symbolic capital seems to have risen: many companies, and in the meantime even nations, have become aware of the fact that, in a world characterized more and more by mobility, virtuality, and mediality, the promise

---

[1] To offer just a short overview of contributions that directly or indirectly deal with authenticity and the Blues, with no claim to comprehensiveness: Stephen Henderson (1982, 22-30); Tom Kuntz (1995, sec. 4, 7; Charles Shaar Murray (2013); Jeff Sharlet (2007); Meghan Winsby (2012, 155-67); Daniel Lieberfeld (1995, 217-21); Lisa Hollenbach (2015, 301-16); Edward E. Waldron (1971, 140-49); Marybeth Hamilton (2000, 132-60); David Chinitz (1996, 177-92); Lorenzo Thomas (1997, 409-16).

of an "authentic" experience has become something like the gold standard of successful marketing. Branding, for example, heavily depends on it.[2]

It was against this striking discrepancy that I and a few colleagues from Switzerland started an interdisciplinary research project with the name "Theory and Practice of Authenticity in Global Cultural Production." And although the Blues was not part of it, I realized that one of the outcomes of that project, a semiotic model of authenticity, proved to be perfectly applicable to many of the academic and non-academic discussions in which the concept was invoked that we read in the Blues seminar.

I would like to first introduce this semiotic model–or rather, the two models–of authenticity and then illustrate its value for a critical assessment of its hardnosed existence in discussions about the Blues. In its light, I will address two "myths of origin" that have taken centre stage in the debate surrounding the Blues–W.C. Handy's story about the ragged black man that he heard playing the Blues in Tutweiler, Mississippi, and the legend surrounding Robert Johnson–to then address the dangerous implications and conceptual contradictions that these entail.

Please allow me quickly to introduce what might look, at first glance, as a very complex model. Our theoretical analysis of the concept of authenticity started out from several premises:

1) There is no authenticity *without an act of authentication*, and thus without an authenticator. Self-authentication is an empty gesture, and requires, to work, the recognition of at least one other person. Thought of in terms of semiotics, self-authentication is the equivalent of a completely transparent sign, in which the signified and the signifier are entirely congruent to each other–which, as we know since Saussure, is impossible.

2) Said authentication has to presume a point of origin (PoO) against which the claim to authenticity is then being measured. This point of origin, however, is necessarily arbitrary.

3) Authentication is then granted or withheld according to the degree of (impossible) congruence of the Claim for Authenticity and the Point of Origin by someone who assumes the authority to make such a judgment.

4) What authentication is based upon is the total negation of time–or rather, *the negation of history as contingent force of change, as all change will by default threaten the congruence between signifier and signified.* And this holds true not only about the relationship between

---

[2] On this, cf. Alessandro Ferrara (2019), forthcoming.

the PoO and the CfA, but also as regards the highly arbitrary nature of the PoO as such–which might in many cases easily be claimed to be located before or after.

5) This holds true not only with regard to the time relationship between the PoO and the CfA, but also that between the CfA and the act of authentication (AoA). As the authenticator necessarily has to be someone different from the claimant for authenticity, another act of reading is involved that threatens to undermine a second layer of assumed congruence, this time between the claimant and the authenticator.

6) In order to achieve the authority to grant or withhold authentication, however, the authenticator him- or herself needs to be recognized as such, and be granted the authority to do so; and again, with reference to his expertise about the PoO.

This is the first model:[3]

Figure 10.1: Semiotic Model of the Process of Authentication

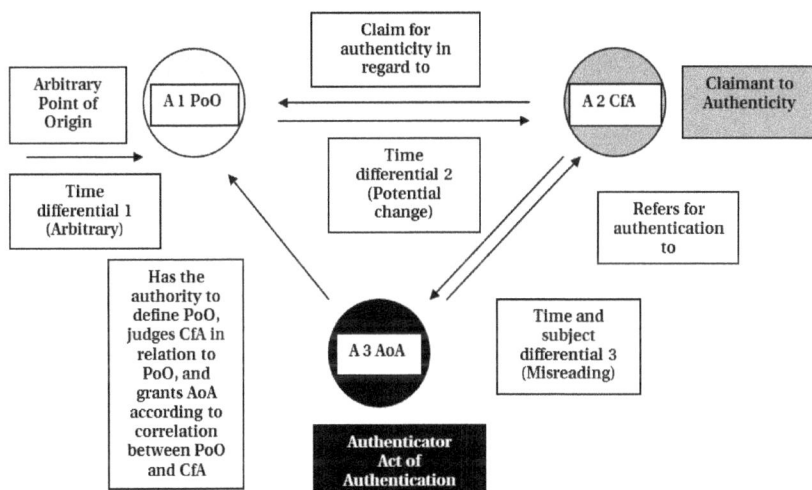

---

[3] The model is derived from the distinction made by the linguist Ferdinand de Saussure in his 1905 *Course on General Linguistics* between the signified (the mental concept that we have of a thing) and the signifier (the material sign or sound used to represent it), and applies it to the process of authentication. In contrast to former models that mostly work with a dual model, however, it features a triangular schema, as it takes into account the necessary role of a third factor: the authenticator. For a full comprehensive and detailed presentation of this model, as well as its implications, cf. Thomas Claviez (2019), forthcoming.

This leads, as the second diagram can show us, not only to the defiance of historical time as contingent, but also to a perpetuation of a system of authorization and/of authentication. The first diagram (Circular first order semiotic system) illustrates what I have called the circular– and thus, in the last instance, empty claim of self-authentication.

Figure 10.2: Circular First Order Semiotic System of Self-authentication

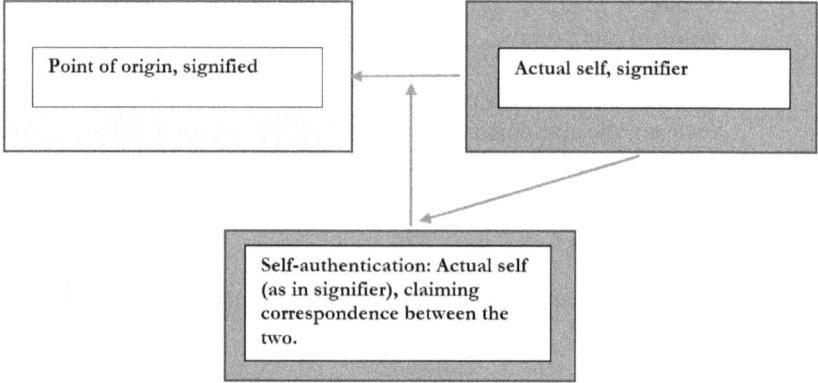

The second one (Second order semiotic system) shows us the considerably more complex, but unavoidable one of authentication through an external authenticator. Not only might I "read" the PoO differently from the latter; the latter has to read both myself (as relation between a signifier and a signified), but to read my claims for authenticity against a PoO that, in turn, is also differentiated. This potentially opens up an abyss of misreadings–the claimant misreading the PoO, misreading him/herself in relation the PoO; the authenticator misreading the claimant, reading the PoO differently, and consequently the relation between the two.

The third one (Third order semiotic system) shows the self-perpetuating structure of the system of experts and authenticators who authenticate the authenticators, but who also compete as to their authority as to what constitutes the relevant PoO. This PoO is, on the one hand, always highly arbitrary but, structurally speaking, achieves in this model of authentication the status of this unthinkable thing: a transcendental signified, which defies the contingency of time. The reason being that the authority of the authenticator is immediately connected with, because dependent upon, his or her assumptions and alleged expertise as regards the PoO, which other "authorities" in the field can dispute.

Allow me then to recapitulate the major insights of this model: the assumption of any kind of authenticity depends on a caste of self-perpetuating experts, who might compete with other experts as regards their authorization through differing PoOs, but who share, no matter where this

PoO is being arbitrarily located, the denial of time or history as being a force of change and contingency, because this contingency might be potentially threatening as regards their own authority.

Figure 10.3: Second order semiotic system

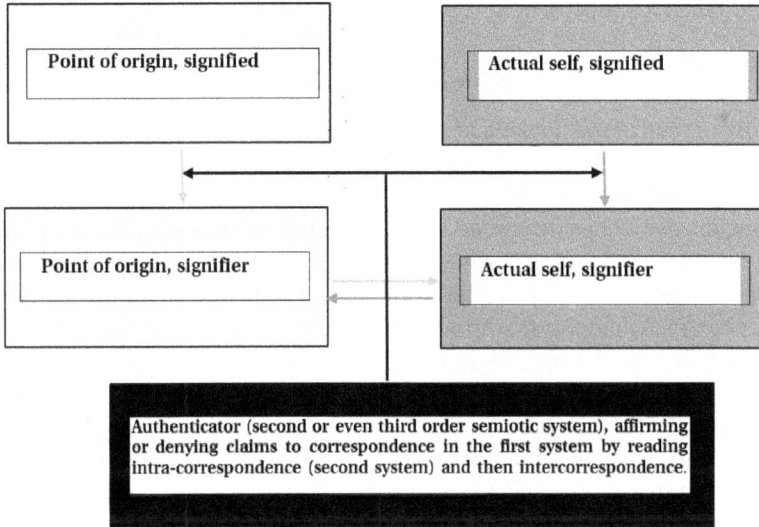

Point of origin, signified	Actual self, signified

Point of origin, signifier	Actual self, signifier

Authenticator (second or even third order semiotic system), affirming or denying claims to correspondence in the first system by reading intra-correspondence (second system) and then intercorrespondence.

Figure 10.4: Third Order Semiotic System

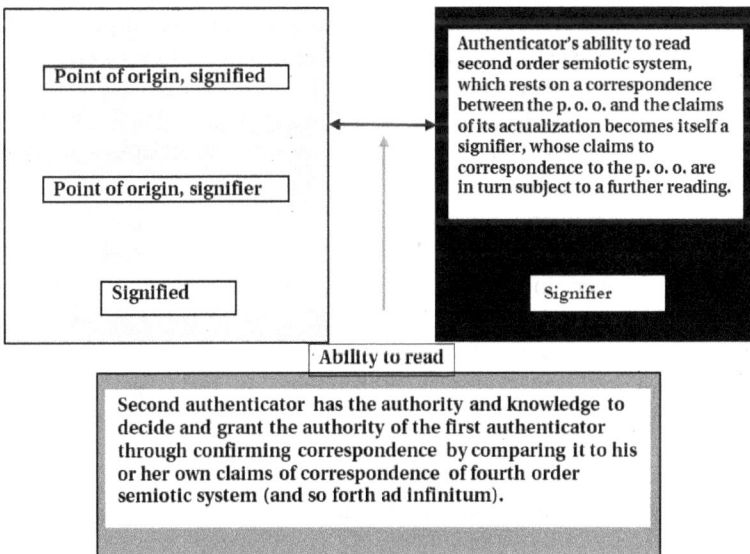

Point of origin, signified

Authenticator's ability to read second order semiotic system, which rests on a correspondence between the p. o. o. and the claims of its actualization becomes itself a signifier, whose claims to correspondence to the p. o. o. are in turn subject to a further reading.

Point of origin, signifier

Signified

Signifier

Ability to read

Second authenticator has the authority and knowledge to decide and grant the authority of the first authenticator through confirming correspondence by comparing it to his or her own claims of correspondence of fourth order semiotic system (and so forth ad infinitum).

Let me mention another final and important aspect of this model of authenticity: the consequences of such a transcendental signified–or, to put it in another way, the empty centre of such an episteme–are that other PoOs, and thus, other options to claim authenticity, are being excluded, or at least made considerably more difficult. Now, what does all of this tell us about the hotly debated authenticity as regards the Blues?

The myth of the origin and the origin of myth

As mentioned above, looking at the debate surrounding the Blues, one hardly encounters a single contribution in which the issue of authenticity is not raised, whether ex- or implicitly. Let me add at this point that I cannot claim the status of an objective observer in this matter, because I have been playing the Blues for over forty years now–and I have been playing it with both white and black people alike. Thus the assumption that I am a potential member of the class of "white boys" who allegedly cannot play it "authentically" has a certain relevance for me. Let me add, by means of a caveat, two things: I never encountered, in my life as a musician who had the opportunity to play the Blues in L.A., New Orleans, and even at the Checker's Lounge in Chicago, any reservations in this regard. For most musicians, you either play it well or you do not, no matter the colour of your skin. Second, my own "point of origin"– that is, my initiation into the Blues–was "tainted" in as much as it happened to be the album *Nothing But the Blues* by Johnnie Winter that, when hearing it, propelled me into learning how to play. And the albino Johnnie Winter, being the "whitest" of Blues musicians you could possibly pick as a point of reference, probably destroyed any opportunity for me to ever play the Blues "authentically"–at least in the light of all the essentialist categories used to decide who allegedly can or cannot play it. However, scholarship on the Blues has often enough repeated that a true "point of origin" a) cannot be located, and that b) even the assumption that it emerged at a localizable point in time collides with the fact that it is a genuinely "hybrid" genre; one that owed its existence to a confluence of both Black and White traditions, techniques, available instruments, and other historically contingent factors such as the conditions of slavery in which it emerged. Still, the appeal of the concept of authenticity seems to be too strong to be laid to rest.[4] There seems to be too much at stake to let go of it, too much symbolic and other capital connected to it, and for too many different stakeholders at that. There are "vested interests" involved, many authorities affected by it; too many careers depend

---

[4] For the "myth of origins" as regards the Blues, cf. Henry Louis Gates (1988), esp. chapters 1 and 2; David Evans (1999, 8-13).

on where you locate yourself and others in this regard. Not only do problems of "cultural imperialism" pop up; questions of who can play the Blues, how to play it, economic success or failure. Questions as to who holds the "sovereignty of definition" in what context: academia, popular journals, the culture industry, all of which–if for different purposes and different goals–vie for the right to define what counts as authentic and what not.

One of the best contributions to date in this regard is still Marybeth Hamilton's seminal essay "Sexuality, Authenticity and the Making of the Blues Tradition." In meticulously juxtaposing the myths of the alleged authenticity of some versions of the Blues to historical facts, and drawing out the ideological stakes involved in the debate, she successfully deconstructs most of the "origin stories" that surround it; and, as is authenticity, many myths–or, rather, mystifications–are about origins.[5] Without resorting to a full-fledged model of authenticity as developed above, Hamilton unveils the exclusionary force of the alleged "points of origin" that inhabit any claims to authenticity: the exclusion of the urban, and mostly female-dominated vaudeville shows in favour of the rural country Blues; closely connected to this the exclusion of sexually charged lyrics in favour of the alleged "innocence" of the original Blues texts. This, in turn, feeds into the commodification argument, in which the attempt to titillate and please (white) audiences leads to the selling out of the Blues. Moreover, Hamilton clearly points out both what is at stake in the notion of authenticity (and the class of expert authenticators that perpetuate it), as well as the romantic desire at its roots:

> For twentieth-century academic folklorists, authenticity claims were a means to legitimate their discipline, rooted in a scientific training that gave them the tools to distinguish the real from the spurious and police the boundaries of popular art (Hamilton 2000, 137).

She adds, however, the following caveat:

> If authenticity quests are bids for cultural power, they also constitute admissions of vulnerability, impelled by a conviction that something precious in the human soul is threatened by the urban industrial order, and that creating or salvaging authentic culture is a key step towards getting it back (Hamilton, 138).

---

[5] This is not the place here to open up a detailed theoretical discussion about myth theory. Suffice it here to say that Roland Barthes famous *Mythologies Today* has done a royal disservice to the debate in hopelessly mixing up myth – which was Claude Lévi-Strauss' main concern – with mystification for ideological purposes. As I have shown elsewhere (Claviez 1996), these two concepts are at odds, since myth is based upon an inclusive logic of both, whereas ideology follows an exclusive logic of either/or. This leads to the fact that, at a certain point, in Barthes' model the two are bound to clash.

The assumption that there is something "precious" that is threatened, however, is part and parcel of the Romantic ideology that inhabits the quest for authenticity in the first place, and thus a tautology ensues. In order for there to be an authentic artefact, there has to exist a PoO in relation to which the authenticity can be established. In fact, the entire Romantic enterprise strongly depends on the assumption that authenticity does–must–exist.

The "precariousness" of this alleged "point of origin" lies, as I have argued, as much in its inherent significance for any concept of authenticity, as it does in its equally inherent arbitrariness. This, as Hamilton shows, holds equally true for the famous anecdote already mentioned above: W. C. Handy's encounter with a ragged old Blues man using a knife to emulate a slide guitar in the absence of a bottleneck. Hamilton quotes Eric Lott's comment on the significance of this origin story: that it allegedly reveals "the object of study in the moment of its emergence, the pure thing (unadulterated by later, superfluous changes)" (Hamilton, 141). The romantic tinge of this assessment cannot be ignored; it begs, however, several questions:

1) While this might have been Handy's "initiation" into the Blues, what about this can be considered "pure"? It is a highly contingent snapshot that might have served as the personal PoO for Handy's further preoccupation with the Blues; but why would it have any relevance for the "emergence" (another processual term) of the Blues itself?

2) Only if we buy into this questionable purity logic, however, do other terms even make sense; or rather, betray their senselessness: why would any change have to be both "adulterating" and "superfluous"? What we see clearly reflected here is the allergic reaction of the authenticators against the contingency of time, and the change it by default implies.

As Hamilton correctly argues, this PoO has clear ideological implications as to what "counts" as authentic and what not: "Handy's story has drawn Blues scholars because it matches their perception of the music's authentic contours: rural, male, non-commercial, and permeated by sorrow" (Hamilton, 141). What happens here is exactly what I have tried to capture in what I have called the "Third order semiotic system": the story does not only serve to authenticate Handy himself; it is also made to serve a set of authenticators to in turn authenticate both Handy *and* themselves.

Moreover, if the protagonist of his anecdote is turned into a PoO, then everything that he is *not* will inevitably fail to live up to the litmus test of authentication: that is, every non-male, every non-Black, every non-rural, and, eventually, every non-poor and non-suffering person, every non-acoustic Blues player will by default fail to match the criteria of authenticity.

Which means that every female, white, urbanized, successful and electrified person would infallibly fail such a test.

But obviously, to fight the tide of historical contingency proves to be a rather challenging task, as the encounter between the Lomaxes and Leadbelly has shown: caught between the attempt to preserve the "unadulterated purity" that the former so cherished when they heard the latter sing for the first time in Louisiana's Angola Prison in 1934, and their vested interests in making this phenomenon known to a wider public, the Lomaxes found themselves in a "trap," as Benjamin Filene points out: their "political goals demanded that they strive for as wide a hearing as possible, but as the singers adapted their music to reach popular audiences, purists denounced them for selling out their heritage" (Filene 1991, 609). And, as Alan Lomax has to admit, authenticity suddenly becomes "relative": "Lomax described Leadbelly's 1940 recordings as "not complete authenticity, but I believe the nearest thing to it that could be achieved away from the prison farms themselves" (Filene, 611). Ideally, so the perverse logic of authenticity goes, Leadbelly, in order to preserve his "purity," should have stayed in prison; instead, he became a mixture between the Lomaxes sidekick as chauffeur and servant, and the golden calf whose revenues they retained mostly for themselves, marketing him as the "real thing." Moreover, his role within the political agenda of the Lomaxes made him, as Filene argues, not to "perform" himself, but actually to serve as a synecdoche for someone else: "In publicizing Leadbelly…, the Lomaxes portrayed him as a populist spokesman–a mouthpiece who vented, unmediated, the hopes and fears of the masses" (Filene, 613). Strangely enough, in such a scenario, Leadbelly actually disappears: he becomes the "unmediated/unmediating medium" for an anonymous mass that he himself is not a part of.

Leadbelly's story sheds an interesting light upon a special facet of authenticity: that of "performative" authenticity. In my model offered above, if the authenticity of the *performance* of an artist is not measured according to the "truthfulness" of what is being played in relation to an earlier style or quality of the music, but according to the truthfulness of the expression of the artist's "true self," then the first axis–that between PoO and AoA–simply collapses, or approaches zero. In Leadbelly's case, however, this is not truly the case: in fact, another axis opens up: that between a "former" Leadbelly and a later one. As the Lomaxes insisted that Leadbelly "performs" himself– often having him wear, *against his own will*, his old prison outfit–the "performance" of authenticity becomes just that: a per-form, a substitute for something that is emphatically *not* present.

In light of what has been said, then, Charles Shaar Murray's question, in his article "Can there be such a thing as 'real Blues' in the 21st century," acquires significance: "So at what point should we demand that the music stand still and be flash-frozen or freeze-fried"? (Murray 2013). This inquiry, in a nutshell, captures almost everything that is to say about the arbitrariness of what I have identified as the PoO, upon which any assumption about authenticity relies. However, should not, in light of what I have said, the question rather be: "*Why* should we demand that the music stand still and be flash-frozen or freeze-fried?" Anything flash-frozen and freeze-fried is one thing for sure: dead.

If all of what I have said tells us anything, it is that the reference to authenticity–which, as we know, is an invention of "white Romanticism" following in the traces of its Godfather, Jean-Jacques Rousseau–can serve many masters. However, some of these masters–aka as experts–are dependent upon this concept in order to either sell themselves, sell artists, or sell records. Moreover, we all know that Romanticism has a very specific view on history: every development away from the Golden Age of the beginning can only be a step in the wrong direction. That is, history as contingency is always also a history of decay. In contrast to European culture, however, the Blues is based–among other things–upon the very orality of its performance. That includes, amongst other things, the changeability of the story: the fact that, since there is no (written) "original" to emulate as closely as possible, the storyteller is free to "improvise." To improvise not, as Adorno calls it, to make "stumbling the rule," as he puts it in his notorious essay on Jazz (Adorno 1936, 256), but to acknowledge history and time as contingent and changing. This is exactly what authenticity denies, but what Adorno–ironically the author of a book with the title *The Rhetoric of Authenticity*–totally misses in what would probably have to count among his worst, since most unreflected essays ever. An essay published, by the way, under the pseudonym Hector Rottweiler–and the relentlessness of his attacks on Jazz in this essay makes this name (Greek warrior meets German attack dog) a good choice. It is the only instance of Adorno's writing that I know that is driven almost exclusively by emotions; one of them being the hatred for the culture industry. A hatred also for the masses that seemed to be duped, in his perspective, into acknowledging an alternative to the sublimity that he accorded to the 12-tone music of Berg and Schönberg; and a contingency that he, the musical sociologist and fervent, if disillusioned Romantic-believer-in-the-Enlightenment, wasn't prepared to grant gypsies and African-Americans.[6]

---

[6] Interestingly enough, behind his entire argument that Jazz only "performs" the authenticity of both syncopation and authentic improvisation makes only sense when he presupposes that something like "genuine" authenticity can exist. At one point in his essay, he even talks about a "collective immediacy" (*kollektive Unmittelbarkeit*, 248) that characterizes "autonomous art". It is almost ironic that he himself warns the reader about the inherent Romanticism that lurks in considering "the usability of Jazz ... as a corrective to the

If, as I have claimed, stories in the oral tradition are able to acknowledge the contingency of time, it might be worth looking at one of the other "founding" stories of the Blues. Much has been written about the lore engulfing Robert Johnson and his alleged encounter with the devil at the Crossroads; and it is not my intention to review this debate in its entirety.[7] Enough is known to subvert any claim about the "authenticity" of the story, or of Robert Johnson: a) It is actually ascribed to Tommy Johnson; b) Robert Johnson's recordings might have been sped up, which changed both Johnson's voice and the speed of his playing; etc. What I find so striking about it, however–and what has, to my knowledge, not been commented upon–is one of the story's most important narrative features: while Robert Johnson, as many commentators have pointed out, has become one of the reference points as regards the Blues (and its authenticity), nobody seems to be too preoccupied with the fact that he, in order to achieve this prowess on the guitar, had, according to the Faustian plot, to sell his soul to the devil. Now the question that I would like to raise is: *how on earth can someone who has sold his soul to the devil possibly be "authentic"*?

References

Adorno, Theodor W. (alias Hector Rottweiler). 1936. "Ueber Jazz." *Zeitschrift für Sozialforschung* 5, 235-259.

Claviez, Thomas, Britta Sweers, and Kornelia Imesch. 2019. *Critique of Authenticity.* Wilmington: Vernon Press. Forthcoming.

Claviez, Thomas. 1996. *Grenzfälle: Mythos – Ideologie – American Studies.* Trier: wvt.

Claviez, Thomas. 2019. "A Critique of Authenticity and Recognition." In *Critique of Authenticity*, edited by Thomas Claviez et al. Wilmington: Vernon Press. Forthcoming.

Ferrara, Alessandro. 2019. "The Dual Paradox of Authenticity in the 21st Century." In *Critique of Authenticity*, edited by Thomas Claviez et al. Wilmington: Vernon Press. Forthcoming.

Filene, Benjamin. 1991. "'Our Singing Country': John and Alan Lomax, Leadbelly, and the Construction of an American Past." *American Quarterly* 43, 602-624.

Hamilton, Marybeth. 2000. "Sexuality, Authenticity and the Making of the Blues Tradition." *Past & Present* 169 (Nov.), 132-160.

---

bourgeois isolation of autonomous art" (238, translation mine.). And to think that the improvising amateur could actually embody the "unencumbered and fresh, whose originality asserts itself against the routine of the business" should, according to Adorno/Rottweiler, be "delegated into the realm of the Negro story" (247; translation mine).

[7] For an overview of the most important contributions to this debate, cf. Jonathan Stewart (2013).

Further Reading

Barthes, Roland. 2013. *Mythologies Today.* New York: Hill and Wang.

Chinitz, David 1996. "Literacy and Authenticity: The Blues Poems of Langston Hughes." *Callaloo* 19:1, 177-192.

Evans, David. 1999. "Demythologizing the Blues." *ISAM Newsletter* 29:1, 8-13.

Gaates, Henry Louis. 1988. *The Signifying Monkey.* New York: Oxford University Press.

Henderson, Stephen. 1982. "The Blues as Black Poetry." *Callaloo* 16, 22-30.

Hollenbach, Lisa. 2015. "Phonography, Race Records, and the Blues Poetry of Langston Hughes." In *A Companion to the Harlem Renaissance.*, edited by Cherene Sherrard-Johnson, 301-316. Chichester: Wiley & Sons.

Kuntz, Tom. 1995. "Word for Word / Blues Journals; Down at the Crossroads, There's a Devil of a Debate." *The New York Times*, 5 March, sec. 4, 7.

Lieberfeld, Daniel. 1995. "Million-Dollar Juke Joint: Commodifying Blues Culture." *African-American Review* 29:2, 217-221.

Murray, Charles Shaar. 2013. "Can There Be Such a Thing as 'Real Blues' in the 21st Century?" *The Blues* 5 (Feb.). https://www.loudersound.com/features/can-there-be-such-a-thing-as-real-Blues-in-the-21st-century. Last accessed 24 January 2019.

Sharlet, Jeff. 2007. "Keeping it Unreal." *New Statesman*, 16 April. (Review of Hugh Barker's and Yuval Taylor's book *Faking It*).

Stewart, Jonathan. 2013. "If I Had Possession Over Judgment Day: Augmenting Robert Johnson." *M/C Journal* 16:6. http://journal.media-culture.org.au/index.php/mcjournal/article/view/715. Last accessed 24 January 2019.

Thomas, Lorenzo. 1997. "Authenticity and Elevation: Sterling Brown's Theory of the Blues." *African American Review* 31:3, 409-416.

Waldron, Edward E. 1971. "The Blues Poetry of Langston Hughes." *Negro American Literature Forum* 5:4, 140-149.

Winsby, Meghan. 2012. "Lady Sings the Blues: A Woman's Perspective of Authenticity." In *Blues-Philosophy for Everyone*, edited by Jesse R. Steinberg and Abrol Fairweather, 155-167. Chichester: Wiley & Sons.

11.

I'm goin' away to a world unknown: a corpus study of classic Blues lyrics[1]

Jean-Charles Khalifa

University of Poitiers, France

The idea in this paper is to apply the methodology already used in Khalifa (2007) and Khalifa (2010). Compiling a vast corpus of lyrics and analysing it quantitatively, by means of a concordancer, gives us a sound statistical base of frequencies, sorted by parts of speech (adjectives, nouns, verbs, prepositions), which then allows qualitative interpretation bringing out collocations and various interesting patterns. It will also allow for most revealing comparisons with a white corpus (Old-time, Bluegrass and Early Country). What I am really trying to do is uncover what might be termed the 'unconscious' behind the lyrics, which in the final analysis reaches into fundamental, anthropological dimensions of the genre under scrutiny. For instance, Blues will be found to be characterized by the up / down, or proximal / distal axis, revealing a tension between a familiar world (which is loathed) and profound terror of unfamiliar / unknown remote areas, ambivalently craved and feared.

Introduction and methodology

What I intend to do in this paper is simply apply some simple, even basic tools of corpus linguistics to a large collection of Blues lyrics, and then see if the findings can teach us something about what the Blues is really all about. To put things differently: if, to borrow a phrase from Randolph Lewis (this volume) "Blues speak the truth of America", the main question in this study is, quite simply, do *words* speak the truth of the Blues? Hopefully, the data here presented, mainly but by no means only quantitative, and the related conclusions, will feed more qualitative approaches, whether literary, cultural or historical.

---

[1] I would like to express our thanks to Douglas Ponton and Uwe Zagratzki for making all of this possible, and to two anonymous reviewers for their very helpful remarks.

The corpus compiled simply brings together about 400 Blues songs, all of them pre-war, a choice meant to really get to the heart of the Blues, as it were. Obviously, it is impossible to even approach exhaustiveness: the very idea of a corpus is to be representative, and for the purposes of this paper, the selection will be taken as representative enough. The songs were simply all copied back to back into one single file (which proved to be something of a headache), saved it in .txt format, and run through a concordance programme to see what would happen. As the corpus was untagged, a sophisticated tool was unneeded, so what was used was the same concordance programme as for Khalifa (2007) and (2010), namely *SCP* (version 4.0.8.), developed by Alan Reed (freeware).

The raw data, word frequencies and ranks

To begin with, let's take a look at the raw figures about the file: 145,953 words, and a 5,332 word-vocabulary. There are, of course, a number of ways of viewing those figures; let me just compare this corpus to a corpus of 400-plus Bob Dylan songs analysed in the same way and using the same tools about 10 years ago (Khalifa 2007). The number of words was comparable (111,555), but the vocabulary count (number of types, or different words, to put it simply) was significantly higher (8,170). The Old-Time, Early Bluegrass and Early Country corpus I analysed in the same way had 214,000 words and a 7,494 word vocabulary. One possible explanation for the lower vocabulary count is the repetitive nature of Blues, with its AAB structure where the first line is almost always duplicated, albeit sometimes with very minor variations. However, the vocabulary count for all of these popular, traditional genres should by no means be considered as poor in itself. If we take a couple of British classics to compare, James Joyce's *Dubliners* has 67,000 words, with a 7,600 word-vocabulary, and Daniel Defoe's *Robinson Crusoe*, 121,000 words and a 6,500 word-vocabulary. The next thing our software may provide us with is word frequencies, a much more telling tool for analysis.

Given our experience of analysing a number of corpora, whether musical or literary, using the same tools and methodology, at this preliminary stage the usual results might have been expected, namely that the definite article *the* ranked #1 by far, followed by other determiners such as the indefinite article *a*, conjunctions such as *and*, pronouns, the auxiliaries *have, be* and *do*, all of which routinely crop up as the most frequently used items in the language, hence in specific genres. Which means that all these corpora, at least on this most visible criterion, were definitely aligned with our reference corpus, the Corpus of Contemporary American English (C.O.C.A.). For instance, in C.O.C.A. not only is the definite determiner *the* the #1 item, but it appears with a frequency twice as high as the next item, which is *be*.

In the case of our Blues corpus, however (see table 11.1 below), what appeared was that the 1st- and 2nd-person pronouns ranked 1 and 2. And of course, the picture is even more spectacular for the 1st-person pronoun if items #4 and #6 in the list, *me* and *my*, are factored in. When we look at C.O.C.A., *I* ranks only 11th with a frequency of 8,841 / million and *you* is 14th (freq. 6,847 / million), both admittedly quite frequent, but by no means as prominent as in our Blues corpus, where they are about 5 times more frequent. We will return to this in more detail later in this paper, but let us simply say, at this stage, that this does seem to bear out the oft-mentioned and somewhat trivial idea that the Blues is a highly (inter-)subjective genre, one that is mostly about the 1st-person narrator's state of mind and which involves overt or covert dialogue between him[2] and another protagonist. And indeed, in the whole corpus, it is almost impossible to find a single song where 1st-person pronouns, whether in the subjective or objective case, do not appear. The only one that comes close is *District Attorney*, recorded by Bukka White in 1940, and even there, while the rest of the verses are in the 3rd person, the last verse goes: *The District Attorney sho' is hard on a man / He taken **me** from **my** woman, cause her to love some other man*, the proverbial exception that proves the rule. And other apparent exceptions like *John Henry, Louis Collins* or *Casey Jones* are, in actual fact, more akin to the ballad tradition than to the Blues, but are present in the corpus because songsters like Mississippi John Hurt, whose 1928 recordings feature prominently in our collection, never seemed to make a real difference between those, which was also the case of many of the later pioneers, including of course Leadbelly or Big Bill Broonzy.

Table 11.1: Top 10 items in Blues Corpus and C.O.C.A.

BLUES CORPUS[3]			C.O.C.A.[4]	
1.	I	(47,116)	1.	the
2.	you	(30,638)	2.	be
3.	the	(23,300)	3.	and
4.	my	(20,589)	4.	of
5.	to	(17,817)	5.	a
6.	me	(16,046)	6.	in
7.	a	(15,546)	7.	to
8.	and	(15,500)	8.	have
9.	in	(10,441)	9.	to
10.	baby	(9,571)	10.	it

---

[2] Note that I'm not being politically incorrect here when not using "him or her", as the vast majority of the songs in our corpus are told from a man's point of view, the blatant exception in our collection of songs being Memphis Minnie's compositions.

[3] Frequencies in this table to be read as X per million words.

[4] Frequencies omitted for the sake of clarity; what matters at this stage is only the contrast involving personal pronouns.

However interesting the raw data may be, we need to take a more fine-grained look at our corpus, and the most obvious way to achieve this, as usual in our methodology, is to sort out words by lexical categories.

An analysis of the four parts of speech

Let us start the investigation with lexical nouns; the following is a comparative table, a linguistic hit parade, as it were, of the top ten nouns in our corpus:

Table 11.2: Nouns

BLUES CORPUS[5]			C.O.C.A.		
A	B	C	D	E	F
1. baby[6]	(1243)	9,571	[52] time	(764,657)	1,799
2. lord[7]	(748)	6,021	[54] year	(769,254)	1,810
3. man	(650)	5,005	[62] people	(691,468)	1,626
4. woman	(489)	3,765	[84] way	(470,401)	1,106
5. mama	(437)	3,364	[90] day	(432,773)	1,018
6. home	(432)	3,326	[94] man	(409,760)	964
7. Blues	(422)	3,249	[97] thing	(400,724)	942
8. time	(288)	2,217	[111] woman	(341,422)	803
9. day	(266)	2,048	[114] life	(333,085)	783
10. night	(254)	1,955	[115] child	(333,849)	785

Only three of our top ten nouns (*man, woman* and *time,* highlighted in grey in the table) are common to our corpus and to C.O.C.A., but of course, a simple look at frequencies per million words shows us how massively they are used in Blues lyrics. However, rather surprisingly (or is this really surprising?), the first item, by far, is *baby* (9,571 / million words). Only eight (0.6%!) of those are "real" babies (= newborn children, as in, i.e. *John Henry was a little baby,* etc.). All the rest mean *sweetheart,* of course. And about two-thirds of those (more than 800) are actually forms of address, like shouts or hollers, as in ***Baby,*** *please don't go,* etc., often appearing at the beginning or the end of lines. In

---

[5] Frequencies in this and the next tables to be read as: absolute number of occurrences (in round brackets), frequency per million words (Column C, Column F). Relevant comparisons, of course, only make sense between frequencies per million words. In this and subsequent tables, C.O.C.A. items appear with their absolute ranks (square brackets) in the whole corpus. For instance, noun #1 in C.O.C.A., *TIME*, appears as 52th of all the words in the 420-million word-corpus, irrespective of category, and so on.
[6] Including *babe.*
[7] Including *Lordy.*

the remaining third, 440 to be precise (36%), which are NOT forms of address, about half are subjects and half are objects. This confirms, if anything, the deeply subjective, conversational nature of the Blues. Just for comparison purposes, the noun *baby* is 589th in C.O.C.A. with a frequency of 159 / million (and of course, the overwhelming majority of those are "real" babies!)

It should be noted in passing that the analysis of item #5 on the list, *mama*, would be pretty much the same: 14 only (3%) are mothers, as in Lightnin' Hopkins' *I was born'd on the levee, I'm my mama's baby child*). All the rest are *heavy-hipped mamas, red-hot mamas* and the like. *mother*, incidentally, is 15th in the list of nouns, with a frequency of 1,001 *vs.* 398 in C.O.C.A. (*father* being way down the list with a frequency of 169).

We will not be saying much about item #2, *Lord*, even though it would require a separate paper. What could simply be said is that almost all *Lords* present in the corpus are also forms of address. As a provisional conclusion, indeed the Blues is a highly intersubjective, conversational genre, in which someone seems to be constantly addressing someone else, whether human or divine. We may also mention the fact that, according to whether the music producers meant to push forward the religious segment or the secular one, it was quite frequent for *lord* to simply replace *baby* in the same song, or the other way around. To wit: *I'm gonna buy me a pony can, pay for fox-trot and run / I'm gonna buy me a pony can, pay for fox-trot and run / Lord, when you see me comin', pretty mama, I'll be on Highway 61* ("61 Highway", Mississippi Fred McDowell).

We are indeed more interested in analysing in some detail item #6 on the list, *home*, because it would actually rank #1 if we took away all the forms of address and **man, woman,** which are in the top ten nouns in C.O.C.A. anyway; the other reason why we are most interested in it is that it did rank #1, with a frequency of 4,370 / million, in our country / old-time / bluegrass corpus. To be more precise, the statistics presented conflate the real nominal uses of *home* (as in *I ain't got no home* or *my home in Texas*) and the adverbial uses (as in *go home*, etc.), but as it turns out it really does not affect the point at all. With a frequency of 3,326 / million, it is 7.5 times more frequent than in C.O.C.A. (250th with a 631 / million frequency including adverbial uses). On the other hand, we also have 93 *house* (716 / million words,) double what we have in C.O.C.A. (351 / million words). It is well-known that the word *home* is almost impossible to translate properly in many languages, including French–to the utter and long-standing dismay of the present researcher, also a translator–; this is mostly on account of its multiple connotations, all referring to the concept of unicity and to a kind of deep-rooted, intimate link with individuals. If we take a look at etymology, the root is a very old Indo-European one, in which the salient meaning is one of a dwelling or place in which one feels safe, secure:

Table 11.3: Etymology of HOME

(həʊm) Forms: 1–2 **hám**, 3–5 (7) **hom**, (3–4 **hoom**, 4–5 **hoome**), 4– **home**, 5–7 **whome**, 6 **whom**); north. and Sc. 3–5 **ham**, 4– **hame**, (5 **hem**, 5–7 **hayme**, 6 **heme**, 6, 9 **heame**, 7 **haim**, 9 **haam**). [Com. Teut.: OE. hám = OFris. hém, OS. hém (MDu., Du. heem), OHG. heim (MHG., Ger. heim), ON. heimr dwelling, world, (Sw. hem, Da. hjem), Goth. háims fem., village. Cf. Lith. kẽmas, kaímas, village, homestead, OPruss. caymis village; Skr. kšêmas safe dwelling, f. *ksi to dwell secure.

(Oxford English Dictionary)

But what is most interesting to analyse, in our view, is the associations between *home* and its immediate or less immediate contexts. To cut a very long story short, those associations are very often negative, in the sense that the security/safety symbolized by *home* is simply absent (*lose a home, ain't got no home, ain't nobody home, away from home, a long way from home*, etc.) or else is represented as distant in space and/or time, sometimes a distant dream; indeed 103 (23%) of *home* are associated with *come* (*coming, come back, come on*), as in:

Hey, hey, baby, where you stayed last night
*You didn't **come home** until the sun was shining bright*
("32-20 Blues", Robert Johnson)

This time now baby, just got to let you go
***Come home** tellin' me that you won't get drunk no more*
("Jake Head Boogie", Lightnin' Hopkins)

Your mother treated me like I was her baby child
*That's why's I find it so hard to **come back home** to die*
("Fixing to Die Blues", Bukka White)

and another 107 (23% again) with *go, hurry, walk*, etc. Which brings us to our next table, that of lexical verbs:

Table 11.4: Lexical verbs

BLUES CORPUS			C.O.C.A.		
A	B	C	D	E	F
1. go	(1157)	8,908	[19] say	(191,5138)	4,506
2. know	(850)	6,545	[35] go	(115,1045)	2,708
3. come	(503)	3,873	[39] get	(992,596)	2,335
4. get	(481)	3,703	[45] make	(857,168)	2,016
5. want	(426)	3,280	[47] know	(892,535)	2,100
6. tell	(389)	2,995	[56] think	(772,787)	1,818
7. see	(367)	2,825	[63] take	(670,745)	1,578
8. take	(299)	2,302	[67] see	(663,645)	1,561
9. leave	(266)	2,048	[70] come	(628,254)	1,478
10. cry	(240)	1,848	[83] want	(514,972)	1,211

We will not insist too much on the verbs, for lack of space, and also because lexical verbs are a little less interesting in our view, seven out of ten being also in the top ten verbs in C.O.C.A. *tell* is indeed further down the list in C.O.C.A. (yet not too far down, 15th in the verb category with a frequency of 803 / million). However, *leave* is quite significant for our purposes here, for the verb is almost four times as frequent in the Blues corpus as in C.O.C.A., where it ranks only 26th with a frequency of 534 / million. The situation is even more spectacular for *cry*, which has a frequency of only 62 / million in C.O.C.A., where in addition a number of these occurrences mean *shout* and not *weep*. We will return to this further down, but let us now turn our attention to the motion verbs *go* and *come*, which of course are also present on the right-hand side, but *go* is three times more frequent and *come* 2.6 times more frequent in the Blues corpus. The Blues is beginning to emerge as a landscape in which the 1st-person narrator/protagonist is involved in a lot of coming and going, either in the literal sense or in an idealized sense, and where the fixed point of reference in all that coming and going is the safety represented by *home*, and most often construed as a point forever out of reach. Add to this that there's also a lot of "leaving" involved, and that the point of reference is massively again the 1st-person narrator, who is being left in 27% of cases (71) and actually does the "leaving" in another 20% of cases (34) (*leave* **you**, *leave* **my baby**, *leave* **my home**, *leave* **town**). Those represent almost half of the occurrences of the verb. The overall picture that emerges is definitely one in which the Blues seems to be generated by all that instability, whether spatial or emotional (the latter being, for our purposes here, a metaphor of the former).

Let us now turn to adjectives:

Table 11.5: Adjectives

BLUES CORPUS			C.O.C.A.		
A	B	C	D	E	F
1. good	(350)	2,695	[75] other	(547,799)	1,288
2. old	(337)	2,594	[88] new	(435,993)	1,025
3. little	(274)	2,109	[110] good	(353,973)	832
4. sweet	(157)	1,208	[141] high	(255,936)	602
5. bad	(156)	1,201	[152] old	(236,577)	556
6. wrong	(150)	1,155	[160] great	(225,005)	529
7. last	(140)	1,078	[162] big	(227,169)	534
8. poor	(131)	1,008	[176] American	(214,968)	505
9. black	(113)	870	[203] small	(185,463)	436
10. lonesome	(97)	746	[221] large	(175,611)	413

The picture is here reversed, in the sense that only two of these (as it turns out, the top two) are common to the Blues corpus and C.O.C.A. The last three items undoubtedly draw a remarkably accurate picture of the condition and state of mind of black folks in those days; *black* has a frequency of 354 / million in C.O.C.A., less than half what we have in our corpus; *poor* is way down the list with 126 / million. And *lonesome* is not even in the top 5,000 words![8]

But let us return to the top two; we will ignore *good*, which is too polysemic to be really exploitable in a qualitative analysis. But #2, *old*, is worth a few words of comment. What is striking is that very few of those actually mean *"old in years"*, as in:

> *I'm satisfied, tickled too, **old** enough to marry you...*
> ("I'm satisfied", Mississippi John Hurt).

In other words, the relevant opposition or semantic axis is not *old / new* or *old / young* as in C.O.C.A.[9] or any other general English corpus (as a matter of fact, *new* is far down the list of adjectives in our corpus, with a frequency of 431 / million, to be compared with the 1,025 of C.O.C.A. where it is the 2nd most frequent adjective, and *young* is even further down, with a frequency of 123 / million, *vs.* 376 / million in C.O.C.A.). But most of the time in the corpus, we have examples like:

> *'Cause she loves good old jelly, oh, that good **old** jelly roll*
> ("That Good old Jelly", Sonny Terry and Brownie McGhee)
>
> *You know, I must-a had them **old** walkin' Blues*
> ("Death Letter Blues", Son House)

---

[8] Interestingly, LONESOME (but NOT POOR), also features prominently in the country/bluegrass/old-time corpus, with a frequency twice as high (1,536); this of course does not mean that white folks were feeling twice as lonesome as black folks.

[9] An anonymous reviewer suggested elaborating this point to better demonstrate the contrast between the uses of the adjective in both corpora. Obviously, it would be a formidable task to look at all 236,577 instances of OLD in C.O.C.A., and to date no corpus linguistics tool is sophisticated enough to tease out one meaning from the other automatically. However, there are ways; looking at the left context, for instance, shows that the combination YEARS/DAYS/WEEKS/CENTURIES OLD (always preceded by a figure) represents more than 15% of all occurrences; a simple, heuristic manual look at two random samples of 100 instances each returned only one instance of the 'familiar, reassuring' meaning. But the most reliable of methods is to look at N+1 collocations. A search on OLD + NOUN, for instance, returns the following associations, in decreasing frequency: MAN, WOMAN, DAYS, FRIEND, AGE, LADY, FRIENDS, MEN, WORLD, HOUSE, TESTAMENT, TOWN, CITY, GUY, WAYS. None of these points to anything else than the 'chronological' use of the adjective; moreover, if we just add the occurrences, singular and plural, of MAN/GUY/WOMAN/LADY alone, we find that those that refer to a human being, are as frequent as the next 30 in the list.

*'Cause that **old** girl's mad with me, friends, but I don't care*
("Police Sergeant Blues", Robert Wilkins)

So the meaning we're seeing is overwhelmingly that of ***familiar, customary*** (O.E.D.: *Frequently with reference to a customary pleasure indulged in fully: plentiful, great, enjoyable, memorable. Now merely reinforcing an appreciative adjective, as* good old, grand old, high old, *etc.*)

In such cases, the adjective denotes affection or attachment with an object or an individual for which a privileged relationship is built. The key structuring opposition, in this case, is **familiar *vs.* strange, reassuring closeness *vs.* threatening remoteness**. We can take this even further by looking at the etymology:

The Old English ancestor of the *old* of contemporary English is *ald* (German *alt*) and comes from a form of Gothic *al-an*, "growing up", cognate to old Norse *al-a*, "raise, feed" and to a Latin root *al-era* "feed" (a form of which, *alimentum*, gave a whole family of terms in French, which, incidentally, English borrowed at some point; cf. *Alma Mater*).

Table 11.6: Etymology of OLD

Etymology: Cognate with Old Frisian *ald*, Middle Dutch *out, oud*, regional *olt, alt* (Dutch *oud*), Old Saxon *ald, old* (Middle Low German *ōlt, olt*, German regional (Low German) *oll, old, olt, oold*), Old High German *alt* (Middle High German *alt*, German *alt*), Crimean Gothic *alt*, and further (< the same base with *j* -suffixation) with Gothic *alþeis* < a derivative (apparently originally a participial formation corresponding to ancient Greek forms in -τός, classical Latin -*tus* of the Germanic base of Old English *alan* to nourish, Old Icelandic *ala* to nourish, bring up, Gothic *alan* to feed oneself, to grow up < the same Indo-European base as classical Latin *alere* to nourish (see aliment n.)

(Oxford English Dictionary)

This, of course, very much ties in with the semantic network I described above about *home*. And now, to end this guided tour of the corpus, a brief look at prepositions.

Two striking examples (we will just ignore *in, of* and *on*, none of which being likely to be very instructive for our purposes):

- *BACK*: 3,465 / million as opposed to 817 in C.O.C.A. (four times as many). And incidentally it is also of interest to note the high proportion of ***BACK HOME***: 79 / 446 (≈18% of all instances of *HOME*)
- *AWAY*: 2,125 / million as opposed to 340 in C.O.C.A. (6.2 times as many), most of which are associated with *come, go* and other verbs of motion (*RIDE, DRIVE*, etc.)

What seems to be going on here is most consistent with the semantic networks already construed with *old* and *home*: again, the fundamental instability or imbalance which generates the Blues is closely associated to a deep-rooted tension between the place (again, whether understood as spatial or metaphorical/emotional) where you are and the place where you want to be. This is further corroborated by a simple look at two more prepositions, *down* and *up*:

Table 11.7: Down and Up

	COUNTRY CORPUS		BLUES CORPUS		C.O.C.A.
	A	B	C	D	E
DOWN	(941)	4,328	(880)	6776	775
UP	(562)	2,585	(425)	3272	1,871

At this stage, I really could not resist comparing the Blues corpus and the country/old-time/bluegrass corpus analysed in Khalifa 2010, that is black music and white music. What was really striking in the analysis of the country corpus a few years back was the prevalence of *down* over *up*. As table 7 shows, *up* is twice as frequent as *down* in a standard corpus like C.O.C.A., and in all other general corpora of English. But the proportion was reversed in the country corpus. And not only was it reversed, but both prepositions were found to be incredibly numerous, as the figures show (Column A). And what is even more spectacular is that both *down* and *up* are even more numerous in the Blues corpus. Now of course, as any native speaker of English knows, the relevant meaning is not verticality, but horizontality: in other words, *up* refers to a movement **towards** some reference point, and *down*, on the opposite, to a movement **away from** that reference point, in other words, what linguists call the proximal / distal axis.

This obviously completes and reinforces the semantic networks we have seen being construed. What generates the Blues is this series of tensions/contradictions between what is here and what is not here, what is familiar, reassuring and even nurturing and the sense of void one may feel when pushed or torn away from it. We might even, tentatively, go one step further. Given what we know of the social/economic condition of black folks in pre-Second World War days, the familiar world, for all its reassuring nature, is also loathed; and on the other hand, there is also considerable ambivalence in feelings for unfamiliar / unknown remote areas, a mixture of profound terror and profound desire, inasmuch as there might be something different at the end of the journey. This is, of course, best summarized by Charlie Patton's famous line, which was borrowed for the title of this paper: *I'm goin' away, to a world unknown / I'm worried now, I won't be worried long.*

A conclusion?

In actual fact, the conclusion to this paper is, academically speaking to be found in the previous two paragraphs. Let us then consider the few lines that follow as some sort of epilogue, or maybe as the beginning of another research paper to come. If we just return to what was said above in Part 1 of the highly subjective, conversational nature of the Blues on the basis of the very high frequency of 1st- and 2nd-person pronouns in the corpus, we might wonder whether this is really a unique feature of the genre. But as it turns out, a single look at the figures below (Column D) against those of our country/bluegrass corpus (Column B) – again black music *vs* white music – shows, somewhat unexpectedly, that frequencies were in fact exactly (for the 1st-person pronoun) or almost exactly (for the 2nd-person pronoun) the same. The only discrepancies were for 3rd-person pronouns, the masculine being a little more frequent in C.O.C.A. than in our two corpora, and the feminine being over-represented in both the Blues corpus and the bluegrass/country corpus. This might suggest that even though separated, white folks and black folks were sociologically, if not culturally, very close, close enough to show the same sort of linguistic patterns in their music. This indeed would deserve another separate study.

Table 11.8: Personal pronouns in black and white traditional music

	COUNTRY CORPUS		BLUES CORPUS		C.O.C.A
	A	**B**	**C**	**D**	**E**
I	(10,313)	47,439	(6,119)	47,116	8,841
You	(6,156)	28,317	(3,979)	30,628	6,847
HE	(1219)	5,107	(615)	4,735	6,465
SHE	(1315)	6,049	(1,005)	7,738	3,300

Further Reading

Khalifa, J.-C. 2007. "A semantic and Syntactic Journey through the Dylan Corpus". *Oral Tradition* Vol. 22: 1. Website: http://journal.oraltradition.org/issues/22i/khalifa.

Khalifa, J.-C. 2011. "Country-conservatisme, blue-fascisme ? Les musiques américaines à base traditionnelle et l'ordre établi." In *Langue, musique, identité,* edited by Jeremy Price, Licia Bagini, Marlène Belly, 73-84. Paris: Édition Publibook.

12.

The devil's music–a critical discourse analysis-based study of the lyrics of Robert Johnson

Giulia Magazzù

University "Gabriele D'Annunzio", Chieti-Pescara, Italy

The Blues is a musical form whose origins and early development are inextricably tied up with the history and geography of the United States. Contrary to popular opinion, it is not a branch of jazz, nor is the opposite true, and the two types of music, though mixing readily, evolved in different geographical centres with entirely different social and cultural demographics. The musical roots of the Blues can be traced back to points of origin as diverse as the work songs of slaves, sea shanties, nineteenth-century English ballads and traditional African griot songs. When a recognisable musical Blues genre appeared is open to dispute, but it is generally considered to have a relatively late genesis at some point between the turn of the century and the outbreak of World War One. As a recorded form, it was popular from the 1920s onwards (Trynka 1996). Early Blues was generally performed on guitar, banjo, mandolin, and harmonica and, in urban areas, piano, either in a solo or ensemble format, most readily in the form of ad hoc 'jug bands'. Blues of the post-war period will be recognisable to most listeners as having the same structures, rhythms and sound as rock and roll, which was the name given to Blues music when record companies wanted to sell it to white audiences. Musically, it is characterised by simple chord progressions, typically involving 12 bars of music using the tonic, sub-dominant and dominant chords of a key. Unusual guitar tunings may be used, such as the Hawaiian "slack-key", which allows for the use of a slide or bottleneck to fret the strings instead of the fingers, and a use of the "blue note", the flattened 5th note of a major scale, which gives it an ambiguous tonal centre, being neither major or minor (Charters 1999). The other defining feature of Blues music is the lyrics. Different scholars suggest including various extra musical aspects in musical discourse analysis, such as psychological, personal factors, social and historical environment, stylistic conventions, artistic aims and so forth (De Nora 2000; Roy 2010).

The aim of this paper is to distinguish types of lexical units and semantic structures peculiar to the musical discourse of the Blues and explain their use from the point of view of the social context; thus, I applied a qualitative social analysis to the lyrics of Robert Johnson, possibly the most famous of all Blues musicians and one of the few musicians whose entire body of work has been annotated and is available for analysis. After reviewing the literature in this field, the methodology section describes the corpus used for this analysis, while Section four identifies key themes in the Blues and examines features of the Blues performer's relationship with his contemporary audience. There follows a focus on the work of the pre-war Blues artist Robert Johnson, which examines the relationship of his lyrics with the genre as a whole.

Background: some publications in Blues scholarship

Samuel B. Charters' *The Country Blues*, the first study of Blues singers and their music, was published in 1961 and set the pattern for the following fifty years of scholarship related to the genre. Charters divided his analysis into biographical chapters of individual Blues men and women, giving an outline of their life and times, which he used to dissect particular songs. Subsequent studies have often, however, over-emphasized the biographical aspect, in the sense that they fail to acknowledge the potential difference between the Blues man and the speaker presented in the lyrics. In doing so, there has been a tendency to try to see all lyrics as autobiographical, almost as if they were diary entries, and to give them a one-dimensional aspect. This is particularly true of studies which investigate the work of one artist, Guralnick's *Searching For Robert Johnson* (1998) being a good example.

The background knowledge for this study comes from a range of texts and there are two non-linguistic areas which have formed part of the research. The first is the relevant history of the USA and of the African-American population. Key texts exposing and analysing the ideological standpoints of the day range from *The Most Southern Place on Earth: the Mississippi Delta and the Roots of Regional Identity* (Cobb 1999), *A History of the South* (Simpkins and Pierce Roland 1972) and *The Enduring South* (Reed 1986), which provided a backdrop for the era which spawned the Blues, to anthropological studies like *From Plantation to Ghetto* (Meier and Rudwick 1970) and *Black Self-Determination* (Franklin 1984), which provided examples of African-American attitudes of the time and also gave statistical information about population and migration figures.

The second area comprises those studies of the Blues which do not have their basis in literary analysis. Lomax's famous *The Land Where the Blues Began* (Lomax 1993) and *Portrait of the Blues* (Trynka 1996) are amongst the texts which provided an insight into the realities of life for black Americans in the north and south. The lyrics examined are all from male Blues singers, due to the geographical and historical nature of the study. Though female Blues singers were generally more prolific in their recordings, they operated in an entirely different way to the male Blues singers, especially before the war. Whilst male singers would be found within rather limited geographic areas, often constrained to counties or even single villages and operating with a first-hand knowledge of the locality, "female Blues singers toured the black vaudeville circuits or performed in nightclubs; that is, they all performed in comparatively protected venues" (Lomax 1993, 139).

Where there seems to be a gap in all the works already cited, is in an analysis of a large body of Blues lyrics which can be used to objectively test, in linguistic terms, the critical theses already posited. Courlander's study (1966) gives an example of the problem. In his chapter on the Blues, he seeks to define the style and use of the form. In doing so, he covers the thematic areas the Blues deals with. The absence of a large corpus of Blues lyrics means that there is no quantitative information or analysis about different eras of the Blues or, indeed, the relationship between individual Blues performers and their genre as a whole. These are gaps which I seek to address within this study.

In *English Corpus Linguistics*, Aijmer and Bengt explain that corpora provide ideal ways of exploring the "quantitative and probabilistic aspects of the language" (Aijmer and Bengt 1991, 2). Through various collected articles, the construction of corpora and their use are dealt with in great detail. Of particular relevance to this study was Greenbaum's (1991) description of how the international corpus of English was developed, as, although its purposes were quite removed from our own, it gave an idea of how large corpora can be created by collating various sub-corpora. Stenstrom's "Expletives in the London-Lund Corpus" (1991), in the tabulation of linguistic figures and the use of percentages and fractions within a text to discuss language, offered some guidance for my own writing.

However, in terms of the already identified problem within Blues research, that is, the problem of a gap between qualitative analysis and quantitative evidence, Paul Baker's *Using Corpora in Discourse Analysis* (Baker 2006) offered a method of integration which I adopt in this analysis. Corpora can be used as effective tools in examining language at quantitative and qualitative levels and allow for the use of other methodologies, such as discourse analysis, which relate directly to my own questions of how the language of the

Blues reflects or exposes ideological tensions of the times. Given the fact that Blues songs in general had not been subjected to a corpus assisted analysis, the study may also be valuable in highlighting issues connected specifically to a linguistic type or genre.

Methodology and corpus

In order to examine a large body of Blues lyrics, I adopted a corpus assisted approach (Partington 2006). This involves comparing a specific language sub-set, in this case Blues lyrics, against a larger body of more general language called a reference corpus. A software program called Wmatrix (Rayson 2009) processes the language and provides statistical information concerning the frequency of individual words and phrases and also their "keyness" compared to the reference corpus. The Wmatrix programme is capable of accessing several different reference corpora. Ideally, as our sub-corpora consist of Blues lyrics from the nineteen-twenties to the nineteen-sixties, a reference corpus would perhaps consist of contemporary American English from the same period and possibly from the same regions under discussion. As this was not available, a "best fit" (Baker 2006, 19) had to be found. In fact, it has been suggested that, as long as it is large enough, a bad reference corpus cannot be found (Hoey et al. 2007, 46). With this in mind, I used the 982,712-word "British National Corpus Spoken Sampler" as the closest fit, despite its use of British English, due to the fact that the Blues is essentially a vernacular form evolved from an oral tradition, and displays features of general spoken language. It is also the case that this is the largest corpora that was available for use. Once the reference corpus had been decided upon, the Blues corpus was compiled. The lyrics were all taken from an online source called "Harry's Blues Lyrics Online".[1] This database was chosen for the wide variety of Blues artists represented and also for the consistent formatting which helped facilitate collation into a form which could be used with Wmatrix.

Consisting of 104,579 words, the Blues corpus created represents thirty-five different male artists from the nineteen-twenties to the nineteen-sixties and includes 795 separate songs. This "Full Blues Corpus" was further subdivided into a pre-war corpus, consisting of 55,264 words (333 songs from 22 Blues men) and a post-war corpus of 49,315 words (462 songs from thirteen artists). This meant that, just as the "Full Blues Corpus" could be checked against the "British National Corpus Spoken Sampler" for any statistically salient features, so the pre- and post-war corpora could be checked against the "Full Blues

---

[1] http://Blueslyrics.tripod.com/, last accessed 10/10/2018.

Corpus". For the purpose of this study, I created a sub-corpus limited to the lyrics of Robert Johnson.

Linguistic features of the Blues

This section will use the initial, quantitative data from Wmatrix to examine the "Full Blues Corpus" for defining features of the Blues genre and then will focus on the lyrics of Robert Johnson. Keyness results from Wmatrix indicate that the main preoccupation of Blues lyrics is Men, Women and Relationships. Half of the key semantic fields relate to this area and include:

a. personal names
b. people: female
c. people: male
d. relationships: intimacy and sex.

Further to this, seven of twenty key words link to the theme: "love", "mama", "man", "woman", "babe" and "loving". Looking at these key points in conjunction with one another allows the nature of the topic to be delineated and investigated. That "baby" ranks as the top lexical word and forms the bulk of the semantic field "b. people: female" is significant for two reasons. Firstly, it heralds the preoccupation with the female figure within the lyrics of Blues men and secondly it gives us a typical example of the way in which women were conceptualised by these men. There are 1685 occurrences of "baby" in the corpus and the majority are synonymous with the word "woman". Examining the concordances of "baby" shows the full range of uses of "woman" within Blues lyrics: 31% of lines treat "baby" as the possession of the speaker. The top collocate involving "baby", "My baby", also reveals patterns that configure the relationship between the speaker and the woman in terms of possession. The details of the relationships between the speaker and the female figures vary between lyrics, but the structure usually configures the speaker as the subject and the female as the object. Additionally, the relationships presented polarise into positive and negative camps. These positive and negative poles are defining features of the relationships presented in the lyrics. In 27% of concordances, "baby" is part of a construction which represents a positive relationship with the speaker. This can be in the form of praise, "I love you so much baby, I love you better than I love myself" or an expression of the desirability of "baby" in lines like "I can't stop loving my baby". However, in 42% of concordances "baby" is couched in an explicitly negative context. In lines like "my baby stay out all night long, keeps me worried all the time" and "I work hard for my baby and she treats me like a slave", a grammatical trend showing a dominant male voice is revealed, which is evident throughout almost all the lyrics. Generally, the figure "I" is agentive in Blues lyrics and so by extension, it is the male voice which is dominant, and which has control in the vast majority of lyrics. When referring to a relationship, the familiar dyad "where men are active, women must be passive" (Cameron 1992, 84) is adhered to. What is important to note, then, is that, as in the examples above, when the female is agentive, the action is one which has a negative effect upon the speaker. This notion is repeated throughout the corpus to the point where male agentive lines like "I love you, baby" are inverted into negative portrayals when the female is agentive exemplified by the often repeated "you done made me love you". In 31% of lines using the pronoun "me", the speaker is constructed in this way, the victim at the hands of a woman. By comparison, in only 7% of lines where the female is agentive is "me" used in a positive context. Relationships throughout the Blues lyrics, both pre- and post-war, tend to fit these patterns where either the male is dominant and the female is an object of desire and something which can be controlled, or she is agentive and almost exclusively capable of acts of unkindness or infidelity. Whilst "baby" is the most frequent item used to describe women, the semantic field "people: female" reveals a number of synonyms, including "woman", "woman", "gal", "girls" "mama" and even "thing". Additionally, of course, there is the huge number of referents "she" and "her". Relatively rarely is a female dignified with a name, and the use of "baby" and the like is a dehumanising feature of the Blues, subjugating "woman" to a set of distinct archetypes which the Blues man uses to define the speaker or the speaker's condition. Allied to this is the prolific use of qualifying adjectives used to classify the female. By far the most frequent are the infantilising "little" and "sweet"–the top three collocates of "little" across the whole corpus are "girl", "woman" and "baby". Similarly, "sweet" collocates with "mama" and "she's". Expanding on this, there are a number of typical categories which, again, occur throughout the corpus. Lyrics mention "no good women", "love making mama" and "brownskin gal". The habit of describing sexual profligacy and proficiency is one which will be explored in more detail later, though it is pertinent to mention here that a woman can be portrayed entirely in terms of her sexual attractiveness or potential as perceived by the speaker, that is, in terms of her "fruit" or her "lovin' ways".

Robert Johnson: at the crossroads

Robert Johnson is possibly the most well-known of all Blues musicians. As such, he is one of the few musicians whose entire body of work has been annotated and is available for analysis. The size of his canon, twenty-nine different songs and variations on those songs, makes for a manageable body of work for the purposes of this paper. Sources for the date of Johnson's birth vary, but his death certificate shows he died in 1938 at the age of 27 (Wardlow

1998, 87). His actual life is almost a complete mystery, inspiring many grail type studies like Guralnick's *Searching For Robert Johnson* (1998) and virtually nothing is known about him. Unlike many of the other Blues artists who were regularly photographed and interviewed during their recording career, there are only two photographs of Johnson, and there is little primary evidence of his existence beyond anecdotes and his actual legacy–his recordings. Accounts suggest that he travelled widely around the South and sometimes beyond, that he was a solitary figure and that the few people who knew anything about him were the women who "kept" him in various towns throughout the South. Between the 23 November 1936 and 20 June 1937, he recorded all his tracks for the Vocalion label. Only one achieved any popularity, "Terraplane Blues", and most contemporary musicians or audiences did not regard him as being particularly special. Johnson's legacy practically sank without trace apart from two songs, "Sweet Home Chicago" and "Dust My Broom", which were performed by Elmore James in the 1950s. Johnson's music was the focus of much debate and very quickly came to be seen as the missing link between the pre-war, acoustic "down home" Blues and electrified and sophisticated post-war Blues in terms of his guitar and vocal style.

Semantic fields and key words

After uploading the corpora to Wmatrix, each individual word goes through a process of "tagging", i.e. the computer program assigns every item with a part of speech (POS) tag and a semantic domain (USAS) tag. For example, the name "Ida Belle" is given a POS tag of NP1, indicating a singular proper noun, and a USAS tag of Z1, indicating the semantic domain "personal names". Wmatrix also provides information about the number of times the word is used and its frequency relative to the corpus as a whole and also gives a log-likelihood (LL) value. This is a figure that shows the relative saliency of the word when compared with the reference corpus (Gries 2008). Any figure with a critical value of 15.13 gives a 99.99% probability that the item is 'key'. "Ida Belle" has an LL value of 9.35, suggesting that the word in itself is not statistically important enough to warrant further investigation. However, Wmatrix is able to compare not just words but types of words. The software shows that, whilst "Ida Belle" is of little significance itself, it belongs to the semantic domain Z1. This has a huge LL value of 1920.60, meaning that the use of "personal names" in the Blues is likely to be a key feature. In addition to providing the above statistical information, Wmatrix helpfully organizes the results by ranking them in terms of the log-likelihood value. This proved a critical feature as many of the log-likelihood values were extremely high.

Using only the log-likelihood values would have meant examining over ninety key semantic fields in the "Full Blues Corpus" alone. Using the rankings, I limited this to a manageable ten key items for USAS and POS tags and twenty-four words, given that these can be sub-divided into lexical and functional groups. Once the key words, USAS and POS fields had been decided, I used Wmatrix to examine concordances of the selected items. By clicking on a word, Wmatrix shows me a list of all of its uses in their contexts, displayed as concordance lines.

For the most part, the semantic field data relating to Johnson show a top ten composed of concrete figures in common with the pre-war Blues corpus (PreBC). One point to note here is that analysis of such a small corpus reveals high LL values for items which have a relatively low frequency. So, whilst the semantic domain "substances and materials" is listed as salient in key domain table, the frequency of items within this domain is only %0.12 in Robert Johnson (RJ) corpus, or just seven mentions. Indeed, the concordances in this field were generated by the word 'stuff', used in just one of Robert Johnson's songs (see Table12.1).

Table 12.1: Semantic field data in Robert Johnson Corpus and Pre-War Blues Corpus

Key Domain	No. in RJ	% in RJ	No. in PreBC	% in PreBC	LL
Discourse Markers	260	4.50	803	2.02	108.35
Temperature: Hot/on fire	61	1.05	60	0.15	10.28
Vehicles and transport on Land	62	1.07	151	0.38	39.94
Business: selling	41	0.71	83	0.21	34.35
Drinks and alcohol	33	0.57	73	0.18	24.54
Objects generally	69	1.19	243	0.61	21.06
Personality Traits	8	0.14	4	0.01	18.82
Unethical	25	0.43	56	0.14	18.26
Getting and possession	172	2.97	822	2.07	17.30
Substances and materials	7	0.12	4	0.01	15.55

Johnson's work replicates the overall obsession with relationships and women and much of his presentation of these themes follows exactly the same lines as those demonstrated in the Blues corpus as a whole. In fact, all but one of Robert Johnson's songs, "Preachin' Blues (Up Jumped The Devil)", involves a woman or relationship in at least one of the verses and for the majority of his songs relationships are the focal point. Common to the rest of the Blues, females are objectified in Johnson's lyrics. In both versions of "Come On In My

Kitchen", the female is explicitly reduced to the level of a commodity in the following lines: "the woman I love, took from my best friend / some joker got lucky, stole her back again". Again, "my baby" is a prominent construct and synonyms and qualifying adjectives abound. Johnson categorises females as: "sweet woman", "no-good women", "little sweet rider", "little girl", "no good doney", "little woman", "good girl", "biscuit roller", "evil-hearted women", "kind-hearted woman", "gamblin' woman", "fair brown", "Miss So-and-So", "pretty mama", "Saturday night women", "brown skin woman" and "close friend". These references in themselves reveal the attitudes Johnson takes towards females in his songs, and are seen to vary from the positive to the negative.

The majority of Johnson's songs adhere to the familiar tropes already discussed. When the male is agentive, the female is the object of the speaker. When the female has an agentive role, the male is portrayed as the victim. As in a number of pre-war Blues, there is a propensity for the speaker to resort to violence and make threats towards the female, often for a reason which is not made clear in the song. Four songs, "32-30 Blues", "Stop Breakin' Down Blues", "Me and the Devil Blues" and "If I Had Possession Over Judgement Day" employ violent or threatening imagery. The verses of "32-20 Blues" are little more than reiterations on the fact that the speaker is going to kill his women if she doesn't obey him. Starting with the ominous "If I send for my baby, man, and she don't come / All the doctors in Hot Springs sure can't help her none", the speaker moves on to detail the calibre of weapon he will use against her (32-20 refers to a gun), subsequently upgrading his pistol for a Gatling gun in order to "cut her half in two". The charm does not end here. In "Me and the Devil Blues", the speaker, in a verse which seems on the literal level to have little to do with the rest of the narrative, interjects with "I'm going to beat my woman until I get satisfied". One outstanding feature of Johnson's Blues is the fact that these outbursts of aggression are countered in some lyrics with an affection not seen elsewhere in the pre-war Blues. In "Come On In My Kitchen", the conceit for the relationship is one where the speaker offers shelter from the rain to a female. There seems in these songs to be a genuine attempt to create a lyric which conforms to ideas of a love song, in a way which other pre-war Blues do not share. These songs, however, are outstanding in the Johnson canon and the majority do conform to the prescribed format of "male in charge" or "male as victim".

Johnson continues the tradition of observing the world around him, incorporating occasional place names. Some of these apply to specific localities, but in a departure from many other rural Blues, these are not central to the meaning of the song and appear as peripheral items. In "Travelling Riverside Blues", for example, Johnson mentions several place names. One line goes "I got women's in Vicksburg, clean on into Tennessee / But my Friar's Point rider, now, hops all over me". The place names are only relevant in terms of highlighting the fact that the speaker has a lot of lovers in different places and it is not important to know where these places are. Johnson's lyrics play out in a world which is for the most part made up of universally understood signifiers. Perhaps this is the reason that Johnson's songs, twenty years after his death, were accepted so readily by a new audience that was totally removed from Johnson's world on almost every count–racial, generational, economic and geographical. Johnson's songs, to a twenty-first-century reader, are easy to understand with very little previous knowledge about Blues or the environment that created it, and very little deciphering is needed. It may well have been that Johnson's contemporary audience also benefited from this universality of reference, but contemporary accounts of Johnson's standing within the music community, "just an unknown Blues singer trying to make a buck" (Wardlow 1998, 141), his lack of commercial success at a time when Blues music was relatively popular, and the subsequent disappearance of his legacy suggest his lyrics did not make much of an impression.

"Drunken Hearted Man" is an example worth looking at as it is typical of both the structure and progression of Johnson's songs:

I'm a drunken hearted man, my life seems so misery.
I'm a drunken hearted man, my life seems so misery.
And if I could change my way of living, it would mean so much to me

I'm a drunken hearted man, and sin was the cause of it all.
And the day that you get weak for no-good women, that's the day that you bound to fall.

(Johnson 1938)

The first verse offers us an abstract which essentially summarises both the narrative and highlights the depressing tone of the song: the speaker is lamenting his condition and wishing for a way out. The first and second verses complement each other and aid in the orientation stage–we learn something of the history of the speaker and there is some explanation for the causes of his problem. The complicating action, in the sense that this is the point of "maximum suspense" (Johnstone 2003, 638) is actually contained within the abstract at the beginning. The conditional clause of line three keeps us in suspense throughout the song as we wait to see if the speaker is actually able to change his way of living. The final verse presents the result or resolution, where we see the drunken man left in the same position, unable to do anything but blame his bad luck with women and love for his situation.

The fact that Johnson's canon, as I mentioned earlier, is preoccupied with women and relationships to the exclusion of almost everything else furthers the sense that the key figure across the canon is Johnson, or the Blues man, as the speaker. All in all, Johnson seems intent on expressing himself rather than his community. I would argue that, in content at least, this is much more in keeping with the post-war Blues. The expression of personal feelings about love and rejection, which do not seem to transcend the basic female-male relationship, are prevalent in both.

God and the Devil

In all but one song, "Crossroad Blues", which contains the line "I asked the Lord above for Mercy", Johnson uses the Lord exclusively as an interjection. "Preachin' Blues" makes no mention of the church but instead gives a sermon personifying the Blues, "worried Blues, give me your right hand", where the speaker relates what it feels like to have the Blues.

Johnson's lyrics are distinctive in the fact that they not only mention the devil but in that the devil and hell become integral to the songs. The oddly structured "Hell Hound Blues", which defies the usual AAB verse pattern and instead seems to be a series of floating lines, contains the verse "and the days keeps on worryin' me, there's a hellhound on my trail / hellhound on my trail, hellhound on my trail". In the third verse, such as it is, we get the sense that the speaker has been cursed by a woman, metaphorically speaking, as she has "sprinkled hot foot powder, mmm, mmm, all around my door", which, the speaker explains, leaves him unable to focus and doomed to keep moving. It is the final verse which is strange, however. It is added almost as an aside or spoken thought: "I can tell the wind is risin' / the leaves trembling on the tree". In the sense of a narrative, we are given nothing, but instead, the lyrics create a sense of anxiousness, doom, not knowing exactly what is coming with the wind, but we assume it is the hellhound catching up with Johnson.

Modern listeners associate Johnson with the devil, but this seems to be an excellent example of the unfortunate interpretation of lyrics as bibliographic facts. There is a crossroads legend where Johnson supposedly sold his soul to the devil in return for his musical abilities (Guralnick 1998) and this story seems to garner more interest than the songs themselves. Lyrically, it seems he uses the devil and superstition as a way, not of forming a superstitious narrative, but as a way of conveying a mood and explaining the psychological or spiritual state of the speaker. It is perhaps, however, important to see his songs, as with the other pre-war Blues, as being in direct opposition to the idea of the church in general.

Conclusion

Using Wmatrix as a tool to help uncover the salient features of the Blues allowed me to identify several key themes in Blues lyrics.

First and foremost was the broad theme of relationships. Examination of the concordances highlighted a preoccupation with male and female relationships and showed, in particular, consistent patterns in the way females are presented; they are both the object of desire and of derision and there are distinct differences in the way the agency of the male speaker or female character is characterised. Female agency is consistently negative, often putting the male speaker into the position of the victim, whilst male agency configures the female as a passive object. This objectification of the female is emphasised by the use of female archetypes and belittling qualifying adjectives. The constant need for control expressed by the speakers suggested that the extent to which the Bluesman was a mouthpiece for the community was a little harder to ascertain, as the initial findings from Wmatrix showed an absence of pronouns normally associated with efforts to outline a sense of community, namely figures like "we", "us" and "our". However, this study was able to identify patterns in the concordances which relate specific, individual experience to expound a universal "truth".

Johnson's lyrics display elements prevalent in both the pre- and post-war Blues corpora. He uses metaphors to create innuendo and the general obsession with male and female relationships reaches a peak in Johnson, with all but one of his songs touching on the theme. However, the heavy use of paralinguistic features such as "uh" and "mmm" and the structure of the verses, are all features in common with post-war Blues lyrics. In terms of individuality, I point to Johnson's creation of a speaker who seems to be one and the same throughout almost the whole canon, as something which distinguishes his lyrics. In fact, due to the restricted themes, he touches on and the rambling speaker who appears again and again, I suggest that Johnson creates an archetypical Bluesman. Certainly, the common image we have now of pre-war Bluesmen seems to owe a lot to that speaker Johnson presents through his lyrics. The relative simplicity of his lyrics, or, rather, the lack of a need for top-down processing, may have something to do with his modern-day appeal. In fact, we might see Johnson's songs as being on the cusp of a change in wider modes of expression that remain today as

> the centrality of the singer's individual persona, the highly personalised subject matter of the songs, the thematic shifts toward the material world and the pursuit of pleasure were all characteristic of an emergent modern ethos (Hunter 2000, 203).

The evidence I have presented shows Johnson's work embodying elements of both eras and it seems reasonable to think of him, lyrically, as a bridge figure between the pre- and post-war Blues. In terms of individuality within a genre, Johnson does not present lyrics which contain paradigmatic figures: there is nothing particularly outstanding or odd about any of his songs beyond the few unusual references to the devil. Where Johnson's canon reveals its peculiar traits are in the syntagmatic figures that can be identified: the heavy emphasis on the individual, the almost exclusive use of the first person singular in narratives that are themselves almost exclusively about relationships and the repetition of a particular verse format to the exclusion of others. The deviant feature seems to be how typically "Bluesy" in the stereotypical sense Johnson's lyrics seem to be. Though the fact that Johnson's lyrics seem to conform so strongly to many of the elements associated with the Blues does not have any bearing on the quality of his music, it does perhaps offer further evidence as to why Johnson has been so readily accepted as a key figure in the genre.

References

Aijmer, Karin, and Bengt Altenberg. 1991. „Introduction." In *English Corpus Linguistics*, edited by Karin Aijmer and Bengt Altenberg, 1-7. London: Longman.

Baker, Paul. 2006. *Using Corpora in Discourse Analysis*. London: Continuum.

Cameron, Deborah. 1992. *Feminism and Linguistic Theory*. Basingstoke: The Macmillan Press.

Hoey, Michael, Michaela Mahlberg, Michael Stubbs, and Wolfgang Teubert. 2007. *Text, Discourse and Corpora: Theory and Analysis*. London: Continuum.

Hunter, Tera W. 2000. "The Blues Aesthetics and Black Vernacular Dance." In *Major Problems in African- American History*. Vol. II, edited by Thomas C. Holt and Elsa Barkley Brown, 202-209. Boston: Houghton Miflin Company.

Johnstone, Barbara. 2003. "Discourse Analysis and Narrative." In *The Handbook of Discourse Analysis*, edited by Deborah Schiffrin, Deborah Tannen and Heidi E. Hamilton, 635-649. Oxford: Blackwell.

Lomax, Alan. 1993. *The Land Where The Blues Began*. London: Methuen.

Wardlow, Gayle. 1998. *Chasin' that devil music: searching for the blues*. San Francisco: Miller Freeman Books.

Further Reading

Barkley Brown, E. 2000. *Major Problems in African-American History*. Boston: Houghton Miflin Company.

Bluesman Harry. "Harry's Blues Lyrics Online." Available at http://Blueslyrics.tripod.com/, Accessed 18 June 2019.

Charters, Samuel B. 1961. *The Country Blues*. London: The Jazz Book Club.

Cobb, James C. 1999. *The Most Southern Place on Earth: The Mississippi Delta and the Roots of Regional Identity*. New York: Oxford University Press.

Cohodas, Nadine. 2000. *Spinning Blues Into Gold*. London: Aurum Press.

Courlander, Harold. 1966. *Negro Folk Music, U.S.A.* London: Columbia University Press.

De Nora, Tia. 2000. *Music in everyday life.* Cambridge: Cambridge University Press.

Franklin, Vincent P. 1984. *Black Self-Determination: a Cultural History of the Faith of the Fathers.* Westport: Lawrence Hill.

Greenbaum, Sidney. 1991. "The Development of the International Corpus of English." In *English Corpus Linguistics*, edited by Karin Aijmer and Bengt Altenberg, 83-91. London: Longman.

Gries, Stefan Th. 2008. "Dispersions and adjusted frequencies in corpora." *International Journal of Corpus Linguistics* 13 (4), 403-437.

Guralnick, Peter. 1998. *Searching for Robert Johnson.* London: Pimlico.

Labov, William. 1972. "The Transformation of Experience in Narrative Syntax." In *Language in the Inner Cities: Studies in the Black English Vernacular*, edited by William Labov, 354-400. Philadelphia: University of Pennsylvania Press.

Labov, William, and Joshua Waletzky. 1967. "Narrative Analysis: Oral Versions of Personal Experience." In *Essays on the Verbal and Visual Arts*, edited by June Helm, 3-38. Seattle: University of Washington Press.

McIntyre, Dan. 2007. "Deixis, Cognition and the Construction of Viewpoint." In *Contemporary Stylistics*, edited by Marina Lambrou and Peter Stockwell, 118-130. London: Continuum.

MacIntyre, Dan, and Beatrix Busse. 2010. *Language and Style.* Basingstoke: Palgrave Macmillan.

Meier, August, and Elliot M. Rudwick. 1970. *From Plantation to Ghetto.* London: Constable and Co.

Partington, Alan. 2006. "Metaphors, Motifs and Similies Across Discourse Types: Corpus-Assisted Discourse Studies (CADS) At Work." In *Corpus-Based Approaches to Metaphor and Metonymy*, edited by Anatol Stefanowitsch and Stefan Gries, 267-304. Berlin: Mouton de Gruyter.

Pettigrew, Thomas F. 1964. *A Profile of the Negro American.* Princeton: Van Nostrand Reinhold.

Rayson, Paul. Wmatrix: a web-based corpus processing environment, Computing Department, Lancaster University. http://ucrel.lancs.ac.uk/wmatrix/. Accessed 14 June 2019.

Reed, John Shelton. 1986. *The Enduring South: Sub-Cultural Persistence in Mass Society.* Chapel Hill: The University of North Carolina Press.

Renshaw, Patrick. 1996. *The Longman Companion to America in the Era of the Two World Wars 1910-1945.* Harlow: Longman.

Roy, William G. 2010. *Reds, Whites and Blues: Social movements, folk music, and race in the United States.* Princeton: Princeton University Press.

Schiffrin, Deborah, Deborah Tannen, and Heidi E. Hamilton. 2003. *The Handbook of Discourse Analysis.* Oxford: Blackwell.

Simkins, Francis Butler, and Charles Pierce Roland. 1972. *A History of the South.* New York: Alfred A. Knopf, Harlow: Longman Group.

Stenstrom, Anna-Brita. 1991. "Expletives in the London-Lund Corpus." In *English Corpus Linguistics*, edited by Karin Aijmer and Bengt Altenberg, 239-253. London: Longman.

Stockwell, Peter. 2002. *Sociolinguistics: a Resource Book for Students*. London: Routledge.

Toolan, Michael. 1998. *Language in Literature*. London: Arnold.

Trynka, Paul. 1996. *Portrait of the Blues*. London: Hamlyn.

Weinstein, Allen, and Frank O. Gatell. 1970. *The Segregation Era: 1863-1954. A Modern Reader*. Oxford: Oxford University Press.

Williams, Raymond. 1977. *Marxism and Literature*. Oxford: Oxford University Press.

Williams, Sherley A. 1999. "The Blues Roots of Contemporary Afro-American Poetry." In *Write Me A Few Of Your Lines: A Blues Reader*, edited by Steven C. Tracy, 445-455. Amherst: University of Massachusetts Press.

13.

How blue is our Blues? The validation of Blues in the 21st century and the role of technology and social media in its progression

Jack Dandy

University of East London, UK

Emiliano Bonanomi

University of East London, UK

"The things that´s going on today is not the Blues"

- Howlin' Wolf 1969 (Burnett 1969)

Introduction

With the death of Blues legend B.B. King in 2015, leaving only Buddy Guy as the "last bastion of the Blues" (Scancarelli 2018) and as we continue advancing into the age of technology, it would seem that music immersed in as much history and struggle as Blues, could not possibly continue. Yet in 2019, an age of supposed social and political advancements, where some believe Blues has "no real future" (Oliver, quoted in Rudinow 1994, 127), we are still creating and performing Blues music of varying styles and approaches. This spurs the questions, is the Blues music at the cutting edge of the twenty-first century any less valid than the Blues music of the early 1900s, and if Howling' Wolf made the above statement in 1969, how far away from that are we now? To best explore this, we will need to take a multi-faceted approach to how we holistically view Blues music. In an attempt to find validation for this contemporary Blues music we must first analyse various angles of authenticity to determine if there is a singular true "authentic Blues" (Lindholm 2008, 34) and if not, what can be considered "authentic Blues"? We will then dissect the defining musical and metaphorical parameters of Blues music and show how they unify and underpin a new 'metagenre-world' model, with the intent to give fresh insight into the categorisation of Blues music. Finally, we will observe our current social and political climate (the UK), reflecting upon the potential societal issues the twenty-first century brings with it and if these issues give us cause to have 'the Blues', therefore requiring a relevant form of Blues music to express them. The aim is to determine if the validity of this Blues music is diminished by the technologies and methods used to express the Blues of today and if in fact it truly is "impossible to hear the Blues now" (Kunzru 2017).

This is a musicological study, which has recourse to metaphorical and technological ideas to provide fresh insight into what can be considered Blues music, and if the use of technology diminishes the validity of Blues in the twenty-first century. Using a qualitative approach, we analyse themes and concepts from existing texts such as Théberge (1997) and McLoughlin (2008), as well as investigating common practises of contemporary Blues musicians for performing, recording, marketing and communicating.

The role of technology in supporting the development of Blues in the twenty-first century is both fascinating and challenging. The latest evolutions of digital devices for music performers and producers, and the pivotal role played by social media platforms like Facebook, Instagram, etc., leave us with some urgent questions. How can we still maintain an "authentic" sound today using digital instruments? Is it possible for Blues musicians, in the twenty-first century, to stay true to the original message and keep the Blues alive in the way they promote their music and build a fanbase today? This paper aims to offer fresh insight into the grounding of twenty-first-century Blues music in musicological and metaphorical foundations while determining if utilising the sound, technology and media tools of one's own time and environment, allows for the preservation and demonstration of authenticity and validity for Blues musicians in the twenty-first century.

The validation. Authenticating twenty-first century Blues

The initial quote could be seen to refer to "Blues" as music and "the Blues" as a feeling, both of which will be addressed throughout this study. It implies that "the Blues" and Blues music of today is not real, suggesting it is "tainted goods" (Davis 2003, 14). Twenty-first century Blues encompasses all Blues music still performed today, which includes those who utilise more traditional approaches to Blues music, as they are either isolated from or chose not to embrace technology. In this context, "modern" or "contemporary" could be taken simply to mean performed in a modern context, which all such Blues is, no matter how traditional the approach. In this study, unless stated otherwise, "modern" or "contemporary" will refer to those approaches that embrace the technologies and tools the twenty-first century has to offer, such as 'Neo-Blues' (a term defined later), as they provide the strongest antithesis to the opening quote.

When it comes to Blues discourse, the topic of authenticity quickly arises. What is, or is not authentic is far from as finite as purist ideologies may suggest, and a level of subjectivity must be considered when discussing it. There are many facets and positions to consider when exploring authenticity, too many to fully investigate within the scope of this study. The aim is instead to demonstrate the possibility of finding authenticity within contemporary Blues approaches, centred around ideas of key writers on the subject. One such writer is Charles Lindholm, who lays out two broadly encompassing categories for defining how authenticity is found within music, the first being of a "genealogical or historical (origin)" nature (Lindholm 2008, 2). Raymond Leppard describes this as attempting to recreate the "exact conditions, the precisely duplicated ways and means of the music's first appearance" (Leppard 1988, 73). Those sharing this view believe that only once this is achieved can its true authentic content and message be revealed. Lindholm's second category for authentication is "identity or correspondence (content)" (Lindholm 2008, 2). This angle "seeks the widest creative freedom" (Leppard 1988, 73) possible, acknowledging that music needs constant revision and reinterpretation to "keep pace with the present as much as to keep faith with the past" (Leppard 1988, 77).

Lindholm's first category presents a restrictive view, seeming to reflect the ideas of the opening quote, limiting authenticity to finite musical moments. Leppard explains why searching for authenticity in this way could be deemed futile, due to the fact that "it is we who are different" (Leppard 1988, 74). We are so far removed as listeners and performers from the original circumstances that we are unable to fully digest the "authentic message" in the same way. All we can do is "attempt to understand…the text that is left to us…and subsequently, make as our prime objective a translation of that into our own time" (Leppard 1988, 75).

It is this translation that begins to provide plausible authentication for modern Blues approaches. Here "our own time" refers to the twenty-first century and all its technological innovations and developments. Contemporary Blues musicians can only truly "represent the culture" which they come from (Gilbert and Pearson 1999, 104-105), if they are utilising the technologies and methods, it makes available to them as a vehicle, to express individual and societal troubles with "honesty" (Middleton 1990, 127). So, who judges the validity of a performer's honesty? Sarah Rubidge tells us that this depends on who "we" are (Rubidge 1996, 219); we, as an audience, can ascribe authenticity. Therefore, those who relate to and connect with the sounds of modern Blues music may authenticate it. However, Moore tells us that any Blues music can be authenticated by a "particular group of perceivers" (Moore 2002b, 220), providing an 'authentic blanket' for all styles of Blues music, suggesting that modern approaches to Blues are as valid as any other, to certain audiences.

From this observation, it would appear that the use of technology could be seen to strengthen the authenticity of modern Blues approaches. As long as the musicians provide "real and pure" (Lindholm 2008, 2) portrayals of themselves, and there is an audience that seeks comfort from it, then it is possible for these contemporary approaches to be seen as valid, although it is not within the scope of this study to determine which modern Bluesmen are truly honest and which are not. We will now analyse the musical parameters these musicians use to keep faith with the past and the metaphorical parameters they use to "speak the truth" (Gilbert and Pearson 1999, 104-105).

The musicological

One is reluctant to use rigid analytical criteria when it comes to analysing Blues, as doing so might confirm accusations of elitism, which it is our intention to challenge. However, if we are to determine if traditional approaches hold greater validity over contemporary approaches, we must understand the parameters within which we are working and how malleable they can be. Although "the Blues" is a "feeling" (Williams, quoted in Ferris 1984, xii), emotional expression is a "vital part of every musical genre" (Lehmann, Sloboda and Woody 2007, 85), consequently there have to be defining musical traits. Therefore, we have to consider both musicological (Blues music) and metaphorical parameters (the Blues) when analysing it.

The parameters below are considered standard when classifying Blues music. Recognisable musical traits are important, as they produce an "identifiable sound" (Shuker 2016, 96); traits that no matter how contemporary an approach, one must adhere to in some variation to be considered Blues.

Figure 13.1: Musicological Parameters (a table consisting of the recognised parameters consistently found within Blues music).

MUSICOLOGICAL PARAMETERS
TWELVE BAR 'I IV V' CYCLICAL STRUCTURE
REPEATED VOCAL PHRASES
FLATTENED 3^{rds} AND 5^{ths}
SYNCOPATION

Figure 13.2a: Score excerpt from "Human" by Rag 'n' Bone Man

Figure 13.2b: Score excerpt from "Kind Hearted Woman Blues" by Robert Johnson

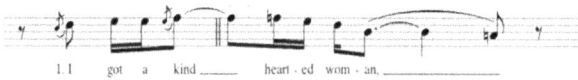

The above are examples of repeated phrases that can be heard in "Human" by Rag 'n' Bone Man and "Kind Hearted Woman Blues" by Robert Johnson.

Figure 13.3a: Score excerpt from "Human" by Rag 'n' Bone Man

Figure 13.3b: Score excerpt from "Kind Hearted Woman Blues" by Robert Johnson

The above are examples of syncopation that can be heard in "Human" by Rag 'n' Bone Man and "Kind Hearted Woman Blues" by Robert Johnson. In these examples, we see similar parameters employed in songs written nearly one hundred years apart, if the full score was to be analysed here you would find similar cyclical structures and use of flattened thirds and fifths. However, Blues is not just "a matter of…form" or rhythm (Erlewine 1999, v).

The metaphorical

Shirley McLoughlin's "Blues metaphor" (McLoughlin 2008, xiv) helps to define Blues beyond musicological parameters. This metaphor transcends race, class and gender, providing fresh insight into Blues music that steers away from the preliminary quote. The metaphor allows for malleability of the musical parameters and recognises this flexibility as one of the "important components" of Blues (McLoughlin 2008, xv). This implies changes and developments are a part of Blues and vital to its development.

The metaphor applies to the content of the lyrics and the lives of performers. Davis states that a Bluesman is a "middle age black man whose clothing and hairstyle are a decade or more out of date" (Davis 2003, 254), restricting who can identify as a Bluesman. The metaphor suggests it is in the "minds and bodies" and actions of individuals (Holt 2007, 2), implying that if key themes of the Blues metaphor are embodied in mind and performance, anyone can be a valid Bluesman.

Figure 13.4: Metaphorical Parameters (a table of the themes Shirley McLoughlin believes a musician should address and demonstrate if they are to be considered as a Blues musician who embodies the Blues).

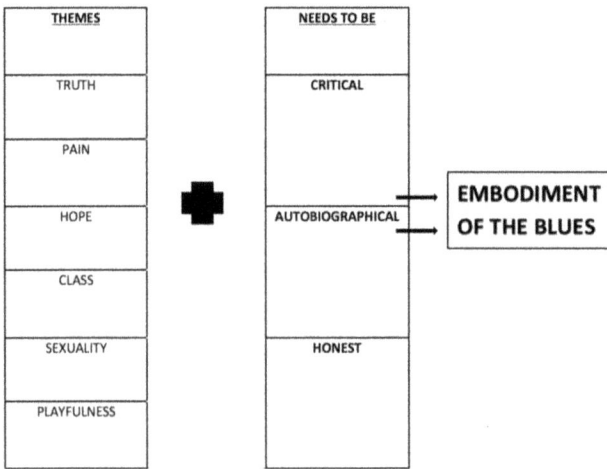

THEMES
TRUTH
PAIN
HOPE
CLASS
SEXUALITY
PLAYFULNESS

NEEDS TO BE
CRITICAL
AUTOBIOGRAPHICAL
HONEST

EMBODIMENT OF THE BLUES

Figure 13.5a: Score excerpt from "Human" by Rag 'n' Bone Man

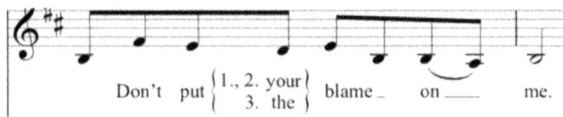

Don't put {1., 2. your / 3. the} blame on me.

Figure 13.5b: Score excerpt from "Kind Hearted Woman Blues" by Robert Johnson

My ba-by don't love me.

The above are examples of pain demonstrated in the lyrics of "Human" by Rag 'n' Bone Man and "Kind Hearted Woman Blues" by Robert Johnson.

Figure 13.6a: Score excerpt from "Human" by Rag 'n' Bone Man

1. May - be   I'm   fool - -   ish,   may - be   I'm   blind.

Figure 13.6b: Score excerpt from "Kind Hearted Woman Blues" by Robert Johnson

my   life ____ don't   feel   the   same. __

The above are examples of autobiographical content demonstrated in the lyrics of "Human" by Rag 'n' Bone Man and "Kind Hearted Woman Blues" by Robert Johnson.

By examining the same pieces again, through the Blues metaphor we catch a glimpse of evidence that the Blues is embodied within both pieces. These themes reflect embodiment and unification across all the varied approaches to Blues, for as long as they are grounded in this metaphor then "the Blues" behind the music is valid. It is beyond the scope of this study to determine if, this study merely identifies the potential of embodying `the Blues´ even ninety years later,

Metagenre-world

What we are left with is a music that is deeply rooted in both musicology and the lives of those who perform it. Therefore, when defining Blues, we must consider a model that recognises that it is "music sharing distinctive musical characteristics" as well as being centred in a strong "social context" (Shuker 2012, 146) and "cultural nexus" (Shuker 2016, 95).

For this study, the idea of "metagenre", which is an "umbrella" term for music that shares social and cultural origins as well as a broad musical identity, resulting in stylistic and international diffusion (Shuker 2012, 148), has been combined with the concept of "genre world". "Genre world" refers to the "complex interplay of musicians" and "listeners" within a piece of music such as Blues (Frith 1998, 88). When these ideas are brought together with McLoughlin's Blues metaphor at its core, a new 'metagenre-world' model can be formed to provide fresh insight into how Blues could be holistically viewed:

Figure 13.7: Metagenre-world Model: a holistic model for viewing Blues music and its varying approaches.

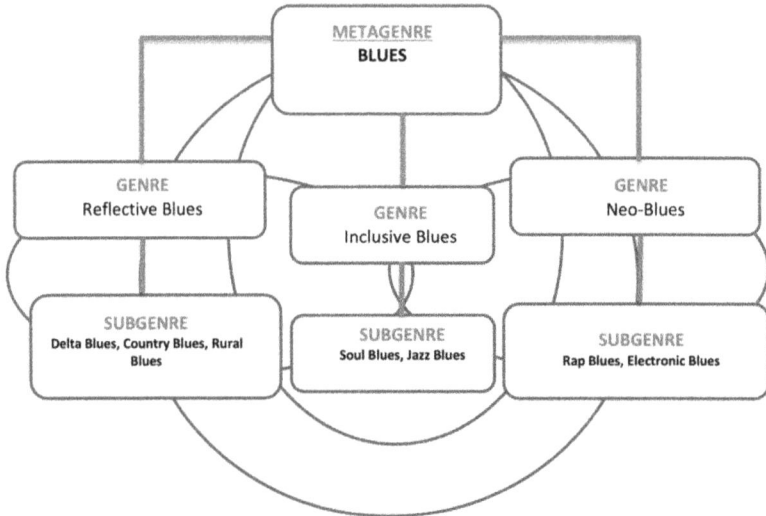

The network of this 'metagenre-world' is made up of a "constellation of styles" (Holt 2007, 18), where style is used to refer specifically to how the musical parameters are delivered. The model demonstrates how the musicological and metaphorical parameters unify and are at the heart of all styles, depicted by the thick dark lines. The varying styles are dependent on the geographical, historical and social context, and it is through the people within these contexts that the "major genres and subgenres" emerge (Shuker 2012, 148). The thin lines that are interwoven throughout this model represent the interplay between musicians and listeners across the cultures that surround each style and how this interaction, across location and through time, influences new players and gives rise to new sounds with the parameters at their core. This reinforces the idea of a "constant" within Blues music, moving away from a "Blues today" and a "Blues back then".

The varying styles can be encompassed by the three "genre" divisions, as shown above. This is determined by how each style presents the musicological parameters, to what extent they utilise the technology of the twenty-first century, and their place in time. Firstly, we have 'Reflective Blues', which seeks to keep Blues music as close to its origins as possible. Although this is a model for viewing Blues throughout history, which is why the subgenres presented in Reflective Blues are of a traditional nature, because they have been removed from their original context, any performance of them now has to be considered 'reflective'. Secondly, there is "inclusive Blues", which employs certain Blues parameters enveloped in other musical styles, and finally "neo-

Blues". Neo-Blues utilises the technology and musical influences of the current day to produce Blues music reflective of the digitalised culture many people live in.

What this model has shown us is that no matter the context or setting, all Blues music is united by musical and metaphorical parameters. This suggests it is one entity, not individualities, providing validation for Neo-Blues as any style can be seen as just a different means to the same end, the expression of the human experience.

Blues today

At the cutting edge of the twenty-first century, Neo-Blues seems to present itself as a direct target for Howling' Wolf's opening quote and as the antithesis of the Blues music he is referring to. However, if we analyse Neo-Blues within the scope of the musical and metaphorical parameters, validation can still be found.

Hari Kunzru agrees with Burnett and believes it is "impossible to hear the Blues now" (Kunzru 2017), implying that 'the Blues' were only felt within a certain context and time and no other society or culture can have 'the Blues'. The Blues metaphor lays out the themes at the heart of 'the Blues', some of which are truth, pain and class (see figure 13.4), that are still present today. In the UK, 36.7 million people are in relative or low income after housing costs (McGuiness 2018); 83% of people do not believe their political representatives tell the truth (IPSOS 2017), males account for three-quarters of recorded suicides (Manders 2018), and between 2014-2016 there were an estimated 204,000 hate crimes (Office for National Statistics 2017). The technological advances of the twenty-first century have brought about increased numbers of online platforms such as Instagram, the use of which has been linked to depressive symptoms (Lup, Trub and Rosenthal 2015), with 43% of social media users asked, feeling "bad about themselves if no-one comments on or likes their posts" (SmartSocial 2018). While all of these may seem inconsequential compared to the horrors endured during the conception of the Blues, it is important to remember that "every person's problems are their own worst nightmare. It is different for everyone, and the immensity of each circumstance should not be something to compare" (Mariano 2016). Although these modern issues can be explored through any style of Blues music, Neo-Blues' will remain the focus as it uses cutting edge twenty-first-century methods to reflect twenty-first-century troubles.

We have already seen that even Neo Blues artists, such as Rag 'n' Bone Man, can conform to the musical parameters laid out earlier in this study (see figure 13.1). The concern here is how a lack of "real instruments" (Redhead 1990, 52) impacts an artist's ability to truly express the "human experience" (McLoughlin 2008, 41). Juslin and Sloboda tell us that these mechanical instruments can be used to convey emotions with the "same level of accuracy" as someone playing a 'real instrument' (Juslin and Sloboda 2010, 478). These digital instruments reduce the limitations of "traditional" instruments in the realisation of a "composers (supposedly unbound) sonic imagination" (Dorschel, Eckel and Peters 2012, 1), giving rise to new sounds that may better reflect the issues of our current society, as opposed to more traditional instruments.

These new sounds and instruments serve important purposes for both the performer and the listener. Lindholm believes that for authentic Bluesmen, "only the performer's heart and soul matter" (Lindholm 2008, 34). On the other hand, Juslin and Sloboda believe the important thing about emotion within music is "the sound that reaches the listener, not what the performer is feeling" (Juslin and Sloboda 2010, 478). These new sonic pallets may be more relatable and suitable in alleviating and expressing the troubles of the twenty-first-century performer and listener, where traditional instrumentation may not.

Technology for Blues in twenty-first century

We agree with Paul Théberge when, talking about the relationship between technology and contemporary musicians, he describes it as "one of mutual dependency: technological innovation is, in this sense, not only a response to musicians' needs but also a driving force with which musicians must contend" (Theéberge 1997, 5). This statement may be supported by those who claim that digital tools and social media affect authenticity, thus corrupting the original message intended by the artist and confirming once again that, as Howling' Wolf put it "the things that's going on today is not the Blues". However, to analyse how Blues musicians take on this relationship, we need to consider the three genres within the metagenre of Blues separately.

It might seem easier to classify the Reflective and Inclusive from a sonic prospective, as Neo Blues artists opted to "keep pace with the present as much as to keep faith with the past" (Leppard 1988, 77), thus leaving us with the need of investigating in more detail their choices of equipment for live performances and studio recording. Nonetheless, overcoming the technological limitations of the time to fully implement an artist's idea represents a goal that many other famous world-renowned musicians have pursued before.

To offer an exhaustive analysis, this section focuses on three main subjects:

- Identifying the sonic platforms (analogue or digital) featured in the three genres of Blues to highlight different approaches in delivering the musical ideas of the artist.

- Analysing the profiles of innovative musicians considered historically relevant for their effort in exploiting technology to serve creative goals.
- Introducing how Blues musicians in the twenty-first century use social media to reach and build a fan base, thus getting new opportunities for promoting, selling and distributing their music.

Analog vs. digital

During the international conference GuitCon held in Germany in 2018, which gathered professional guitarists, international gear manufacturers and YouTubers, Pete Thorn asked the panel whether digital devices and simulations of "the real thing" (Thorn 2018) could negatively impact the authenticity of the tone, thus limiting or irreversibly modifying the original musical intent of the artist. Despite revealing different experiences and personal backgrounds, their answers can be synthesised as follows:

- Tone is first of all in the hands, mind, soul of the musician.
- The specific gear used (analogue, digital) comes only second in order of importance for the final result.
- Musicians are always looking for a certain level of responsivity (feedback) from their instruments, in order to "feel alive", enjoying and thus improving their performance in front of the audience.

There is essentially a high demand for the sound to be "true" and the gear to follow and react to the musician's input, because this is what musicians in the twenty-first century are (still) looking for. What does this mean? We can see here a genuine interest for authenticity in the sonic features of those genres where the guitar still represents one of the most prominent voices.

Now, how do Blues musicians deal with digital devices? It is possible to classify each genre according to the equipment used in live performances as follows:

- Reflective: whether it is a band ensemble like Greta Van Fleet or a single act such as Jack Broadbent, they all base their sound on either full acoustic setups or electric instruments with analogue amps and pedals, keeping the setup minimal with no sophisticated effect chains or artificial tone alterations, to better reproduce that original organic sound.
- Inclusive: best represented by Joe Bonamassa, they accomplish their sonic objective by adopting "the best of both worlds" and combining analogue amplifiers and dynamic processors with digital modulations (delays, reverb, chorus etc.) to bring more colours to their sonic pallet.

- Neo: considering for example Rag 'n' Bone Man and Hozier, the need for "being in the moment" is fulfilled by bringing on stage electronic devices to fill in the rhythm section particularly. Electronic drum-kits set the beat, wave samples feed synthesizers and create melody lines, to be put on top of any chord progression that could be generated in real time through loop station pedals.

This might seem to confirm that Neo-Blues artists have abandoned the old sonic conventions, favouring all-digital solutions and adopting new instruments on stage. However, to get a more accurate perspective, it is necessary to further explore their preferences in the recording studio.

Analysing the hit song "Take Me To Church" by Hozier, the producer and engineer Rob Kirwan highlights a willingness to focus on the least commercial aspects of the music. This also translates into a precise opinion about computers and digital devices assisting music production:

> People today focus way too much on the computer...But what I am interested in is the sound of people in a room, and how that affects you emotionally...The computer's capabilities are endless, but you don't necessarily need them, and worse, they can be a major distraction...and this does not necessarily help music at all. (Tingen 2015)

The strong connection of Neo-Blues musicians with the tradition and original features of Blues is also revealed in their musical influences. During an interview with Ethan Sapienza, Rag 'n' Bone Man clearly expressed his reverend appreciation for Muddy Waters, probably his main source of inspiration to start singing:

> Close to my heart is Muddy Waters. I love the way he sang...There's something really magical about his voice, and he taught me how to sing...People like him, and all the great Blues singers, like B.B. King. (Sapienza 2017).

Nonetheless, it is also true that the adoption of digital devices and (new) technology tools might still be questioned. This is why we need to reflect on how many Blues musicians, throughout the decades, found themselves exploring new ways to overcome limitations, particularly at a sonic level, reaching greater success and audience approval in doing so. As history demonstrated, the ultimate goal of these innovators was to bring something new to the sonic conventions of Blues as universally accepted at their time. One case for all, Jimi Hendrix. He was a pioneer of using effects like the wah-wah and the octaver "when few were even willing to try" (Hein 2009). Also, he turned noise feedback into a vehicle for expressing his musical ideas in an original way, instead of treating it like an unwanted effect, as demonstrated in the execution of "The Star-Spangled Banner" at Woodstock in 1969.

If on one side today, both Reflective and Inclusive artists still take full advantage of Hendrix's sound innovations, it is also true that Neo-Bluesmen have taken Hendrix's curiosity and hunger for musical knowledge as a driver for experimentation. As recalled by Miles Davis in his autobiography, Hendrix completely immersed himself in a process of development that allowed him to pioneer the fusing of different genres and influences:

> Jimi...wanted to add more jazz elements to what he was doing...So we started getting together...I would just play it for him on the piano or on the horn, and he would get it...He had a natural ear for hearing music...Then he started incorporating things I told him into his albums. It was great. He influenced me, and I influenced him, and that's the way great music is always made. Everybody showing everybody else something and then moving on from there. (Davis and Troupe 1989, 292)

If a common feature is to be found here connecting past and present Blues musicians, it has to be open-mindedness and a solid perception of the sonic result to be achieved. Once again, we believe this attitude towards technology represents the best way to preserve your own sonic authenticity in the twenty-first century.

It is now time to move the focus away from the performing and recording aspects of Blues music, and ask ourselves: "how do Blues artists manage to get their music heard, thus allowing them to make a sustainable career based on recording, singing and producing new songs today?" To answer this question, the figure of the "travelling musician", originally referred to as the twentieth century "songster" needs to be recalled.

Travelling musicians in the twenty-first century

As described by Kirstin Faucett, the "songsters", twentieth-century predecessor of Bluesmen, and then Bluesmen themselves, were "itinerant musicians, or street corner musicians who played a variety of tunes in order to make a little money from passers-by" (Fawcett 2014). To get a living from performing, they used to carry "their songs from community to community by railroad, by steamboats, by wagon and even by foot" (Moore 2002a, 5).

We need to look at the way Blues musicians operate nowadays to reach an audience, build a fan base, create new opportunities to make their music heard and get a sustainable career out of their art. The focus is mostly on upcoming artists in need of marketing their product with a small budget and no deal with labels or traditional managers to support them.

Despite the previous classification of Blues, which led to the definition of three distinct genres, we can trace a common path followed by every contemporary Blues musician when it comes to promoting and distributing music. This channel is called "social media", while "social media marketing" embodies the techniques used on platforms like Instagram and Facebook to promote music, spread "brand awareness" and therefore build a fan base of "followers". Although there can be negative impacts using these platforms, as mentioned earlier, if used correctly, they can be very beneficial. Blues musicians seem to commit especially to Instagram posts. Accounts like "Blues is everything", with 234 followers as of February 2019 (Guitar Tricks 2019), offer the perfect place for both upcoming new artists and established ones to be found, appreciated and get their music shared (for free) by old and new Blues enthusiasts.

Counting exclusively on pictures and one-minute long videos, artists need to engage on a daily basis with a world-wide audience, being aware of how relevant its role is in their career. Thanks to technology, listeners and viewers transitioned "from being passive television viewers and radio listeners as receiver of mediated messages" to becoming "active consumers of media content as users and producers" (Stewart 2013). Blues musicians must consider this aspect thoroughly. Most of all, they need to plan a social media strategy to satisfy this request properly, as explained below.

Social media strategy for musicians

It should be evident, at this point, that social media marketing represents an unavoidable subject for musicians to master or, at least, to understand and implement at their convenience. The need for travelling to spread the word of Blues has disappeared, and Bluesmen can make a living from their music stationed in any part of the world, with just a video camera and an internet connection. However, the level of commitment expected has not decreased at all. Gilad Salamander offers honest and practical advice on the subject:

> The only way for them [musicians] to make money is to embrace the marketing tactics of a 'startup'. Whether you like it or not, you and your band are a business and you need to start acting like one, which means developing social media marketing strategies that will grow your fan base (Salamander 2016)

Despite an apparently strong sense of commodification emerging from this description, we found that the "mutual dependency" between musicians and the "driving force" of technology described by Théberge (1997, 5) has been not only addressed but also exploited successfully by artists like Joe Bonamassa. Bonamassa represents the best example of how a Blues musician in the twenty-first century can embrace social media to both ensure himself a consistent and successful career, while at the same time attempting to "keep the Blues alive" for future generations.

Personal branding to keep the Blues alive

Joe Bonamassa demonstrated how an artist can break the boundaries of the old conventional music business thanks to social media and digital music platforms. In 2011 as agreed with his manager, he decided "to work with the public rather than for the radio and music industry" and "to make the digital shift permanent" (Morin 2015). They started their own label and further developed the presence of the artist, "on Facebook and other social media networks, to further increase the fan base" (Morin 2015). This move ended up growing Joe's initial fan base from just over 2000 likes on Facebook in 2008, to a core number of "ambassadors" that "has risen to over 2 million, with over 1.5 million downloads" (Morin 2015). Analysing Bonamassa's approach to engaging with his fans, we find exactly what Salamander recommends about gaining trust and loyalty "to leverage the benefits of social media engagement" (Salamander 2016).

At the same time, it is also true that Bonamassa never missed a chance to give back to the Blues community. This is revealed in two ventures the Blues guitarist set out on with precise and different focuses: "Keeping The Blues Alive" foundation and "Keeping The Blues Alive at sea" cruise ships.

Through the "Keeping The Blues Alive" foundation, he fulfilled a mission "to offset the loss of music education programs by funding music projects, scholarships, and preserving the rich culture and history of the Blues as a true American art form" (Bonamassa 2011).

With "Keeping The Blues Alive at sea" cruise ships, Bonamassa offered his fans unique live performance experiences and artist "meet and greets" while sailing around the world. This allowed him to gain further economic support for himself, and for other artists' careers, and consolidate fans' engagement by giving them the opportunity to share a vacation with their preferred Blues musicians.

In both situations, the Bluesman is looking to offer new opportunities to nurture and promote young Blues musicians to guarantee a future for Blues music in its broadest meaning with no distinction of sort:

> Now...there are a lot of both male and female guitarists, singers, and songwriters. And if you can give one kid the seed, and it grows, and it comes out to be the next big Blues rock star then you know what? I've done my job; I've done what I set out to do so many years ago. Not only have I developed a little career for myself, but I have also helped others the same way BB King helped me when I was 12 years old. And it's a great name, 'Keeping the Blues Alive.' That's what it is. (Bonamassa 2011)

Conclusion

Through the writings of both Lindholm and Moore, we have found that it is possible for twenty-first-century Bluesmen to produce authentic music created in their own time, as a reflection of their own time. In turn, they can be authenticated by those who connect to the music, as can all styles of Blues music be equally validated by a certain group of perceivers. Their creations are further validated by adhering to certain musical and metaphorical parameters, validating both the content of the lyrics and the manner in which they are presented. These parameters underpin the 'metagenre-world' model, unifying all styles of Blues music and demonstrating how they should be viewed as parts of a whole, not separate entities.

We have seen that the use of technology in delivering the musical parameters may not diminish the validity of Neo-Blues, nor any Blues music of today. In fact, it has the potential of providing the best way for Neo-Bluesmen to truly reflect the issues of their time. Much as Blues music was born out of a reaction of the time, with the means those people had available to them, Neo-Blues is a reaction of a time, through the means available; the only difference is how they are presented. These issues, as we have seen, do adhere to the Blues metaphor, which leads us to believe that what's going on today, is indeed the Blues.

We have found that the sonic choices of each genre of Blues, especially in live contexts, can be directly associated with the interpretation of authenticity embodied by the artist. In accordance with the relationship described by Paul Théberge, Neo-Blues musicians have been shown to exploit the driving force of technology to better represent modern struggles on the stage, while at the same time paying tribute to the roots of Blues as their source of inspiration when it comes to recording and producing strategies in the studio. Where technology becomes helpful for Blues musicians of any genre is for promoting new music and reaching an audience. The need for Bluesmen to travel is gone. Nonetheless, contemporary musicians are still required to commit themselves to a different sort of journey, in a digital world. They need to develop a social media strategy in order to market their music, build a fanbase and make a living out of their creative work. In this case, Blues musicians need to successfully exploit the tools technology has to offer not only for personal success but also to guarantee the continuity of the Blues tradition in the future, supporting younger generations of musicians and organising events to keep the Blues alive.

This paper's purpose was to demonstrate the plausibility of Blues musicians in 2019 delivering valid Blues music as long as the aforementioned criteria are met. If the scope of this study was widened, the next steps would be to focus more specifically on investigating the way individual musicians present themselves in both lyrics and performance, and determine if this is an honest

portrayal. We would then analyse in more detail the recording and producing practices of Neo-Blues musicians, to find potential connections between the sonic rendition and the original scope of their creative process. Lastly, social media marketing strategies would be further investigated to reveal how such technological tools impact Blues musicians' career development.

References

Books

Davis, Francis. 2003. *The History Of The Blues.* New York: Da Capo Press.

Davis, Miles, and Quincy Troupe. 1989. *The Autobiography,* edited by Quincy Troupe. New York: Simon and Schuster Paperbacks.

Dorschel, Andreas, Gerhard Eckel, and Deniz Peters, eds. 2012. *Bodily Expression in Electronic Music.* Oxford: Routledge.

Erlewine, Michael, ed. 1999. *All Music Guide to the Blues.* 2nd edn. San Francisco: Miller Freeman.

Ferris, William. 1984. *Blues From The Delta.* New York: Da Capo Press.

Frith, Simon. 1998. *Performing Rites.* Cambridge, Massachusetts: University of Harvard Press.

Gilbert, Jeremy, and Ewan Pearson. 1999. *Discographies: Dance Music, Culture and the Politics of Sound.* London: Routledge.

Holt, Fabian. 2007. *Genre in Popular Music.* London: University of Chicago Press.

Juslin, Patrik N., and John A. Sloboda. 2010. *Music and Emotion - Theory, Research, Applications.* Oxford: Oxford University Press.

Lehmann, Andreas., John A. Sloboda, and Robert H. Woody. 2007. *Psychology for Musicians.* New York: Oxford University Press.

Leppard, Raymond. 1988. *Authenticity in Music.* London: Faber Music.

Lindholm, Charles. 2008. *Culture and Authenticity.* Oxford: Blackwell Publishing.

McLoughlin, Shirley W. 2008. *A Pedagogy of the Blues.* Rotterdam: Sense Publishers.

Middleton, Richard. 1990. *Studying Popular Music.* Buckingham: Open University Press.

Moore, Allan. 2002a. "Surveying the field: our knowledge of blues and gospel music." In *The Cambridge companion to Blues and Gospel music,* edited by Allan Moore, 1-12. Cambridge: Cambridge University Press.

Moore, Allan. 2002b. "Authenticity as Authentication." *Popular Music* 21(2), 209-223.

Redhead, Steve. 1990. *The End-of-the-Century Party.* Manchester: Manchester University Press.

Rubidge, Sarah. 1996. "Does authenticity matter? The case for and against authenticity in the performing arts." In *Analysing Performance: A critical reader,* edited by Patrick Campbell, 219-33. Manchester: Manchester University Press.

Rudinow, Joel. 1994. "Race, Ethnicity, Expressive Authenticity: Can White People Sing the Blues?" *The Journal of Aesthetics and Art Criticism* 52 (1), 127-137.

Shuker, Roy. 2012. *Popular Music Culture-The Key Concepts.* Oxford: Routledge.

Shuker, Roy. 2016. *Understanding Popular Music Culture.* Oxford: Routledge.

Théberge, Paul. 1997. *Any Sound You Can Imagine: Making Music/Consuming Technology.* Hanover: Wesleyan University Press.

Further Reading

Bastin, Bruce. 1986. *Red River Blues.* Urbana: University of Illinois Press.

Sanden, Paul. 2013. *Liveness in Modern Music.* Oxford: Routledge.

Websites

AgrawaL, AJ. 2016. "How Digital Marketing Is Changing the Music Industry". Accessed 25 June 2019. https://www.inc.com/aj-agrawal/how-digital-marketing-is-changing-the-music-industry.html.

Beato, R. 2018. "Big Tube Amps VS Modelers + Pedals". Accessed 25 June 2019. https://www.youtube.com/watch?v=9imzeD5i-t4&feature=youtu.be&t=822.

Bohlinger, J. 2018. "Rig Rundown: Greta Van Fleet". Accessed 25 June 2019. https://www.premierguitar.com/articles/26960-rig-rundown-greta-van-fleet.

Bonamassa, J. 2011. "Keeping the Blues Alive/Founder". Accessed 25 June 2019. https://keepingtheBluesalive.org/founder/.

Fawcett, K. 2014. "Before There was the Blues Man, There Was the Songster". Accessed 25 June 2019. https://www.smithsonianmag.com/smithsonian-institution/before-there-was-Blues-man-there-was-songster-180951863/.

Germanndude. 2018. "Big Tube Amps VS Modelers + Pedals". Accessed 25 June 2019.v https://www.youtube.com/watch?v=9imzeD5i-t4&feature=youtu.be&t=822.

Guitar Tricks. 2019. "Blues Is Everything". Accessed 25 June 2019. https://www.instagram.com/Blues_is_everything/.

Hein, E. 2009. "Jimi Hendrix, electronic musician". Accessed 31/07/2018. http://www.ethanhein.com/wp/2009/jimi-hendrix-electronic-musician /.

IPSOS. 2017. "Politicians-Remain-Least-Trusted-Profession-Britain.". Accessed 25 June 2019. https://www.ipsos.com/ipsos-mori/en-uk/politicians-remain-least-trusted-profession-britain.

Kunzru, H. 2017. "The Blues Still Stands For Authenticity: My Mississippi Road Trip." *The Guardian*, 24 March. Accessed 25 June 2019. https://www.theguardian.com/music/2017/mar/24/the-Blues-authenticity-mississippi-road-trip-hari-kunzru-music, accessed 05/06/2019.

Lup, Katerina, Trub. Leora and Lisa Rosenthal. 2015. "Instagram #Instasad?: Exploring Associations Among Instagram Use, Depressive Symptoms, Negative Social Comparison, and Strangers Followed." *Cyberpsychology, Behavior, and Social Networking* 18 (5). Accessed 25 June 2019. http://doi.org/10.1089/cyber.2014.0560.v

Manders, B. 2018. People Population and Community. Office For National Statistics. Accessed 25 June 2019. https://www.ons.gov.uk/peoplepopulationandcommunity/birthsdeathsand marriages/deaths/bulletins/suicidesintheunitedkingdom/2017registration, accessed 16/10/2018.

Mariano, H. 2016. "Why we need to stop comparing our problems." *The Odyssey*, 3 October. Accessed 25 June 2019. https://www.theodysseyonline.com/stop-comparing-problems.

McGuiness, Feargal. UK. Parliament. House of Commons. 2018. Poverty In The UK: Statistics. House Of Commons Library. SN07096. Accessed 25 June 2019. https://researchbriefings.parliament.uk/ResearchBriefing/Summary/SN07096.

Mental Health Foundation. 2016. "Fundamental Facts About Mental Health 2016." Mental Health Foundation: London. Accessed 25 June 2019. https://www.mentalhealth.org.uk/publications/fundamental-facts-about-mental-health-2016.

Morin, R. 2015. "Personal Branding Lessons From Joe Bonamassa". Accessed 2 November 2018. https://maximizesocialbusiness.com/personal-branding-lessons-joe-bonamassa-22380/.

Office For National Statistics. 2017. "People Population and Community". Accessed 25 June 2019.https://www.ons.gov.uk/peoplepopulationandcommunity/crimeandj ustice/adhocs/007533numberofincidentsofhatecrimebystrandofhatecrimea ndpercentageofthoseincidentsreportedtothepolicecrimesurveyforenglanda ndwalesyearsendingmarch2014tomarch2016combined12monthaverages.

Rag'n'Bone Man, 2016. "Human". (Online Video). Accessed 25 June 2019. https://www.youtube.com/watch?v=L3wKzyIN1yk.

Salamander, G. 2016. "Social Media Strategies for Musicians". Accessed 25 June 2019. https://eclincher.com/blog/social-media-strategies-for-musicians/.

Sapienza, E. 2017. "Rag'n'Bone Man". Accessed 25 June 2019. https://www.interviewmagazine.com/music/ragnbone-man.

Scancarelli, D. 2018. "Buddy Guy Is The Last Bastion Of The Blues." *Forbes*. Accessed 25 June 2019. https://www.forbes.com/sites/derekscancarelli/2018/06/12/buddy-guy-is-the-last-bastion-of-the-Blues/#10265f7975b1.

Smart Social. 2018. "Teen Social Media Statistics 2019 (What Parents Need to Know)". 8 October. Accessed 25 June 2019. https://smartsocial.com/social-media-statistics/.

Stewart M., S. 2013. Artist-Fan Engagement model: implications for music consumption and the music industry. Alabama: University of Alabama Press. Accessed 25 June 2019. https://ir.ua.edu/handle/123456789/1949.

Thorn, P. 2018. "Big Tube Amps VS Modelers + Pedals". Accessed 16 November 2018. https://www.youtube.com/watch?v=9imzeD5i-t4&feature=youtu.be&t=822.

Tingen, P. 2015. "Inside Track: Hozier 'Take Me To Church". Accessed 25 June 2019. https://www.soundonsound.com/techniques/inside-track-hozier-take-me-church.

Audio

Burnett, C. 1969. "Back Door Man." On The Howlin' Wolf Album, Chicago: Cadet Concept Records, vinyl.

Sheet Music

Graham, R., and J. Hartman,. 2016. Human. Sheetmusicplus: Hal Leonard, 2016. https://www.sheetmusicplus.com/title/human-digital-sheet-music/20597244, Digital Sheet Music.

Johnson, R. 1936. Kind Hearted Woman Blues. Sheetmusicplus: Hal Leonard, 1991. https://www.sheetmusicplus.com/title/kind-hearted-woman-Blues-digital-sheet-music/19563630, Digital Sheet Music.

Figures

Figure 13.1Davis, F. 2003. *The History Of The Blues.* New York: Da Capo Press, 4. Ferris, W. 1984. *Blues From The Delta.* New York: Da Capo Press, xii. McLoughlin, S. W. 2008. *A Pedagogy of the Blues.* Rotterdam: Sense Publishers, 41.

Figure 13.2a

Graham, R., and J. Hartman. 2016. Human. Sheetmusicplus: Hal Leonard, 2016. https://www.sheetmusicplus.com/title/human-digital-sheet-music/20597244, Digital Sheet Music.

Figure 13.2b

Johnson, R. 1936. Kind Hearted Woman Blues. Sheetmusicplus: Hal Leonard, 1991. https://www.sheetmusicplus.com/title/kind-hearted-woman-Blues-digital-sheet-music/19563630, Digital Sheet Music.

Figure 13.3a

Graham, R., and J. Hartman. 2016. Human. Sheetmusicplus: Hal Leonard, 2016. https://www.sheetmusicplus.com/title/human-digital-sheet-music/20597244, Digital Sheet Music.

Figure 13.3b

Johnson, R. 1936. Kind Hearted Woman Blues. Sheetmusicplus: Hal Leonard, 1991. https://www.sheetmusicplus.com/title/kind-hearted-woman-Blues-digital-sheet-music/19563630, Digital Sheet Music.

Figure 13.4

McLoughlin, S. W. 2008. *A Pedagogy of the Blues.* Rotterdam: Sense Publishers, 41.

Figure 13.5a

Graham, R., and J. Hartman. 2016. Human. Sheetmusicplus: Hal Leonard, 2016. https://www.sheetmusicplus.com/title/human-digital-sheet-music/20597244, Digital Sheet Music.

Figure 13.5b

Johnson, R. 1936. Kind Hearted Woman Blues. Sheetmusicplus: Hal Leonard, 1991. https://www.sheetmusicplus.com/title/kind-hearted-woman-Blues-digital-sheet-music/19563630, Digital Sheet Music.

Figure 13.6a

Graham, R., and J. Hartman,. 2016. Human. Sheetmusicplus: Hal Leonard, 2016. https://www.sheetmusicplus.com/title/human-digital-sheet-music/20597244, Digital Sheet Music.

Figure 13.6b

Johnson, R. 1936. Kind Hearted Woman Blues. Sheetmusicplus: Hal Leonard, 1991. https://www.sheetmusicplus.com/title/kind-hearted-woman-Blues-digital-sheet-music/19563630, Digital Sheet Music.

Figure 13.7

Frith, S. 1998. *Performing Rites.* Cambridge, Massachusetts: University of Harvard Press, 88.

McLoughlin, S. W. 2008. *A Pedagogy of the Blues.* Rotterdam: Sense Publishers, 41.

Shuker, R. 2012. *Popular Music Culture-The Key Concepts.* Oxford: Routledge, 148.

14.

Black and White Blues:
the sounds of Delta Blues singing

Douglas Mark Ponton

University of Catania, Italy

Introduction

...can a white person play Blues? I say I don't have advantage of a white person. I
only got five fingers. If I had six fingers I could answer you different you know?
And this young man can play![1]

Blues legend Buddy Guy, introducing white prodigy Quinn Sullivan, attempts
to put an end, once and for all, to the well-known controversy within the Blues
world, that only blacks can play the music. Questions of authenticity and
ownership have raged around the Blues at least since the 1960s, when white
musicians, especially in the UK, began to use its musical idioms. British
admirers of Elvis and his black models, such as the Rolling Stones and the
Beatles, began to imitate these quintessentially American/black sounds
during the '60s, an early landmark in the history of British Blues being the
Stones' number one hit in 1964 with the Willie Dixon song "Little Red
Rooster". The debate has even older origins; as more than one critic has
pointed out, the tendency for the hegemonic white culture to absorb
"underclass" black elements into the American cultural/musical mainstream
has been a historical constant, whether the music in question be Jazz, Rhythm
'n' Blues, Rock 'n' Roll, Soul, Rap, or the Blues (see Stallybrass and White 1986,
5, in Daley 2003, 161, Baraka 1987, 259, in Rudinow 1994, 130; also Benzon
1993, Ward 1998).

  The 1980 movie *The Blues Brothers* represented one of the first steps in the
emergence in corporate branding of the Blues as image (Lieberfeld 1995), and
such processes have only accentuated the accusations of cultural imperialism

---

[1] Buddy Guy - Can white people play Blues?
https://www.youtube.com/watch?v=fVICdcbIIIfw, last visit 07/12/2018.

that have accompanied white attempts to perform the music from the first (Born and Hesmondhalgh 2000, 22).[2]

The intention of this chapter, however, is not to engage with the well-worn debate over authenticity (see Claviez, this volume), which has been thoroughly explored over the years (e.g. Rudinow 1994, Baraka 1999, Daley 2003, Young 2008, Jenkins 2012). The idea that only contemporary blacks have a right to sing the Blues because of their share in ancestral suffering under slavery is well answered by Rudinow (1994, 133):

> The access that most contemporary black Americans have to the experience of slavery or sharecropping or life on the Mississippi Delta during the twenties and thirties is every bit as remote, mediated, and indirect as that of any white would-be Blues player.

In point of fact, as Guy's remark indicates, it is widely accepted that certain white performers have mastered the art of playing Blues guitar to similar levels of expertise as their black counterparts. In terms of their skill as instrumentalists, it is indeed arguable that white musicians like Eric Clapton, Johnny Winter or Stevie Ray Vaughan have taken the music to new heights of virtuosity. Whether any are able to sing the Blues like their heroes, however, is another question. As Cory Harris notes in his Blues blog pages, the heart of the Blues is not pyro-technical guitar playing but Blues singing which, he says, is much harder to imitate (Harris 2015). In the voice, say Feld et al. (2004, 323), poetics meets performance. The chapter's aim is to explore these issues, to identify features of traditional Blues singing, and see how far these are reproduced in white performances.

Evolution of the Blues, white Blues

The Blues is a product of black musical and traditional culture, born in the Mississippi Delta and other places across the southern United States, around the turn of the twentieth century. As with most musical genres, it did not remain fixed, but evolved from its early, country origins and simple forms of instrumentation into a sophisticated urban product. Spencer (1992) documents the introduction of electric instrumentation during the "Chicago period", when the Blues, after the population transfer from the Delta to the northern industrial centres, gradually lost touch with its rural roots. The new arrangements featured drums, bass, horn and rhythm sections, and often included long solos from guitar virtuosos. Such was the music as interpreted by the biggest names of the

---

[2] Analogous processes are described by Feld (1994) in his discussion of Paul Simon's supposed 'appropriation' of black musical norms in the Graceland project.

time like B.B. King, Albert King and Buddy Guy. Thus, the profile of the Blues singer also evolved: in the early period they tended to be itinerant figures, roaming the Southern states from party to party, living hand to mouth, struggling to build up reputations that were seldom more than local. Increasingly, they adopted the lifestyles of professional musicians, and the best-known of them became global superstars.

Oliver (1972, 3) refers to the Blues as "the wail of the forsaken, the cry of independence, the passion of the lusty, the anger of the frustrated and the laughter of the fatalist". Gil Scott-Heron says:

> There's the I ain't got me no money Blues;
> There's the I ain't got me no woman Blues;
> There's the I ain't got me no money and I ain't got me no woman,
> which is the double Blues.[3]

It is a music which represents a virile response to "trouble" in its many forms, offering the listener a sense of participation and relief, with effects that may extend to catharsis and healing (Majithia 2012, Stolorow and Stolorow 2012).

Baraka (1987, 259) explores the appropriation of black musical forms by white artists, and there is also widespread recognition of the appeal to early white audiences of the Blues. In popular American music, the impact of the Blues and its derivatives was enormous, starting from the career of Elvis Presley who, as a white performer steeped in black musical lore, was the right man at the right moment to take the music to the world. What he delivered was not so much the Blues as its livelier relation, 'Rock'n'Roll', though his earliest recordings do show him as versed in some of the idioms and features of Blues singing.[4]

Another significant moment in the modern history of the Blues was the appearance of old-timer Skip James, and other veterans such as Bukka White and Son House, at the Newport Folk Festival in 1966. They had an immediate impact on white folk music, influencing stars such as Bob Dylan, John Martyn, Donovan and others; while on the rock scene the impact was even greater, with bands such as Cream, the Who, Fleetwood Mac, Canned Heat, the Rolling Stones, the Doors, John Mayall's Bluesbreakers, and solo artists like Paul Butterfield, Jeff Beck, Johnny Winter and Stevie Ray Vaughan all drawing

---

[3] Gil Scott-Heron, "Watergate Blues" (Winter in America). 1974 Strata-East Records.

[4] E.g. "Milkcow Blues Boogie", "Mystery Train", "That's Alright Mamma", etc. on 'the Sun Sessions', RCA records 1976. One of the comparatively few 'black' Blues covers Elvis recorded during his career was the Jimmy Reed song "Big Boss Man" (RCA records 1967). See also Palmer (1982, 241) on the early Elvis.

inspiration from the old masters' recordings, which began to be re-issued to feed the boom in demand for Delta Blues.

The 1980 blockbuster *The Blues Brothers* represents another milestone, with the Blues reaching a vast audience through the global medium of cinema. The escapades of white brothers Jake and Elwood are accompanied by a type of Blues that is light years away from the down-home sounds of the music's origins (Lieberfeld 1995). Apart from a cameo from John Lee Hooker, the principal Blues offering consists of a version of Robert Johnson's "Sweet Home Chicago" which in the original is a plaintive Delta Blues ballad. It has become, by 1980, unrecognisable, dragged out to over seven minutes by saxophone and electric guitar solos, and can best be described as a catchy foot-tapper. In comparing the two versions of "Sweet Home Chicago" it is hard not to sympathise with Paul Garon's view, that white attempts to play the Blues result in "unauthentic and deeply impoverished" musical artefacts (Garon 1995, see also Halliday, this volume).

White and black Blues

At this point, it must be said that there appears to be no comparable kind of distinct school or cultural tradition to which the abstract label "White Blues" may be attached, one whose songs may be placed alongside "Black Blues" for the purposes of thematic, cultural or lexico-semantic comparison. Rather, white Bluesmen or whites who at times perform the Blues—when they write their own material–appear to do so in an idiosyncratic fashion, generally mixing their Blues songs with some other genre such as Rock, Folk, Rhythm'n'Blues or Jazz. "Steamroller Blues", for example, is James Taylor's affectionate nod in the direction of the tradition, verging towards parody but still, with its vein of tongue in cheek machismo, evoking comparison with similar songs by black singers such as Muddy Waters' "Mannish Boy" or Hooker's "I'm in the Mood for Love".

Of the many possible ways in which black and white Blues could be compared, this study deals briefly with formal and lexical criteria, and in more depth with the technical side of vocal performance. Comments on all these aspects are based on a close listening to the songs in the corpora described below, and the reader must decide how far they apply, more generally, to the vast and varied field of the Blues in its entirety.

In terms of form, it is well known that traditional Blues display characteristic features of lexical and musical construction, and many Blues songs employ the so-called "12 bar" structure, in which the first line is repeated and a third rhyming line, resolving the tension generated by the preceding couplet, completes the verse:

> Now she is a little Queen of Spades, and the men will not let her be
> Mmm, she is the little Queen of Spades, and the men will not let her be
> Everytime she makes a spread, hoo, fair brown, cold chill just runs all over me
>   (Robert Johnson, "Queen of Spades")

It has been suggested that this structure may have African roots (Kubik 1999, 42-43). While white Blues appears to respect this structure fairly rigidly, it is not uncommon for black singers to deviate from it. While many of Johnson's songs follow the pattern, for example, "Walking Blues" does not, simply repeating an initial couplet to complete a four-line verse:

> I woke up this mornin', feelin' round for my shoes
> Know by that I got these old walkin' Blues, well
> Woke up this mornin', feelin round for my shoes
> But you know by that, I got these old walkin' Blues

John Lee Hooker frequently seems to ignore both the constraints of the musical and the lyrical form. In "Hobo Blues", a typical Hooker number in many respects, the verse is intoned seemingly over a single chord and the text makes no attempt to rhyme:

> When I first thought to hobo'in, hobo'in
> I took a freight train to be a friend, Oh Lord
> You know I hobo'd, hobo'd, hobo'd
> Hobo'd a long, long way from home, Oh Lord

The text is given coherence by its use of internal repetition and the line ending "Oh Lord", and these devices, as well as the accompanying strum and the heavy vocal give the piece a hypnotic quality typical of Hooker's style.[5] Listening to early Delta Bluesmen such as Bukka White or Son House, it is not hard to locate Hooker's music within the tradition; by contrast, there are few if any white Blues singers who do anything remotely comparable.

In terms of the lexico-semantic parameter, the themes of Delta Blues tend to be universals such as love, fidelity and betrayal, sex and sensuality, loss and mourning, rootlessness and existential anxiety. Bob Dylan at times produces original Blues songs that stick close to these themes; however, he also brings his own kind of lyrical inventiveness to the form, taking it into new semantic territory. Consider his version of a traditional Blues by Lightnin' Hopkins, which develops a metaphor already explored by Robert Johnson, *woman = car*.[6]

---

[5] See Palmer (1982, 242).

[6] One of Johnson's classic Blues features this as an extended metaphor, concluding: "I'm gon' get deep down in this connection

I see you drivin' round Babe, in your brand new automobile;
You're lookin' happy baby with your handsome driver at the wheel;
In your brand new automobile.

(Lightnin' Hopkins "Automobile Blues")

The Dylan version drops the automobile motif in favour of an item that never featured in any black Blues song, and includes surreal linguistic inventions that evoke the world of Picasso more than that of the Mississippi Delta:

You know it balances on your head just like a mattress balances on a bottle of wine;
Your brand new leopard-skin pillbox hat.

(Bob Dylan "Leopard-skin Pillbox Hat")

Blues singing

Palmer (1982, 18-19) describes some technical difficulties associated with Delta Blues singing:

singing it right involves some exceptionally fine points that few black singers and virtually no white singers [...] have been able to grasp. These fine points have to do with timing, with subtle variations in vocal timbre, and with being able to hear and execute [...] very precise gradations in pitch that are neither haphazard waverings nor mere effects.

While this description offers some insight into the processes involved, it also suffers from the defect of imprecision. For example, "timing" is an essential attribute of all skilful singing white or black, while "subtle variations in vocal timbre" can also be found across the spectrum of white music, from country to choral music. Singing of any kind requires, moreover, nothing if not the ability to execute "precise gradations in pitch". Therefore, Palmer's words do little to explain the phenomenon of instant recognition that allows a listener to "hear", with near certainty, whether they are listening to a black singer or a white one.

The rest of this chapter focuses on a comparative study that identifies features of black Blues singing and then compares to see if white Blues singers reproduce them in their performances. For example, black Blues singers frequently replace the words of a song with sections of "humming", which can be short insertions or long phrases that extend for a whole line or even a verse. Robert Johnson does this in "Come on in my Kitchen", which commences with two lines of verse hummed before singing the refrain. In

---

hoo-well keep on tanglin' with your wires;
And when I mash down your little starter
then your spark plug will give me a fire". ("Terraplane Blues")

"Moaning the Blues", Memphis Minnie hums a whole verse, expressive of her feelings on learning of the death of her partner:

> This morning, setting on the side of my bed
> This morning, setting on the side of my bed;
> They done come brought you a letter, your plumb good man fell dead
>
> Hmmmmm, hmmmmm (etc.)

Both these instances show how an extremely simple technique can be used to express a basic emotion, that of sorrow or grief, which is one of the music's central themes. No doubt white singers would be capable of humming in this way, but they appear not to make use of this technique, at least in the current corpus.

Corpora; methodology

The corpora consist of sixty Blues songs by white and black artists (see appendix). I chose four black singers, all seminal figures in their own way– Robert Johnson, widely regarded as the greatest of all Delta Bluesmen, Lightnin' Hopkins, one of the Blues' most prolific songwriters ever; Muddy Waters, who helped establish the Delta style in its Chicago evolution on the world stage, and Memphis Minnie, the queen of early country Blues.

While it was easy to find songs by black Blues singers, the problem being deciding who to omit, it is hard to find a comparable number of Blues songs by white artists. While many black artists are "Blues singers", whose normal practice is to record entire albums on which every number is a Blues, analogous white figures are thin on the ground. As well as performing other genres, such artists produce cover versions of black Blues songs as much as they write their own material (black artists also perform many covers, but not to the same extent). In 1999, Eric Clapton, one of today's biggest white "Bluesmen" and self-avowed devotee of Robert Johnson, released a retrospective album called "Blues". Of twenty-five tracks, no fewer than eighteen are cover versions of black Blues songs by named artists, three are traditionals from the black tradition, and only four carry Clapton's name as author. One of these, "Wonderful Tonight" is a pop song.[7]

---

[7] http://en.wikipedia.org/wiki/Blues_%28Eric_Clapton_album%29, last access 17/12/2018. In terms of comparing vocal technique alone, it may appear possible to include cover versions, but the problem here is that the white copyist (black Blues singers do not cover white Blues songs, to any extent) will also tend to copy the vocal techniques used by the original, which makes it impossible to identify specific vocal features typifying the two genres.

In an attempt to compare like with like, I decided to focus on the Blues singers who use the conventional, 12-bar format or some version based on it, tending to avoid cover versions in both corpora, thus representing Clapton, for example, not by his most celebrated pieces such as "Crossroads Blues" but by comparatively unknown recordings in the Blues genre. However, some compromises were necessary in order to obtain a numerically equal corpus: in some songs by Bonnie Raitt, the genre is more *pop-rock* than Blues and hence follows a different formal structure, arguably with different generic requirements in the area of vocal technique. The same considerations apply to some pieces by Butterfield (influenced by jazz/rock), Mayall (progressive rock) and Vaughan (rock).

The methodology involved firstly listening to all the songs in the black corpus and making notes of specific features of the performance, then listening to the white corpus and noting instances where they reproduced this feature.

The corpora compared: technical features

In the following analysis of features of black Blues singing, I have gone back to the music and noted features of the performer's style, guided by descriptions such as that of Palmer (1982, 28), who identifies features of Delta Blues singing that derive from African traditions, such as "whooping, or sudden jumping into the falsetto range", and "affected hoarseness, throaty growls and gutteral grunting" (30), and others such as this, by Courlander:

> In most traditional singing there is no apparent striving for the "smooth" and "sweet" qualities that are so highly regarded in Western tradition. Some outstanding blues, gospel, and jazz singers have voices that may be described as foggy, hoarse, rough, or sandy. Not only is this kind of voice not derogated, it often seems to be valued. (Courlander 1963, 23)

However, it must be stressed, that the list of features below (table one) is, in the final analysis, a subjective one, since there is not, as far as I am aware, any authoritative publication on how to sing Delta Blues, from which to derive more reliable criteria.[8]

---

[8] The situation appears to be analogous to that in Gospel music, which has been called the 'sacred counterpart of the Blues' (Allgood 1990, 102). As Williams-Jones (1975, 375) states, there is a lack of researched primary data on the idiom; and it is equally true of Blues music that, as she says of Gospel, transmission appears to be mainly oral.

Table 14.1: Technical features of the corpora (%)

	Technical Feature	Black Corpus (%)	White Corpus (%)
1	Word-breaking falsetto	10	10
2	Falsetto on syllables like 'hoo', 'hee', etc.	23	3
3	Extended use of falsetto for whole lines	1.5	1.5
4	Use of humming/moaning	25	0
5	Extended use of humming for whole lines/verses	6.5	0
6	Singer replaces sung words with spoken words or uses speech	36.5	18
7	'Holler'	21.5	13
8	Intense sound produced by laryngeal constriction	36.5	56.5
9	Imitation of textual feature with instrumental accompaniment	8	1.5
10	Words fade into moaning or drawn out into wordless sound	26.5	10
11	Avoidance of a 'taboo' word by omission	3	0
12	Non-standard pronunciation (e.g. 'ah' for 'I')	40	23
13	Line opens on non-content word ('ooh', 'well', 'yeah', etc.)	43	33
14	Sudden rise/drop in volume of singing	25	50
15	Unusual voice, strange/ silly voice	30	8
16	Sung notes reproduced on accompanying instrument	1.5	0
17	Interjections ('oh Lord', 'Have mercy', etc.)	4.5	0
18	Call/Response	3	1.5
19	Non-content syllable/sound ('woah', etc.)	6.5	26.5

Discussion

The results fall into three groups: firstly, the group in which the feature is more frequently encountered in black singing than in white, secondly those where the proportions are roughly similar, and finally those where the feature is more frequent in the white corpus.

More frequent in black than white corpus

Use of falsetto. 34.5% (black corpus), 14.5% (white corpus).

Viewing the three different types of falsetto collectively, more than one in three songs from the black corpus uses it. However, the great majority of instances occur in the work of Robert Johnson, who uses it to create a plaintive effect. Over a whole line of verse, the effect is to simulate an emotional paroxysm; in the following instance, an attack of jealousy:

> Oh baby, my life don't feel the same / you break my heart when you call Mr So-and-so's name (black corpus 9)

Use of humming. 31% / 0%.

Here, the proportion of black to white occurrences is still more striking. Moreover, this is a technique encountered in all four of the black singers; the effect has already been discussed, above.

Singer replaces sung with spoken words or uses speech. 36.5% / 18 %.

There are differences in the way this technique is used by the two groups. For black singers, the spoken sections contain material that seems to have some textual connection with the subject of the song, e.g. Lightnin' Hopkins, in "Bald-headed woman" breaks off singing to enunciate, very clearly:

> What you want with a woman who ain't got no hair? What's the matter with you girl? (bc 38)

Here, and in other instances in the black corpus, the use of speech provides variety, drawing special attention to the phrases uttered. It also allows the performer to simulate direct, conversational interaction with the audience or with one specific, real or imagined, listener. By contrast, most of the white instances refer to stage phrases, that serve purposes such as encouraging musicians about to play solos, e.g. Paul Butterfield:

> Keep on walkin' honey! (white corpus 10)

Words fade into moaning or drawn out into wordless sound. 26.5% / 10 %.

A technique found in three of the four black singers, again prominent in Robert Johnson, in whose style it seems to add intensity to the delivery, as the clear enunciation of the word is twisted, for example by a prolonged consonant:

> When you got a good /fren.../ (bc 13)

Much less common in the white corpus, it is nevertheless to be found in the most "Bluesy" among these–that is to say Butterfield, Mooney, Morrison, Vaughan, and Mayall.

Imitation of some textual feature with instrumental/vocal accompaniment. 8% / 1.5%.

Black musicians are famous for using instruments to imitate real-world sounds. In this small corpus, the objects imitated include a bell (8), a train (12), a howling wind (14), a corn-mill (48), and clock chimes (51). The Rolling Stones' use of the guitar to imitate the "hounds" mentioned in the song "Little Red Rooster" is an honourable representative of the white corpus in this respect.

Unusual voice, strange/silly voice. 30% / 8 %.

Another technique found mainly in Johnson but also used by two other of the black singers:

> I woke up this mornin', feelin' round for my shoes, everybody know I got these old walking Blues (bc 19)

Here the opening lines are clearly sung in a different style to Johnson's "normal" delivery (e.g. in the opening lines of "When you got a good friend"). "Up" comes out on a sudden crescendo and leaps to an upper register, though not quite falsetto, while the final consonant in "mornin" is drawn out and finishes in a sort of groan. The singer seems to eat some of the words ("shoes", "everybody know", pronouncing them at the back of his mouth, with a sort of "hollow" effect. The phrase "Old walking Blues", by contrast, is produced with constriction. The device is generally used to draw attention to a particular portion of text, but in this number the effect is electrifying.

Holler 21.5% / 13%.

Olmsted describes the field-holler as: "a long, vigorous musical call, climbing then falling, and forcibly entering the falsetto range" (Ohmsted 1853).[9] Included in this category are sounds that satisfy the first part of this description but, since falsetto falls into a separate category, not the second. Something of the field origins of the Blues are heard in such calls as Lightnin' Hopkins gives on the underlined word here:

> If you <u>ever</u> go out in West Texas..." (bc 34)

Non-standard pronunciation (e.g. "ah" for "I") 40% / 23%.

In many cases, both black and white, this seems a feature of conversational style applied to song, as in:

> Yes ah (I) followed the hearse down to the burial ground... (bc 39)

Roughly similar proportions in both corpora

Line opens on non-content word ("ooh", "ah", "well", "yeah", etc.). 43% (black corpus)/33% (white corpus).

---

[9] "A Journey through Texas." Cited in *Au Pays Du Blues.* (my translation).

More prevalent in white than black corpus

Sudden rise/drop in volume of singing 50% / 25%.

This is twice as common in white than black singing as a means, typically, of achieving dramatic emphasis, as in Bonnie Raitt's:

> With me lovin' you, <u>nobody</u> but you…(wc 12)

Non-content syllable/sound (woah, etc.) 26.5% / 6.5%.

In the following instance, from Clapton, the sound seems to release the emotion evoked by the immediately preceding section of text:

> Don't you be surprised to find me with another lover, (oh!) (wc 55).

Intense sound produced by laryngeal constriction 56.5% / 36.5%.

This is so common among white Blues singers that it is tempting to identify it as a key feature of white Blues singing. Apart from Mick Jagger and Peter Green—both represented in the corpus by only a couple of songs—the only white vocalist not using this technique is Bob Dylan, who I discuss below as a special case. In all the other singers, this technique helps give an intense edge to the performance. In the following example, Butterfield bends the consonants of the underlined word, his voice rising towards falsetto, as well as constricting the larynx:

> Train I <u>ride</u> is sixteen coaches long (wc 8)

As the count shows, the technique is also much used by black singers, though the great majority of instances come from Johnson's work.

Conclusion

Even from a rough-grained analysis such as the foregoing, certain important differences between black and white Blues singing seem to emerge. Whether the features, identified in this brief study, constitute integral features of black Blues singing, or whether they are casual devices that simply serve as embellishments, is debatable.

Their relevance to a discussion of what constitutes Blues singing may be appreciated if we compare two singers from the white corpus, Bob Dylan and Van Morrison. Although Dylan clearly drew great inspiration from the Blues, writing many pieces calling themselves Blues and using a 12-bar form, it is clear that, in his hands, the music bears little relation to its original models, especially from the lexical point of view, as pointed out above. As a performer, too, his Blues singing is deficient in the qualities outlined above. There are one or two instances of sudden rising or falling in pitch, and one song, "Bob Dylan's Blues"–significantly, from his earliest recording period–that does use several of the devices. He avoids most of the techniques altogether, however, including laryngeal constriction which, I have surmised, is the favoured white means of achieving emotional intensity. Thus, Dylan appears to be avoiding vocal techniques that most Blues singers, black and white, employ to give emotional depth to their singing. In his case, the emotional impact may result from a combination of his distinctive vocal tone, combined with an unprecedented lyrical inventiveness (Lebold 2007).

By contrast Van Morrison, in one number, "Ramblin' Blues", uses no fewer than seven of the techniques (holler, rise/fall, laryngeal constriction, use of speech, fade into moaning, non-content syllable, line opens on non-content word), and thus shows himself to be a performer whose vocal technique is much closer to the models he is imitating.

Naturally, in a brief chapter like the present, it has not been possible to do more than outline a few of the more obvious vocal techniques displayed by Blues performers, nor provide more than cursory descriptions. Further work is also required to explore the points of cultural and lexico-semantic similarity/difference between white and black Blues. Hopefully, by moving the debate on from the by now familiar tropes concerning ownership, cultural imperialism and–most of all–authenticity, the approach traced above may offer fruitful research pathways to explore the connections between specific vocal techniques and the emotional impact and lasting fascination of the Blues.

References

Allgood, Dexter B. 1990. "Black Gospel in New York City and Joe William Bostic, Sr." *The Black Perspective in Music* 18 (1/2), 101-115.

Born, Georgina, and David Hesmondhalgh (eds.). 2000. *Western Music and Its Others: Difference, Representation, and Appropriation in Music*. London, Berkeley and Los Angeles: University of California Press.

Courlander, Harold. 1963. *Negro folk music, U.S.A.* New York: Columbia University Press.

Feld, Steven. 1994. "Notes on World Beat." In *Music Grooves: Essays and Dialogues*, edited by Charles Kiel and Steven Feld, 257-289. Chicago: University of Chicago Press.

Feld, Steven, Aaron A. Fox, Thomas Porcello, and David Samuels. 2004. "Vocal anthropology: from the music of language to the language of song." In *A companion to linguistic anthropology*, edited by Alessandro Duranti, 321-345. Malden, MA and Oxford: Blackwell.

Garon, Paul. 1995. "White Blues. Race Traitor" (4). Online at: http://racetraitor.org/Blues.html. Last access 18/09/2019.

Harris, Cory. "Can white people play the Blues?" Cory Harris Online at: http://Bluesisblackmusic.blogspot.com/2015/05/can-white-people-play-Blues.html. Last access 10/12/2018.

Kubik, Gerhard. 1999. *Africa and the Blues*. Jackson: University of Mississipi Press.

Lebold, Christophe. 2007. "A Face like a Mask and a Voice that Croaks: An Integrated Poetics of Bob Dylan's Voice, Personae, and Lyrics." *Oral Tradition* 22 (1), 57-70.

Ohmsted, Frederick Law. 1853. "A Journey through Texas." In *Au Pays du Blues*. Online at: http://www.aupaysduBlues.com/t3850-field-hollers. Last access 16/12/2018.

Oliver, Paul. 1972 [1969]. *The Story of the Blues*. London: Penguin Books.

Palmer, Robert. 1982. *Deep Blues*. London and New York: Penguin.

Rudinow, Joel. 1994. "Race, Ethnicity, Expressive Authenticity: Can White People Sing the Blues?" *The Journal of Aesthetics and Art Criticism* 52 (1), "The Philosophy of Music", 127-137.

Spencer, J. M. 1992. "The Diminishing Rural Residue of Folklore in City and Urban Blues Chicago 1915-1950." *Black Music Research Journal* 12 (1), 25-41.

Williams-Jones, Pearl. 1975. "Afro-American Gospel Music: A Crystallization of the Black Aesthetic." *Ethnomusicology* 19 (3), 373-385.

Further Reading

Baraka, Amiri. 1987. *The Music. Reflections on Jazz and Blues*. William Morrow: New York.

Baraka, Amiri. 1999. *Blues People. Negro Music in White America*. New York: Harper Perennial.

Benzon, W. 1993. "The United States of the Blues: On the crossing of African and European cultures in the 20th century." *Journal of Social and Evolutionary Systems* 16 (4), 401-438.

Daley, Mike. 2003. "Why Do Whites Sing Black?: The Blues, Whiteness, and Early Histories of Rock." *Popular Music and Society* 26 (2), 161-167.

Jenkins, Philip. 2012. "The Blues as Cultural Expression." In *Blues Philosophy for Everyone: Thinking Deep about Feeling Low*, edited by Jesse R. Steinberg and Abrol Fairweather, 38-48. Chicester: John Wiley and Sons.

Lieberfeld, Daniel. 1995. "Million-Dollar Juke Joint: Commodifying Blues Culture." *African-American Review* 29 (2), Special Issues on The Music, 217-221.

Majithia, Roopen. 2012. "Blues and Catharsis." In *Blues Philosophy for Everyone: Thinking Deep About Feeling Low*, edited by Jesse R. Steinberg and Abrol Fairweather, 84-95. Chicester: John Wiley and Sons.

Stallybrass, Peter, and Allan White. 1986. *The Politics and Poetics of Transgression*. Ithaca: Cornell University Press.

Stolorow, Robert D., and Stolorow, Benjamin A. 2012. "Blues and Emotional Trauma: Blues as Musical Therapy." In *Blues Philosophy for Everyone: Thinking Deep About Feeling Low*, edited by Jesse R. Steinberg and Abrol Fairweather, 121-131. Chicester: John Wiley and Sons.

Ward, Brian. 1998. *Just My Soul Responding: Rhythm and Blues, Black Consciousnees, and Race Relations.* Berkeley: University of California Press.

Young, James O. 2008. *Cultural Appropriation and the Arts.* Malden, MA, Oxford: Blackwell.

Appendix:
Black and White Blues Corpora[1]

	Black	Artist	White	Artist
1	Crossroads Blues	Robert Johnson	All these Blues	Paul Butterfield
2	Hellhound On My Trail	-	Blues with a feeling	-
3	Milkcow's Calf Blues	-	Born in Chicago	-
4	Honeymoon Blues	-	I Got A Mind To Give Up Living	-
5	Traveling Riverside Blues	-	Last night	-
6	Stop Breakin' Down Blues	-	Love disease	-
7	Little Queen of Spades	-	Love march	-
8	Last Fair Deal Gone Down	-	Mystery train	-
9	Kindhearted Woman Blues	-	Shake your money maker	-
10	I Believe I'll dust My Broom	-	Walkin' by myself	-
11	Sweet Home Chicago	-	Women be wise	Bonnie Raitt
12	Ramblin' on My Mind	-	Sugar mamma	-
13	When You got a Good Friend	-	About To Make Me Leave Home	-
14	Come On In My Kitchen	-	Oh Louise	John Mooney
15	Terraplane Blues	-	Bump and grind	-
16	Phonograph Blues	-	Six o'clock in the morning	-
17	32-20 Blues	-	Need your love so bad	Fleetwood Mac
18	Dead Shrimp Blues	-	Stop messin' round	-
19	Walking Blues	-	Walkin' Blues	Rory Gallagher
20	Preachin' Blues (Up Jumped the Devil)	-	Wanted Blues	-
21	Stones in My Passway	-	Ramblin' Blues	Van Morrison
22	I'm a Steady Rollin Man	-	Good Mornin' Blues	
23	From Four Till Late	-	Little Red Rooster	Rolling Stones
24	Drunken Hearted Man	-	Nature's disappearing	John Mayall -

[1] Recordings of versions available on YouTube at 01/01/2019

25	Me and the Devil Blues	-	Took the car	-
26	Love in Vain	-	My pretty girl	-
27	Katie Mae	Lightnin' Hopkins	Riding on the L & N	-
28	I feel so bad	-	All your love	-
29	Let me play with your poodle	-	It ain't right	-
30	Short haired woman	-	I could cry	-
31	Picture on the wall	-	Ain't no brakeman	-
32	Baby child	-	Don't waste my time	-
33	Some day baby	-	I ain't got you	-
34	Abilene	-	Outlaw Blues	Bob Dylan
35	Jailhouse Blues	-	From a Buick 6	-
36	Last affair	-	It Takes A Lot To Laugh, It Takes A Train To Cry	-
37	Bad luck and trouble	-	Leopard-Skin Pill-Box Hat	-
38	Baldheaded woman	-	Pledging my time	-
39	Cemetery Blues	-	Meet Me in the Morning	-
40	Don't think 'cause you're pretty	-	Dirt Road Blues	-
41	Life I used to live	-	Buckets of rain	-
42	My girlish ways	Memphis Minnie	Bob Dylan's Blues	-
43	Me And My Chauffeur Blues	-	Tombstone Blues	-
44	Nothing in rambling	-	Working Man's Blues	-
45	Bumble bee	-	Texas Flood	Stevie Ray Vaughan
46	Doctor, doctor Blues	-	Tell Me	-
47	When the levee breaks	-	Dirty Pool	-
48	What's the matter with the mill?	-	Tin Pan Alley	-
49	North Memphis Blues	-	Love Struck Baby	-
50	Moaning The Blues		The Sky is Crying	-
51	Meningitis Blues	-	Boot Hill	-
52	My home is in the Delta	Muddy Waters	Empty Arms	-
53	Rock me	-	Life by the drop	-
54	You don't have to go	-	Give me strength	Eric Clapton

55	Trouble no more	-	Bellbottom Blues	-
56	They call me Muddy Waters	-	Groaning the Blues	-
57	Mean mistreater	-	Blues leave me alone	-
58	Howlin' Wolf	-	Same Old Blues	-
59	Got my mojo working	-	Driftin' Blues	-
60	Mannish boy	-	Nobody knows you	-

Author biographies

Emiliano Bonanomi is a professional guitarist and tutor with a genuine interest in music technology and social media. During his Master's Degree in Popular Music Performance at ICMP he further investigated the relationship between contemporary musicians and modern technology. This facilitated his efforts in analysing Blues in the 21st Century, focusing on the two aforementioned aspects. Currently collaborating with the University of Derby on the G.A.S.P. project, he aims to further develop the scholar elements of being a practitioner in popular music, in accordance with the Practice As Research methodology.

Thomas Claviez is Professor for Literary Theory at the University of Bern. He is the author of *Grenzfälle: Mythos – Ideologie – American Studies* (1998) and *Aesthetics & Ethics: Moral Imagination from Aristotle to Levinas and from 'Uncle Tom's Cabin' to 'House Made of Dawn'* (2008). He has co-edited numerous volumes, most recently, with Kornelia Imesch and Britta Sweers, the collection *Critique of Authenticity*, published 2019 with Vernon Press. He is the single editor of the collections *The Conditions of Hospitality: Ethics, Aesthetics and Politics at the Threshold of the Possible* and *The Common Growl: Towards a Poetics of Precarious Community*, both published with Fordham UP in 2014 and 2017. He is currently working on a monograph with the title *A Metonymic Community? Towards a New Poetics of Contingency*, and a collection of essays with the title *Throwing the Moral Dice: Ethics as/of Contingency*, both forthcoming in 2020.

Jack Dandy has been a keen blues guitarist and enthusiast since the age of 14. He channelled this passion into his BA (Hons) Degree in music at the University of Chichester (2012-15). Ready for the next step, Jack undertook a Master's Degree in Popular Music Performance at The Institute of Contemporary Music Performance (ICMP) (2016-17). This enabled him to hone his electric guitar skills and further explore blues in both a practical and an academic sense. Now a working musician and guitar tutor, this is Jack's first publication and he hopes it will not be the last.

Valerio Massimo De Angelis teaches American Literature at the University of Macerata. He is the author of two books (*La prima lettera: Miti dell'origine in The Scarlet Letter di Nathaniel Hawthorne*, 2001; and *Nathaniel Hawthorne: Il romanzo e la storia*, 2004), co-editor of two collections of bio-critical essays on contemporary American authors, of the proceedings of an international conference on Philip K. Dick, and of the proceedings of the 19th International Conference of the Italian Association for North-American Studies (AISNA), as well as a number of articles and essays on historical fiction, romance, abolitionism, feminism, modernism, postmodernism, comics, transatlantic Italian-American relationships, and on authors like Edgar A. Poe, Walt Whitman, Ambrose Bierce, Stephen Crane, Henry James, Langston Hughes, Thomas Wolfe, Dashiell Hammett, Raymond Chandler, Henry Roth, Leslie Fiedler, Doctorow, Stephen King, Leslie Marmon Silko, Margaret Atwood, and Rudy Wiebe. He is Director of *RSA Journal*, the review of AISNA, and Coordinator of the Centre for Italian American Studies at the University of Macerata.

Adriano Elia is Senior Lecturer in English Language and Translation at the Department of Political Science, University of Rome "Roma Tre". He has held teaching and research positions at the universities of Catania, Naples "L'Orientale" and Rome "Roma Tre". His publications include essays on contemporary British fiction, Afrofuturism, Langston Hughes's poetry, W.E.B. Du Bois's short fiction and poetry, Octavia E. Butler's fiction and four books –*La Cometa di W.E.B. Du Bois* (2015), *Hanif Kureishi* (2012), *The UK: Learning the Language, Studying the Culture* (co-author, 2005) and *Ut Pictura Poesis: Word-Image Interrelationships and the Word-Painting Technique* (2002).

Iain Halliday is Associate Professor of English Language and Translation in the Department of Humanities, University of Catania. His research interests include literary translation and, more recently, relations between language and music. His most recent monograph is *Huck Finn in Italian, Pinocchio in English: Theory and Praxis of Literary Translation* (2009), while recent articles include "David Bowie, songwriter, musician and singer" (2017) and "From 'La canzone del sole' (1971) to 'The Sun Song' (1977): more than textual problems in the translation of Battisti's Pop Anthem" (2015).

Jean-Charles Khalifa is Associate Professor of English linguistics and translation at the Department of English Studies, University of Poitiers, France. His research interests include formal syntax, corpus linguistics, the syntax-semantics interface, and professional translation. He has also published papers and given lectures on the folk tradition in the British Isles and in America, and on the Blues. Among his books on linguistics are, *Syntaxe de l'anglais* (2004), *L'Épreuve de grammaire à l'agrégation* (2006), *Perception et structures linguistiques : huit études sur l'anglais* (2010). He is also a musician and a published translator of U.S. novels, including recently: Earl Thompson, *A Garden of Sand* (French title: *Un jardin de sable*, 2018), *Tattoo* (2019), Emil Ferris, *My Favorite Thing is Monsters* (French title: *Moi, ce que j'aime, c'est les monstres*, 2018), Frederick Exley, *Last Notes from Home* (French title: *À la merci du désir*, 2020).

Randolph Lewis is a Professor of American Studies at the University of Texas at Austin. A former contributing writer for *The Brooklyn Rail*, he is the author of four books including *Under Surveillance: Being Watched in Modern America*, *Emile de Antonio: Radical Filmmaker in Cold War America*, *Alanis Obomsawin:*

The Vision of a Native Artist, and *Navajo Talking Picture: Cinema on Native Ground.*

Daniel Lieberfeld started hearing and playing blues as a teenager. He has taught history and international politics at Duquesne University in Pittsburgh, Colgate University, and Bowdoin College. His articles on music and cultural history have appeared in *Rock Music Studies, The Sixties, African-American Review, The Drama Review, The American Scholar, Film Quarterly, Quarterly Review of Film and Video, Logos,* and the *Journal of Popular Film and Television.*

Giulia Magazzù obtained a BA in Modern Languages from the University of Messina, Italy and an MA in Translation Studies from the University of Bologna, Italy. She is completing a PhD in English Studies at the University of Rome Tor Vergata. Her dissertation deals with audiovisual translation and the fansubbing of multilingual TV series. She also works as adjunct lecturer at "Gabriele D'Annunzio" University of Chieti-Pescara, Italy, where she teaches English linguistics and translation at undergraduate level.

Her areas of research are translation studies, audiovisual translation, ESP, and critical discourse analysis. Among her publications are *The Representation of Immigrants in the Italian Press: Exploring visual Discrimination* (in *InVerbis,* 2018); "Dottore, dottore!" Subtitling dialects and regionalisms: the case of "Inspector Montalbano". In Corrius M., Espasa E., Zabalbeascoa P. (eds), *Multilingualism and Audiovisual Translation.* Peter Lang 2019. She is currently working on a book about the language of Donald Trump to be published in 2020 by Cambridge Scholars Publishing.

Chiara Patrizi holds a PhD in American Literature at Roma Tre University and is *cultrice della materia* at Ca' Foscari University of Venice. Her PhD research examines the concept of "wilderness of time" in contemporary American literature, focusing on Kurt Vonnegut Jr. and Don DeLillo. She holds an M.A. from Ca' Foscari University of Venice—her thesis received a special mention at the Lombardo-Gulli Award 2015. She is a member of the American Studies Association of Italy (AISNA). She was Visiting Scholar at Duke University, and has participated in conferences in Italy and abroad, collaborating with the Don DeLillo Society, the Centro Studi Americani (CSA), and the AISNA. Her main publications are "Body and Time in Don DeLillo's *The Body Artist*" and "'A Moth-eaten Shirt': Memory and Identity in Jesmyn Ward's *Sing, Unburied, Sing.*" Her research interests include contemporary American literature, African-American literature, literature and the arts, and trauma studies.

Irene Polimante is a PhD student in Modern Languages and Literatures at the Department of Humanities, University of Macerata. She works on contemporary American poetry with a focus on hybrid and performative poetic forms. She is currently completing her dissertation on performance poetry as a strategy of aesthetic resistance and critical discourse on society from the diasporic perspective of Latin@s, Caribbean, and African-American poets. Her research on texts that lie in-between orality, literacy and performativity (live or digitally mediated) questions and re-negotiates common understandings of poetic textuality through the lens of performance studies, semiotics, and digital humanities.

Douglas Mark Ponton is Associate Professor of English Language and Translation at the Department of Political and Social Sciences, University of Catania. His research interests include political discourse analysis, ecolinguistics, discourse in interaction, applied linguistics, pragmatics, corpus linguistics and critical discourse studies. He has held teaching and research positions at the universities of Catania, Messina and Pisa. His most recent research projects concern representations of Russia in western media, the Montalbano effect on tourism in Sicily, processes of late industrialism and ecological questions in South-Eastern Sicily, and Sicilian dialect theatre. His main publications are *For Arguments Sake: speaker evaluation in modern political discourse* (2011), and most recently *Understanding Political Persuasion: Linguistic and Rhetorical Analysis* (2019). As well as politics, his research deals with a variety of social topics, including legal metaphor, the discourse of mediation, cross-cultural politeness, folk traditions including proverbs and, last but not least, the Blues.

Diana Sfetlana Stoica was born in Baia Mare, Romania. She is a 3rd-year student at the Doctoral School of Philosophy, Sociology and Political Studies of the University of West Timisoara, Romania, conducting research on Sub-Saharan change perspectives in the context of European non-global anti-migration discourse. She graduated in Communication Studies, with a bachelor's degree in Advertising, in 2014. During the master studies in International Development, from which she graduated in 2016, she focused on African studies, inspired by her own interests and her geologist father's dream to climb Kilimanjaro. Her conceptual writing is inspired by intercultural communication and knowledge production. It is founded on a vivid interest in concepts of development, race, and power, as well as their image in the branding of destinations and global knowledge exchange. Her research is based on observations in the field of tourism and air transportation, and participation in high profile exhibitions.

Uwe Zagratzki is Professor of Anglophone Literatures and Cultures and the Chair of Literature at the Institute of English at Szczecin University. He has widely published in Scottish and Canadian Literature and Culture, Cultural Studies (e.g. African-American Music) and War and Literature. He is a co-founder of the Szczecin Canadian Studies Group and has had teaching and research posts at the Universities of Osnabrück and Oldenburg (Germany), Brno (Czech Republic) and the University of West Georgia (US).

His recent publications include *Ideological Battlegrounds–Constructions of Us and Them Before and After 9/11*. Vol. 1 (co-ed. with Joanna Witkowswka, 2014), *Despite Harper. International Perceptions of Canadian Literature and Culture* (co-ed. with Weronika Suchacka and Hartmut Lutz, 2014), *Exile and Migration* (co-ed. with Joanna Witkowska, 2016), *Disrespected Neighbo(u)rs–Cultural Stereotypes in Literature and Film* (co-ed. with Caroline Rosenthal und Laurenz Volkmann, 2018) and *Perspectives on Canada–International Canadian Studies despite Harper and Trudeau* (co-ed. with Barbara Butrymowska, 2018).

Index

S

Scorsese, Martin, 3, 26, 111
sex, 7, 54, 56, 143, 181
Sexuality, 121
Simone, Nina, xv, 63, 65, 66, 67, 68,
    72, 73, 74
singing, xvii, 8, 15, 21, 45, 58, 67,
    68, 101, 105, 106, 166, 167, 177,
    178, 179, 182, 184, 185, 188
slave trade, 15, 18
slavery, 4, 17, 18, 52, 71, 72, 120,
    178
Smith, Bessie, xiii, 39
Syncretism, 16

T

Texas, xiv, 3, 4, 5, 6, 7, 8, 9, 10, 11,
    131, 187, 194, 198
the Beatles, 41, 177
the Devil, xvi, 14, 15, 125, 147, 149,
    151, 193, 194
The Panther and the Lash, 63, 69
The Weary Blues, xv, xvi, 101, 102,
    103, 104, 106, 107, 108, 110
Touré, Ali Farka, xii, xiv, 23, 24, 25,
    26, 28, 29, 30, 31, 32, 33, 34
twelve-bar, 16, 64, 66
twentieth century, 15, 27, 89, 94,
    97, 167, 178

twenty-first century, 148, 155, 156,
    157, 162, 163, 164, 165, 167,
    168, 170

U

University of Catania, xi, 11, 200

V

Vaughan, Stevie Ray, xvii, 6, 178,
    179, 194
vocal technique, xii, 183, 184, 189

W

Waters, Muddy, xiii, 37, 39, 40, 42,
    44, 45, 46, 52, 53, 166, 180, 183,
    194, 195
Weary Blues, 74, 87, 90, 91, 92, 97,
    98, 101, 102, 103, 104, 108, 111
White Blues, xiii, 177, 180, 189, 193
Williams, Raymond, xv, 51, 54
Williamson, Sonny Boy, xiii
Winter, Johnny, 6, 39, 120, 178, 179
Wolf, Howlin', xiv, 37, 39, 42, 155,
    163, 164, 174, 195
Wolof, 15
woman, 5, 6, 9, 17, 18, 47, 51, 52,
    55, 105, 129, 130, 131, 134, 140,
    143, 144, 145, 146, 147, 148,
    149, 174, 175, 179, 181, 186, 194
World War II, 44, 53

www.ingramcontent.com/pod-product-compliance
Lightning Source LLC
Chambersburg PA
CBHW072120020426
42334CB00018B/1663